THE HONOR STUDENT AT Magic High School

Art ◉
Yu Mori
Original Story ◉
Tsutomu Sato
Character design ●
Kana Ishida

7

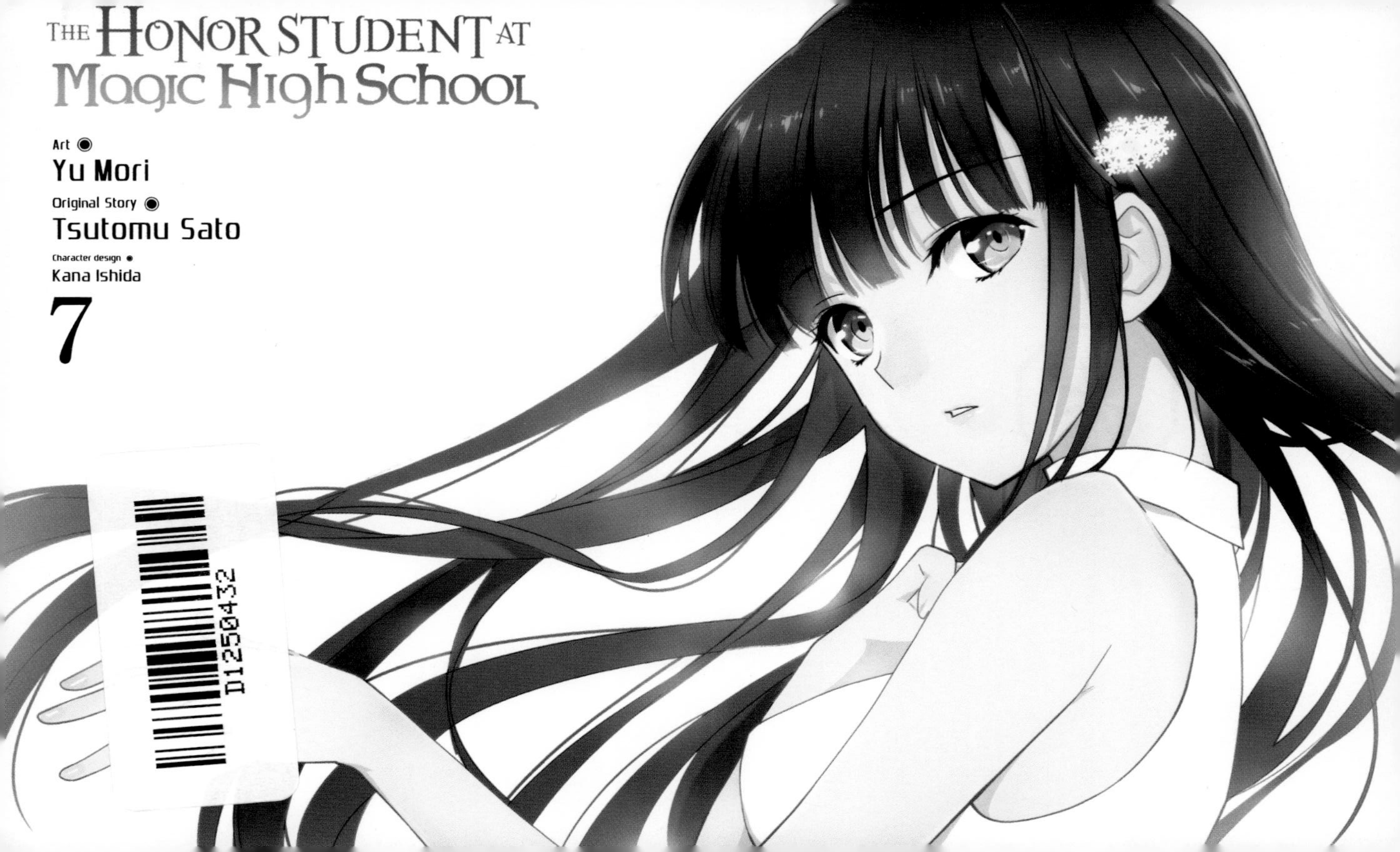

CONTENTS

The Honor Student
at Magic High School

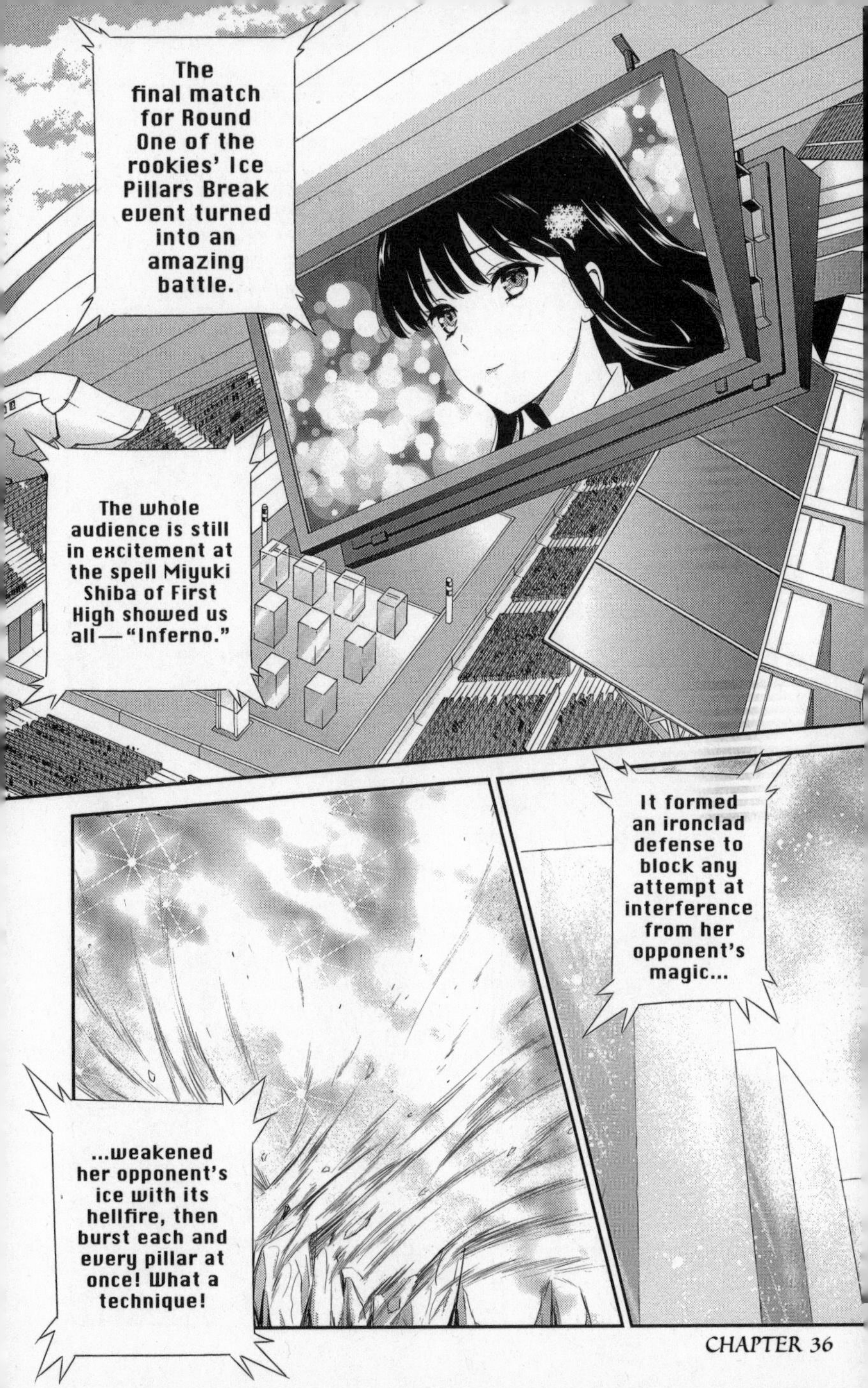
The final match for Round One of the rookies' Ice Pillars Break event turned into an amazing battle.
The whole audience is still in excitement at the spell Miyuki Shiba of First High showed us all—"Inferno."
It formed an ironclad defense to block any attempt at interference from her opponent's magic...
...weakened her opponent's ice with its hellfire, then burst each and every pillar at once! What a technique!

CHAPTER 36

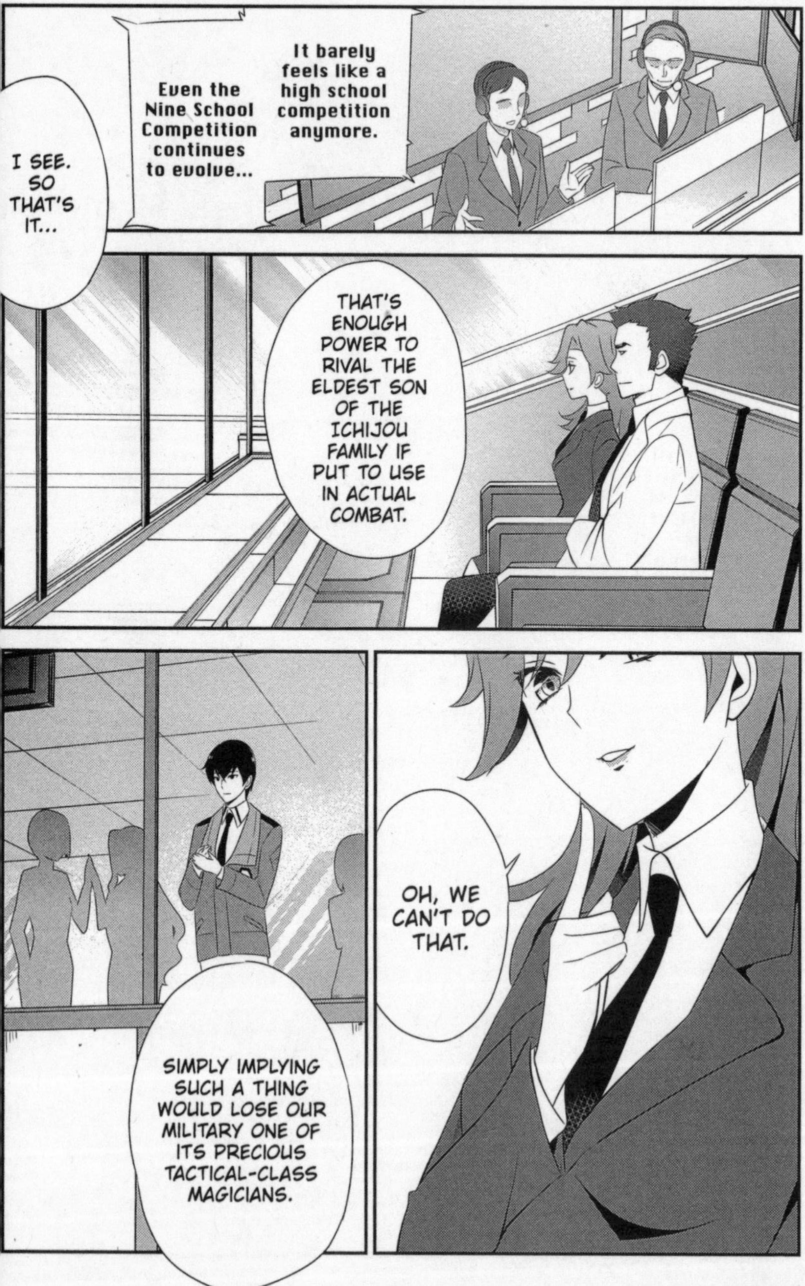
It barely feels like a high school competition anymore.
Even the Nine School Competition continues to evolve...
I SEE. SO THAT'S IT...
THAT'S ENOUGH POWER TO RIVAL THE ELDEST SON OF THE ICHIJOU FAMILY IF PUT TO USE IN ACTUAL COMBAT.
OH, WE CAN'T DO THAT.
SIMPLY IMPLYING SUCH A THING WOULD LOSE OUR MILITARY ONE OF ITS PRECIOUS TACTICAL-CLASS MAGICIANS.

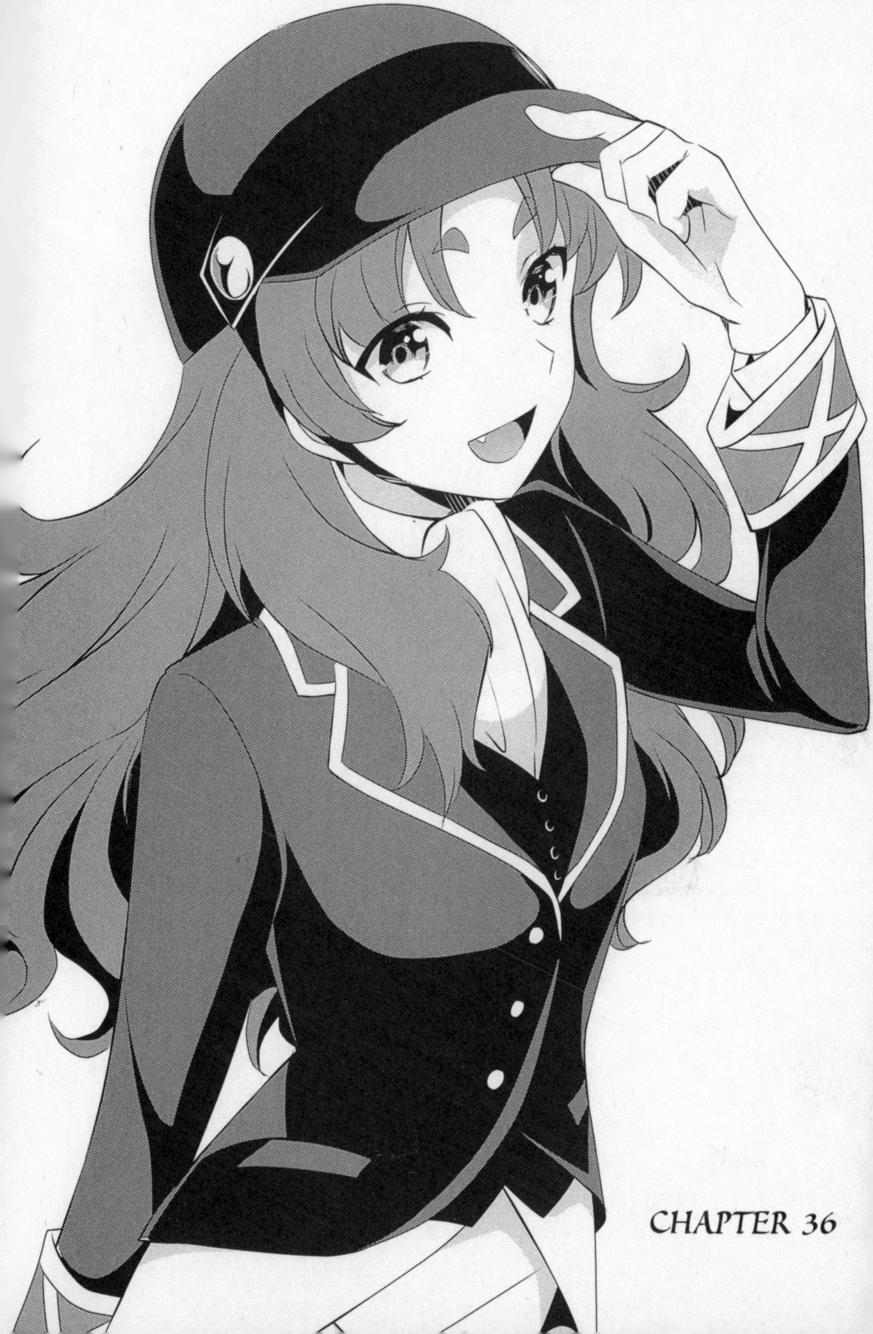

CHAPTER 36

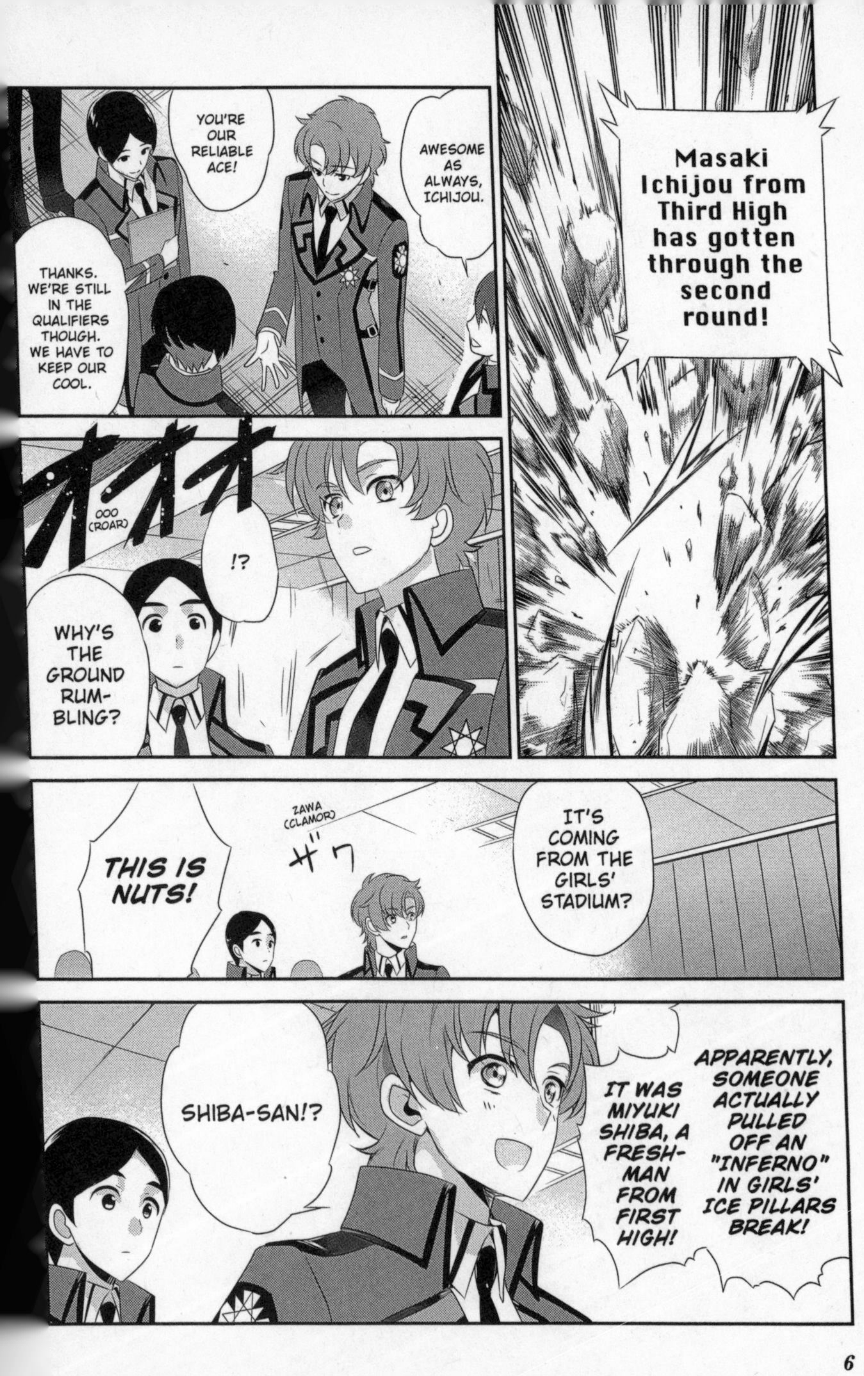
Masaki Ichijou from Third High has gotten through the second round!
AWESOME AS ALWAYS, ICHIJOU.
YOU'RE OUR RELIABLE ACE!
THANKS. WE'RE STILL IN THE QUALIFIERS THOUGH. WE HAVE TO KEEP OUR COOL.
!?
オオオ
OOO (ROAR)
WHY'S THE GROUND RUM-BLING?
IT'S COMING FROM THE GIRLS' STADIUM?
ザワ
ZAWA (CLAMOR)
THIS IS NUTS!
APPARENTLY, SOMEONE ACTUALLY PULLED OFF AN "INFERNO" IN GIRLS' ICE PILLARS BREAK!
IT WAS MIYUKI SHIBA, A FRESH-MAN FROM FIRST HIGH!
SHIBA-SAN!?

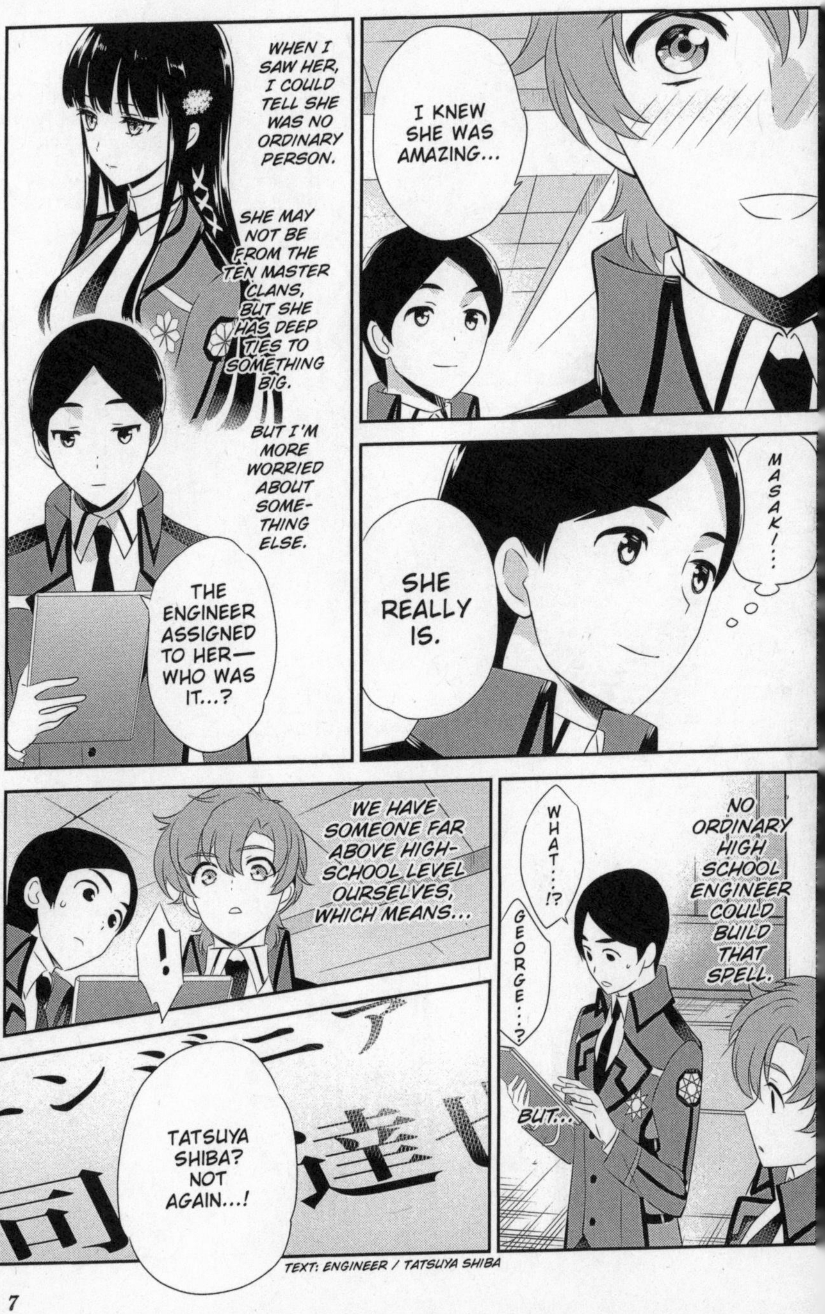
I KNEW SHE WAS AMAZING...
MASAKI...
SHE REALLY IS.
WHEN I SAW HER, I COULD TELL SHE WAS NO ORDINARY PERSON.
SHE MAY NOT BE FROM THE TEN MASTER CLANS, BUT SHE HAS DEEP TIES TO SOMETHING BIG.
BUT I'M MORE WORRIED ABOUT SOMETHING ELSE.
THE ENGINEER ASSIGNED TO HER—WHO WAS IT...?
NO ORDINARY HIGH SCHOOL ENGINEER COULD BUILD THAT SPELL.
WHAT...!?
GEORGE...?
BUT...
WE HAVE SOMEONE FAR ABOVE HIGH-SCHOOL LEVEL OURSELVES, WHICH MEANS...
!
TATSUYA SHIBA? NOT AGAIN...!
TEXT: ENGINEER / TATSUYA SHIBA

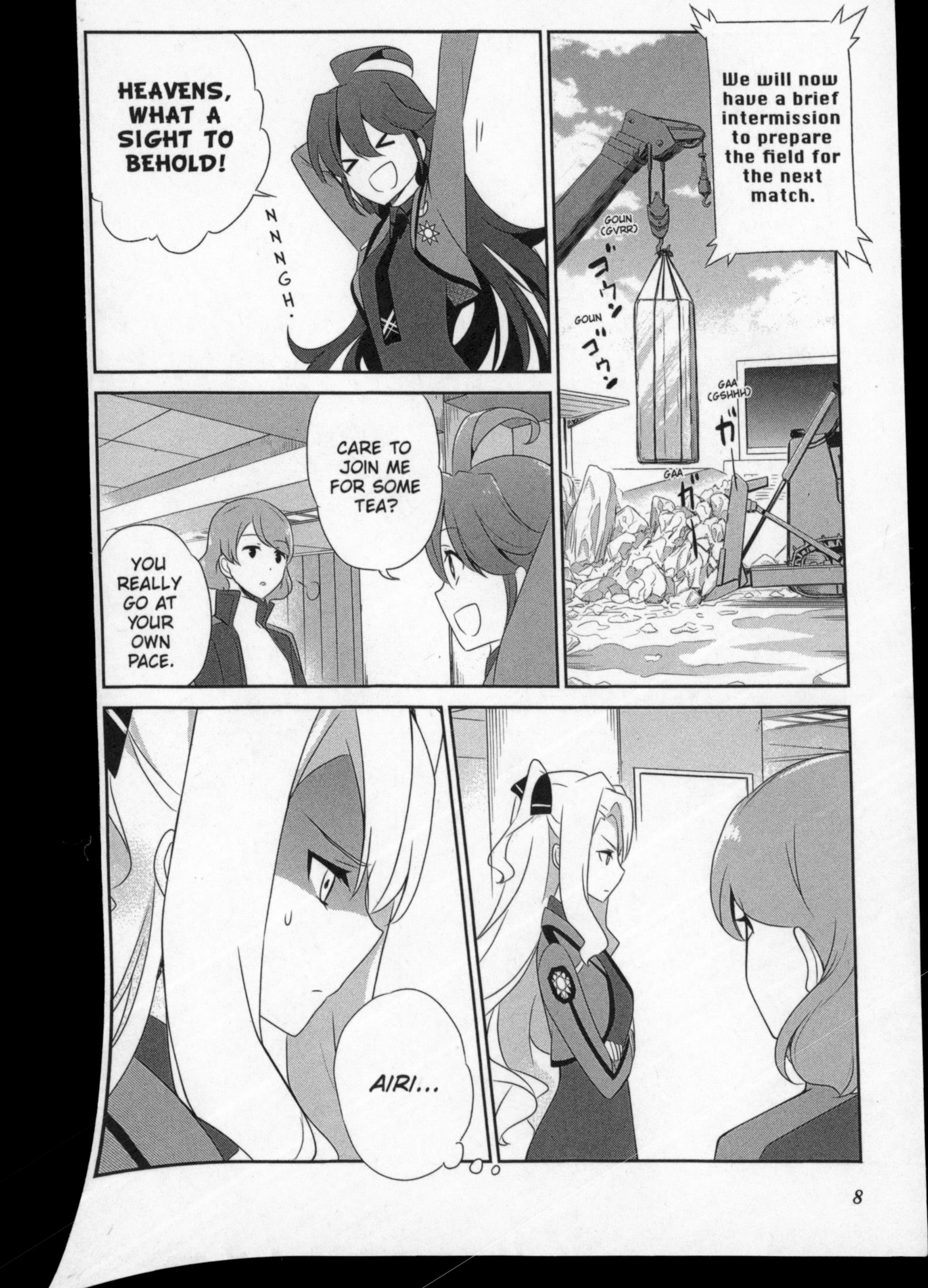
We will now have a brief intermission to prepare the field for the next match.
GOUN (GVRR)
ゴウン
GOUN
ゴウン
GAA (GSHHH)
ガ
GAA
ガ
HEAVENS, WHAT A SIGHT TO BEHOLD!
NNNGH.
CARE TO JOIN ME FOR SOME TEA?
YOU REALLY GO AT YOUR OWN PACE.
AIRI...

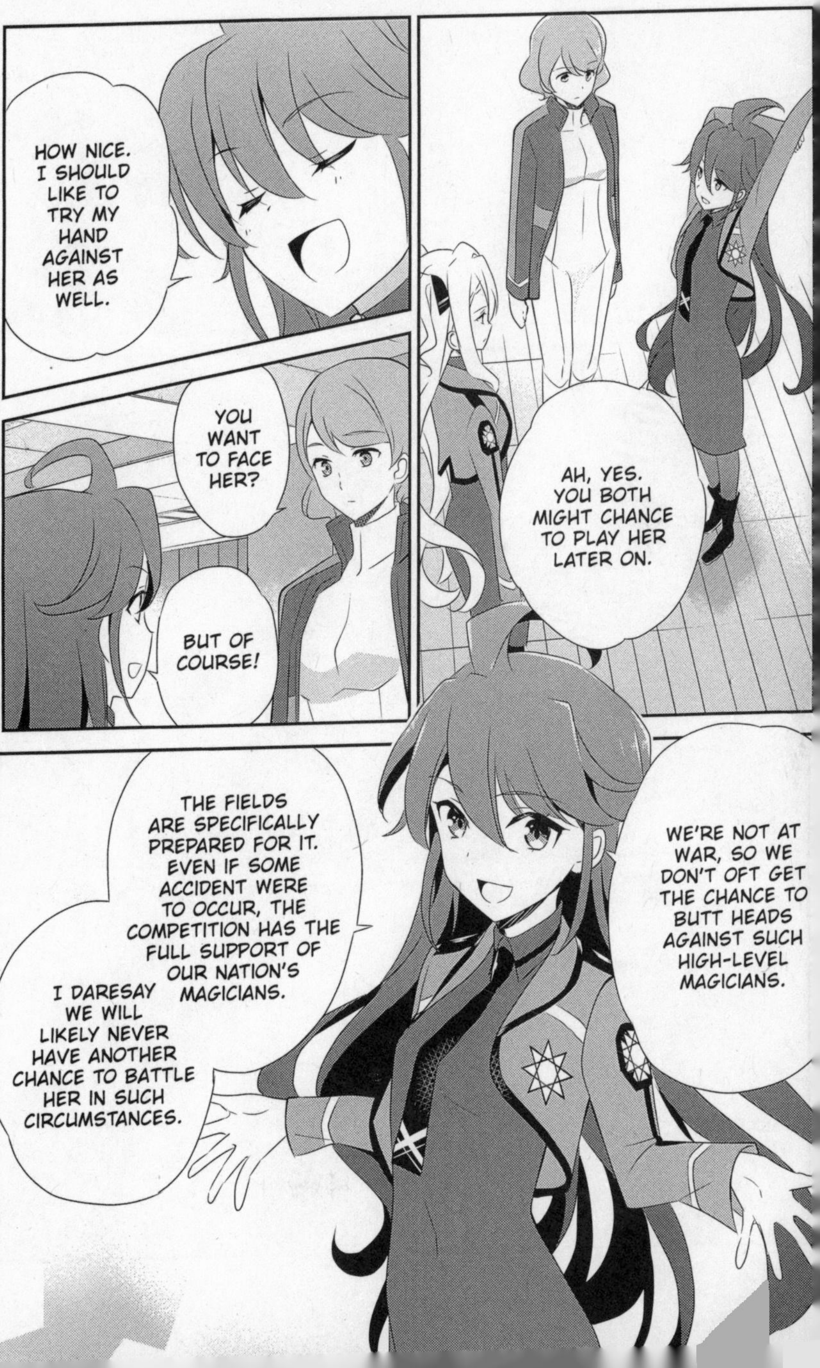
AH, YES. YOU BOTH MIGHT CHANCE TO PLAY HER LATER ON.
HOW NICE. I SHOULD LIKE TO TRY MY HAND AGAINST HER AS WELL.
YOU WANT TO FACE HER?
BUT OF COURSE!
WE'RE NOT AT WAR, SO WE DON'T OFT GET THE CHANCE TO BUTT HEADS AGAINST SUCH HIGH-LEVEL MAGICIANS.
THE FIELDS ARE SPECIFICALLY PREPARED FOR IT. EVEN IF SOME ACCIDENT WERE TO OCCUR, THE COMPETITION HAS THE FULL SUPPORT OF OUR NATION'S MAGICIANS.
I DARESAY WE WILL LIKELY NEVER HAVE ANOTHER CHANCE TO BATTLE HER IN SUCH CIRCUMSTANCES.

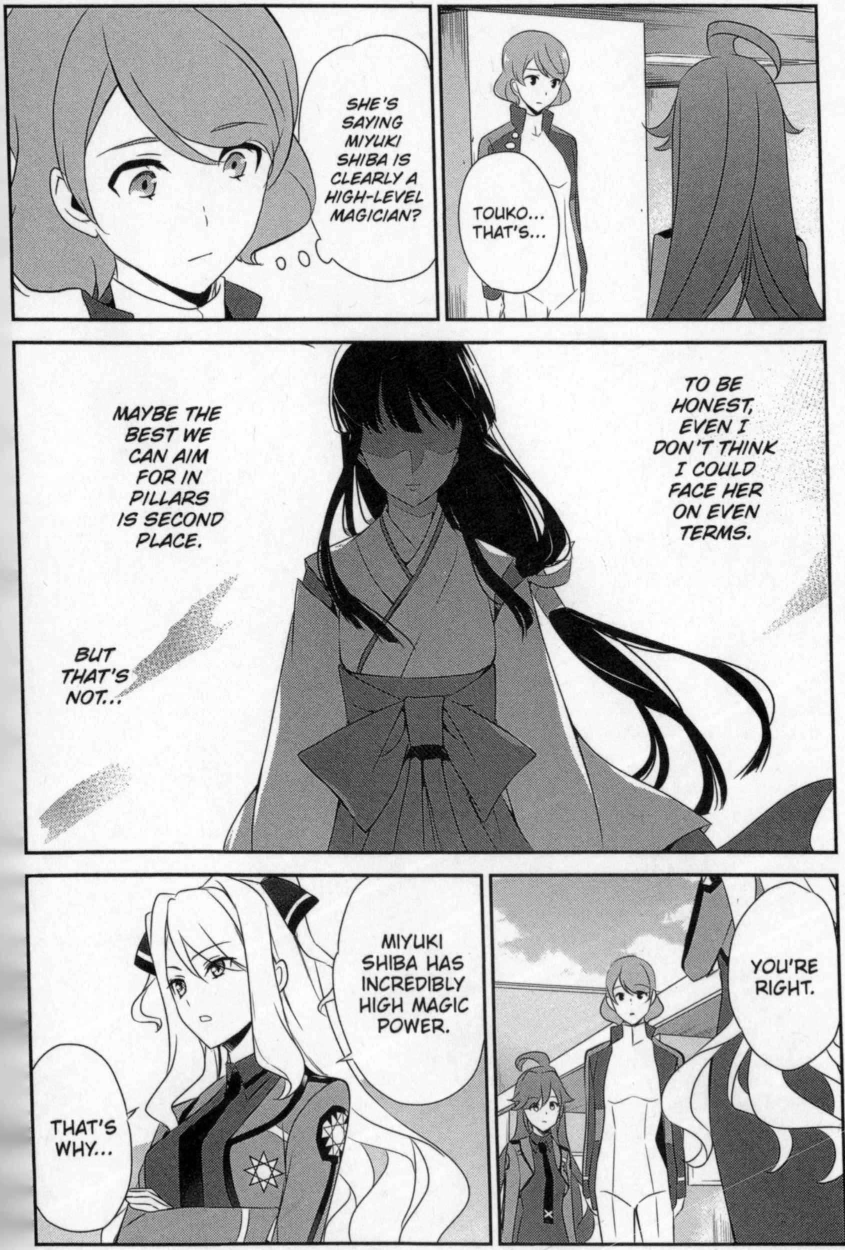
TOUKO... THAT'S...
SHE'S SAYING MIYUKI SHIBA IS CLEARLY A HIGH-LEVEL MAGICIAN?
TO BE HONEST, EVEN I DON'T THINK I COULD FACE HER ON EVEN TERMS.
MAYBE THE BEST WE CAN AIM FOR IN PILLARS IS SECOND PLACE.
BUT THAT'S NOT...
YOU'RE RIGHT.
MIYUKI SHIBA HAS INCREDIBLY HIGH MAGIC POWER.
THAT'S WHY...

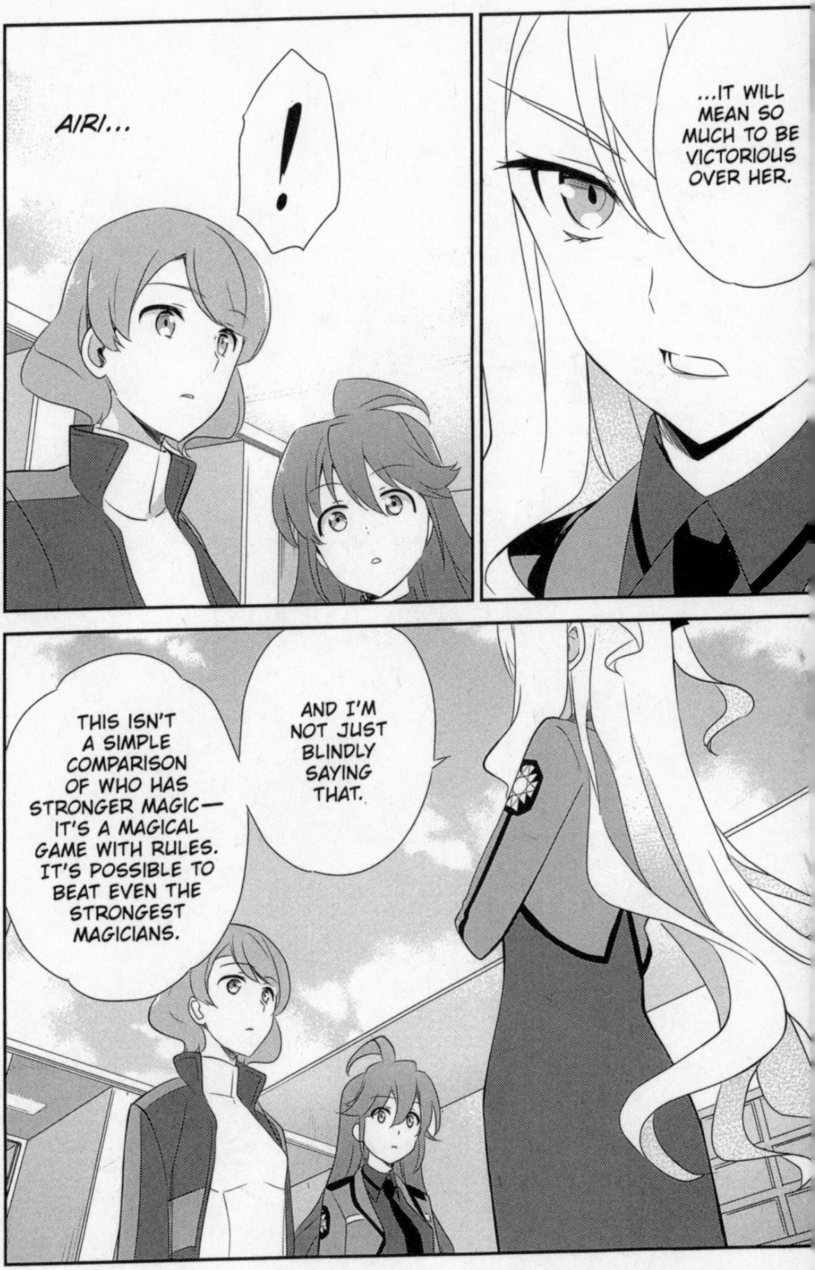
...IT WILL MEAN SO MUCH TO BE VICTORIOUS OVER HER.
!
AIRI...
AND I'M NOT JUST BLINDLY SAYING THAT.
THIS ISN'T A SIMPLE COMPARISON OF WHO HAS STRONGER MAGIC— IT'S A MAGICAL GAME WITH RULES. IT'S POSSIBLE TO BEAT EVEN THE STRONGEST MAGICIANS.

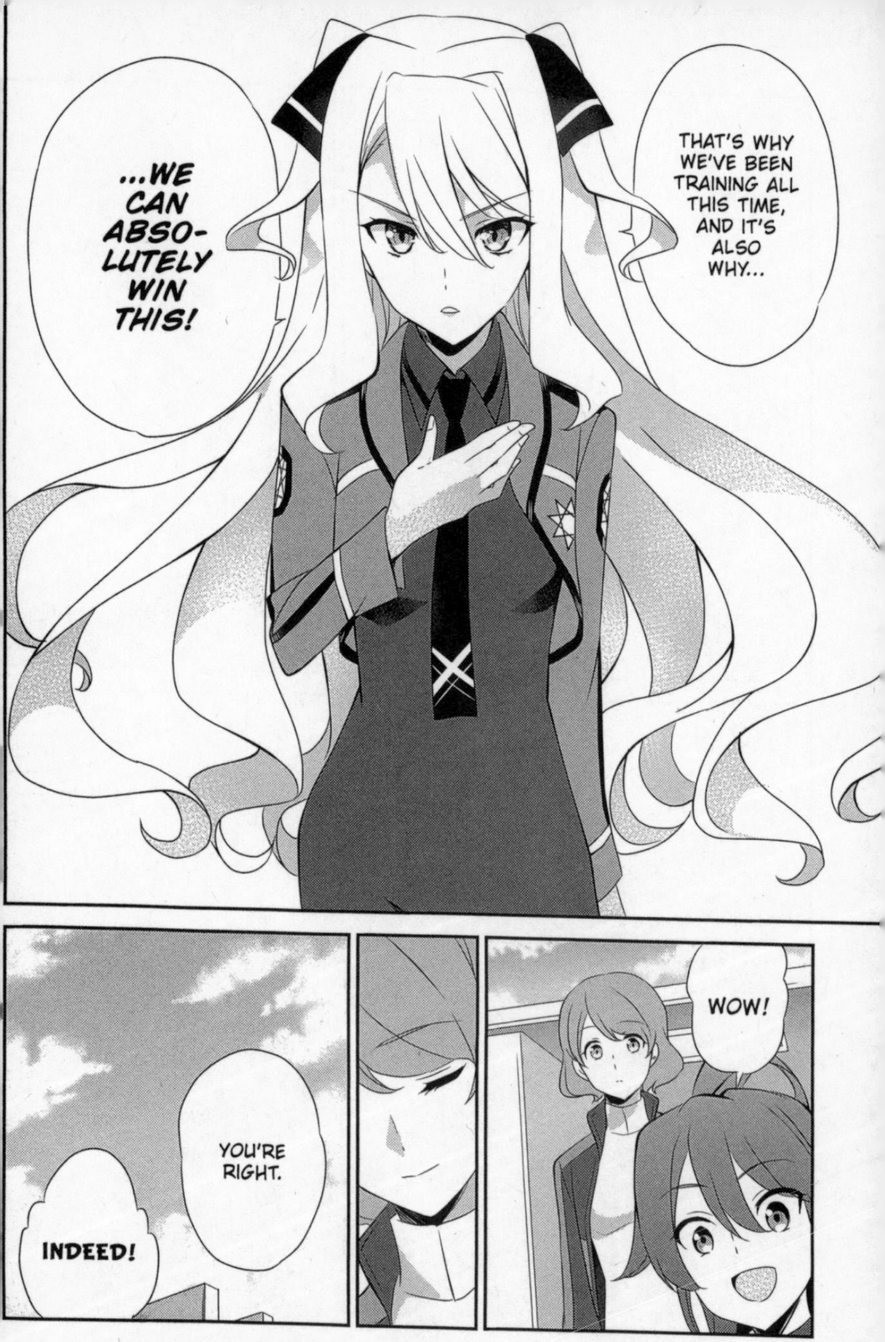
THAT'S WHY WE'VE BEEN TRAINING ALL THIS TIME, AND IT'S ALSO WHY...
...WE CAN ABSOLUTELY WIN THIS!
WOW!
YOU'RE RIGHT.
INDEED!

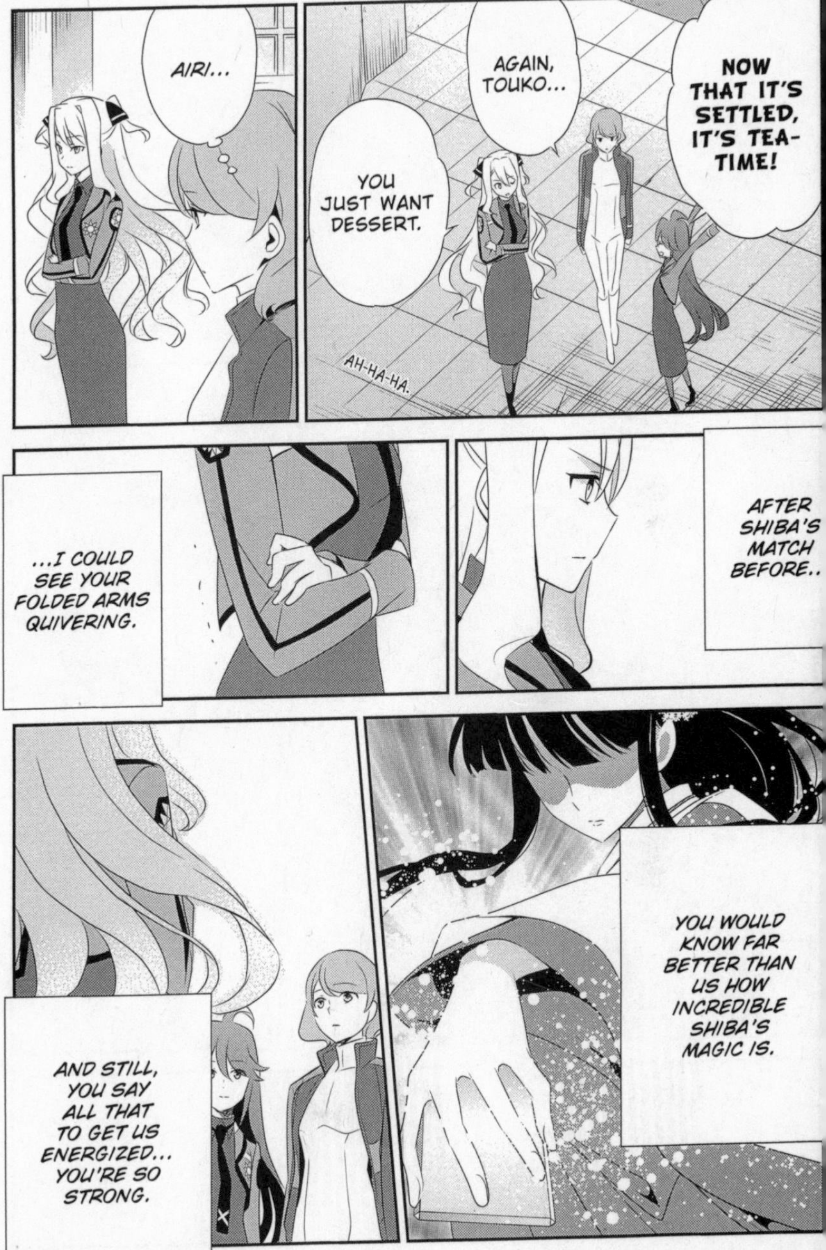
NOW THAT IT'S SETTLED, IT'S TEA-TIME!
AGAIN, TOUKO...
YOU JUST WANT DESSERT.
AH-HA-HA.
AIRI...
AFTER SHIBA'S MATCH BEFORE..
...I COULD SEE YOUR FOLDED ARMS QUIVERING.
YOU WOULD KNOW FAR BETTER THAN US HOW INCREDIBLE SHIBA'S MAGIC IS.
AND STILL, YOU SAY ALL THAT TO GET US ENERGIZED... YOU'RE SO STRONG.

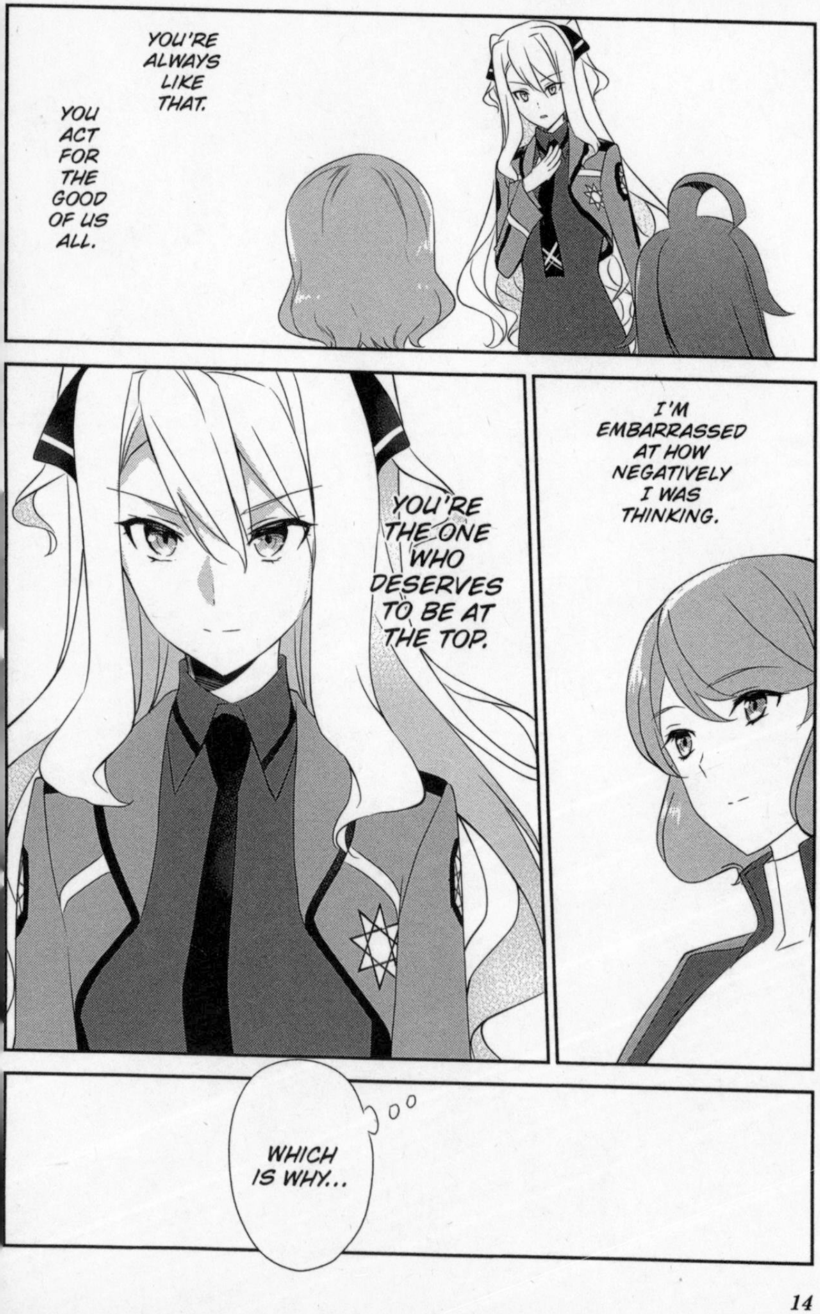
YOU'RE ALWAYS LIKE THAT.
YOU ACT FOR THE GOOD OF US ALL.
I'M EMBARRASSED AT HOW NEGATIVELY I WAS THINKING.
YOU'RE THE ONE WHO DESERVES TO BE AT THE TOP.
WHICH IS WHY...

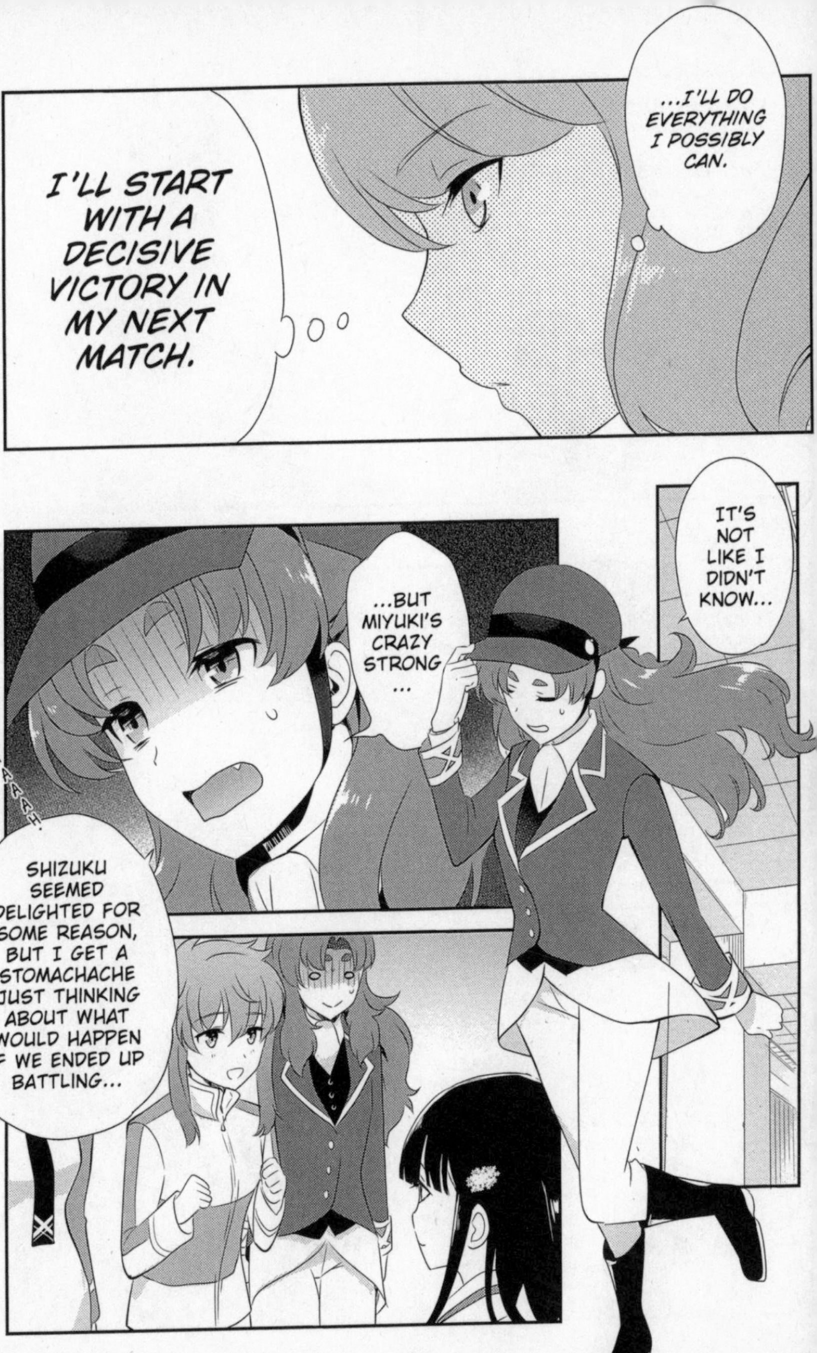
...I'LL DO EVERYTHING I POSSIBLY CAN.
I'LL START WITH A DECISIVE VICTORY IN MY NEXT MATCH.
IT'S NOT LIKE I DIDN'T KNOW...
...BUT MIYUKI'S CRAZY STRONG ...
HAAAAH!
SHIZUKU SEEMED DELIGHTED FOR SOME REASON, BUT I GET A STOMACHACHE JUST THINKING ABOUT WHAT WOULD HAPPEN IF WE ENDED UP BATTLING...

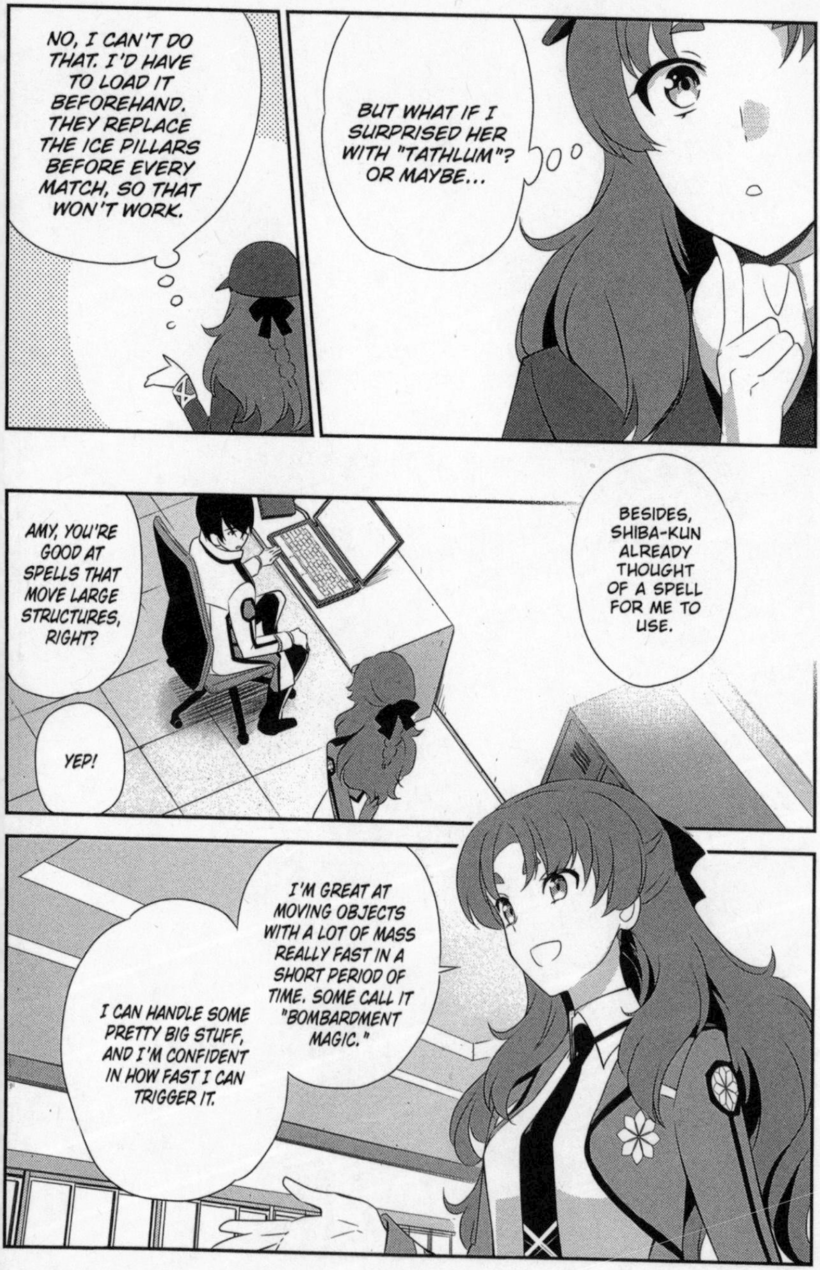
BUT WHAT IF I SURPRISED HER WITH "TATHLUM"? OR MAYBE...
NO, I CAN'T DO THAT. I'D HAVE TO LOAD IT BEFOREHAND. THEY REPLACE THE ICE PILLARS BEFORE EVERY MATCH, SO THAT WON'T WORK.
BESIDES, SHIBA-KUN ALREADY THOUGHT OF A SPELL FOR ME TO USE.
AMY, YOU'RE GOOD AT SPELLS THAT MOVE LARGE STRUCTURES, RIGHT?
YEP!
I'M GREAT AT MOVING OBJECTS WITH A LOT OF MASS REALLY FAST IN A SHORT PERIOD OF TIME. SOME CALL IT "BOMBARDMENT MAGIC."
I CAN HANDLE SOME PRETTY BIG STUFF, AND I'M CONFIDENT IN HOW FAST I CAN TRIGGER IT.

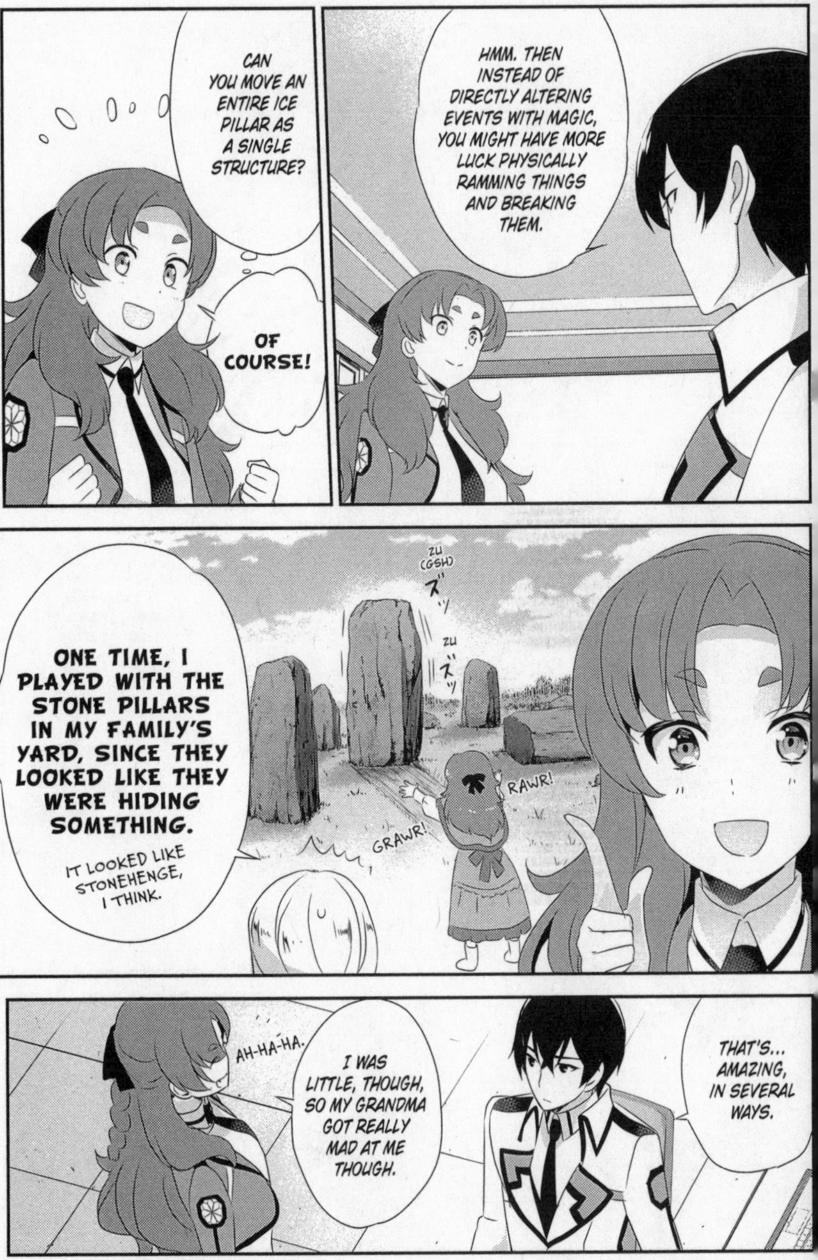
HMM. THEN INSTEAD OF DIRECTLY ALTERING EVENTS WITH MAGIC, YOU MIGHT HAVE MORE LUCK PHYSICALLY RAMMING THINGS AND BREAKING THEM.
CAN YOU MOVE AN ENTIRE ICE PILLAR AS A SINGLE STRUCTURE?
OF COURSE!
ZU (GSH)
ズッ
ZU
ズッ
RAWR!
ONE TIME, I PLAYED WITH THE STONE PILLARS IN MY FAMILY'S YARD, SINCE THEY LOOKED LIKE THEY WERE HIDING SOMETHING.
IT LOOKED LIKE STONEHENGE, I THINK.
GRAWR!
THAT'S... AMAZING, IN SEVERAL WAYS.
I WAS LITTLE, THOUGH, SO MY GRANDMA GOT REALLY MAD AT ME THOUGH.
AH-HA-HA.

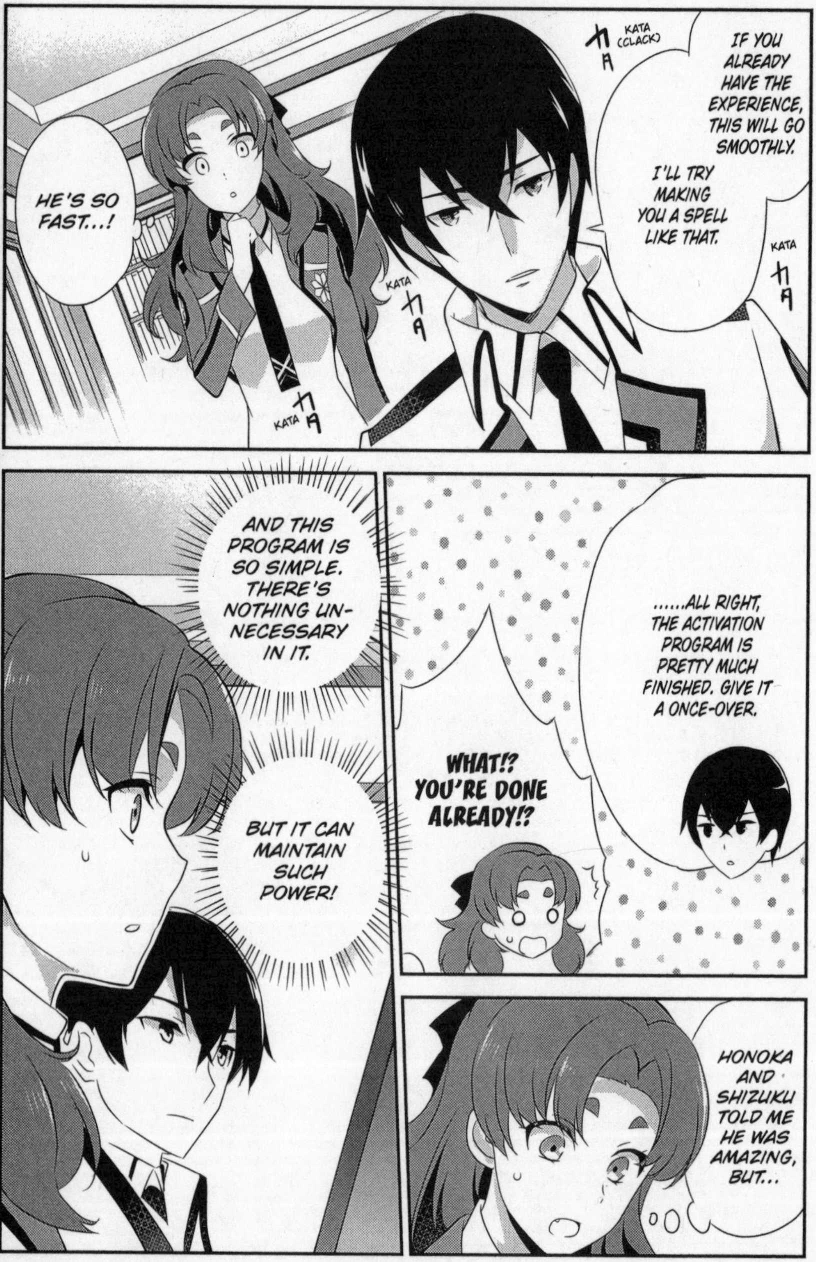
KATA (CLACK)
IF YOU ALREADY HAVE THE EXPERIENCE, THIS WILL GO SMOOTHLY.
I'LL TRY MAKING YOU A SPELL LIKE THAT.
KATA
KATA
KATA
HE'S SO FAST...!
......ALL RIGHT, THE ACTIVATION PROGRAM IS PRETTY MUCH FINISHED. GIVE IT A ONCE-OVER.
WHAT!? YOU'RE DONE ALREADY!?
HONOKA AND SHIZUKU TOLD ME HE WAS AMAZING, BUT...
AND THIS PROGRAM IS SO SIMPLE. THERE'S NOTHING UN-NECESSARY IN IT.
BUT IT CAN MAINTAIN SUCH POWER!

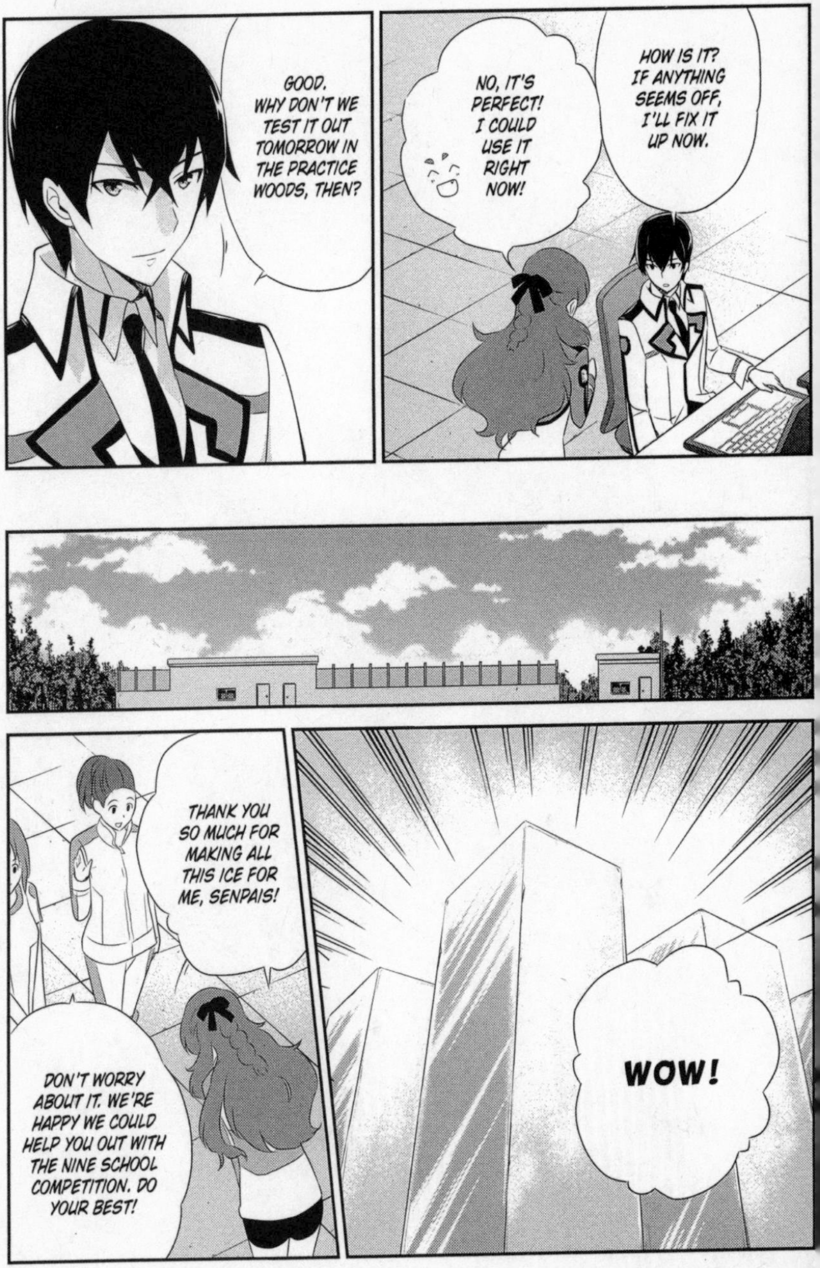
HOW IS IT? IF ANYTHING SEEMS OFF, I'LL FIX IT UP NOW.
NO, IT'S PERFECT! I COULD USE IT RIGHT NOW!
GOOD. WHY DON'T WE TEST IT OUT TOMORROW IN THE PRACTICE WOODS, THEN?
WOW!
THANK YOU SO MUCH FOR MAKING ALL THIS ICE FOR ME, SENPAIS!
DON'T WORRY ABOUT IT. WE'RE HAPPY WE COULD HELP YOU OUT WITH THE NINE SCHOOL COMPETITION. DO YOUR BEST!

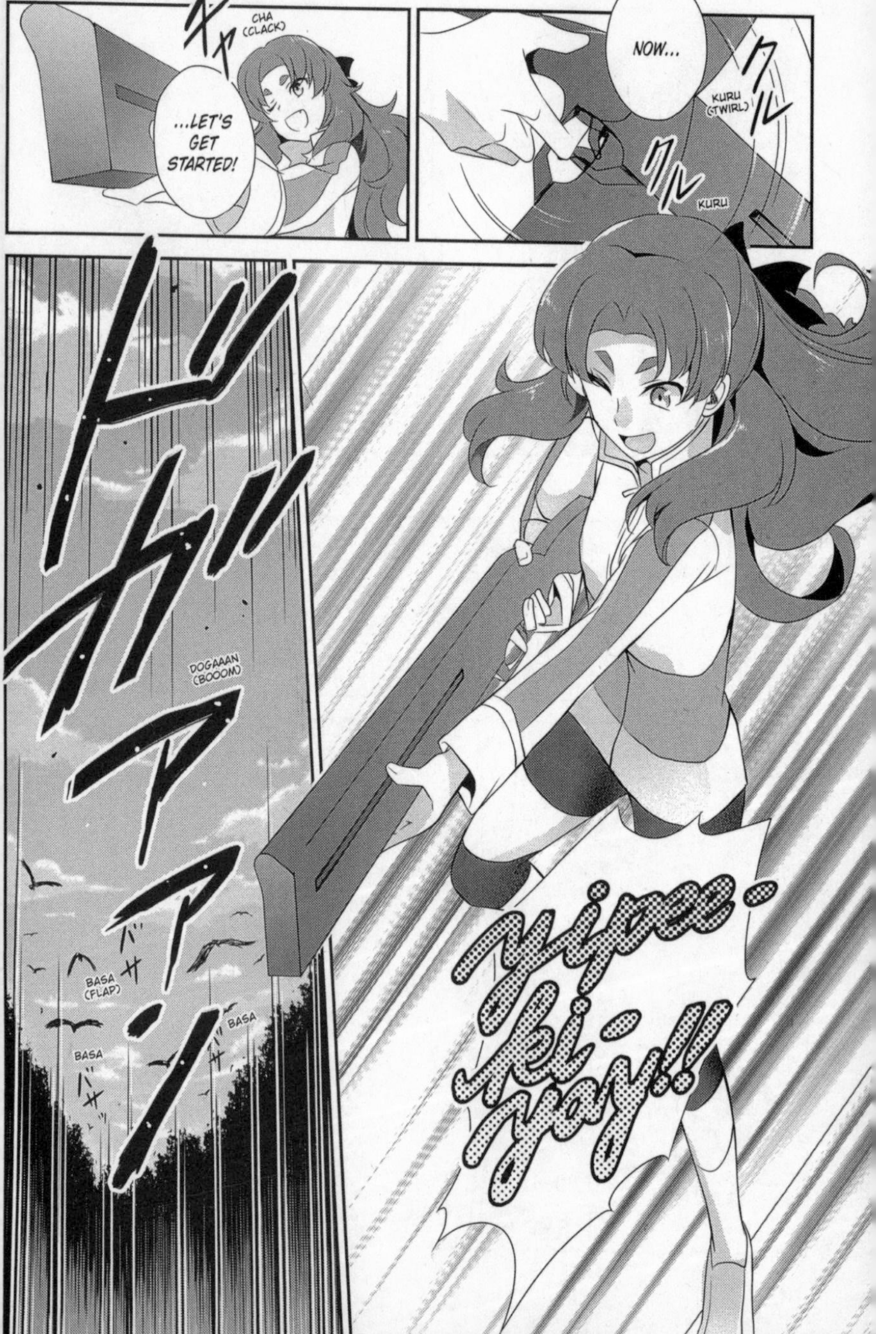
NOW...
KURU (TWIRL)
KURU
CHA (CLACK)
...LET'S GET STARTED!
yipee-ki-yay!!
DOGAAAN (BOOOM)
BASA (FLAP)
BASA
BASA

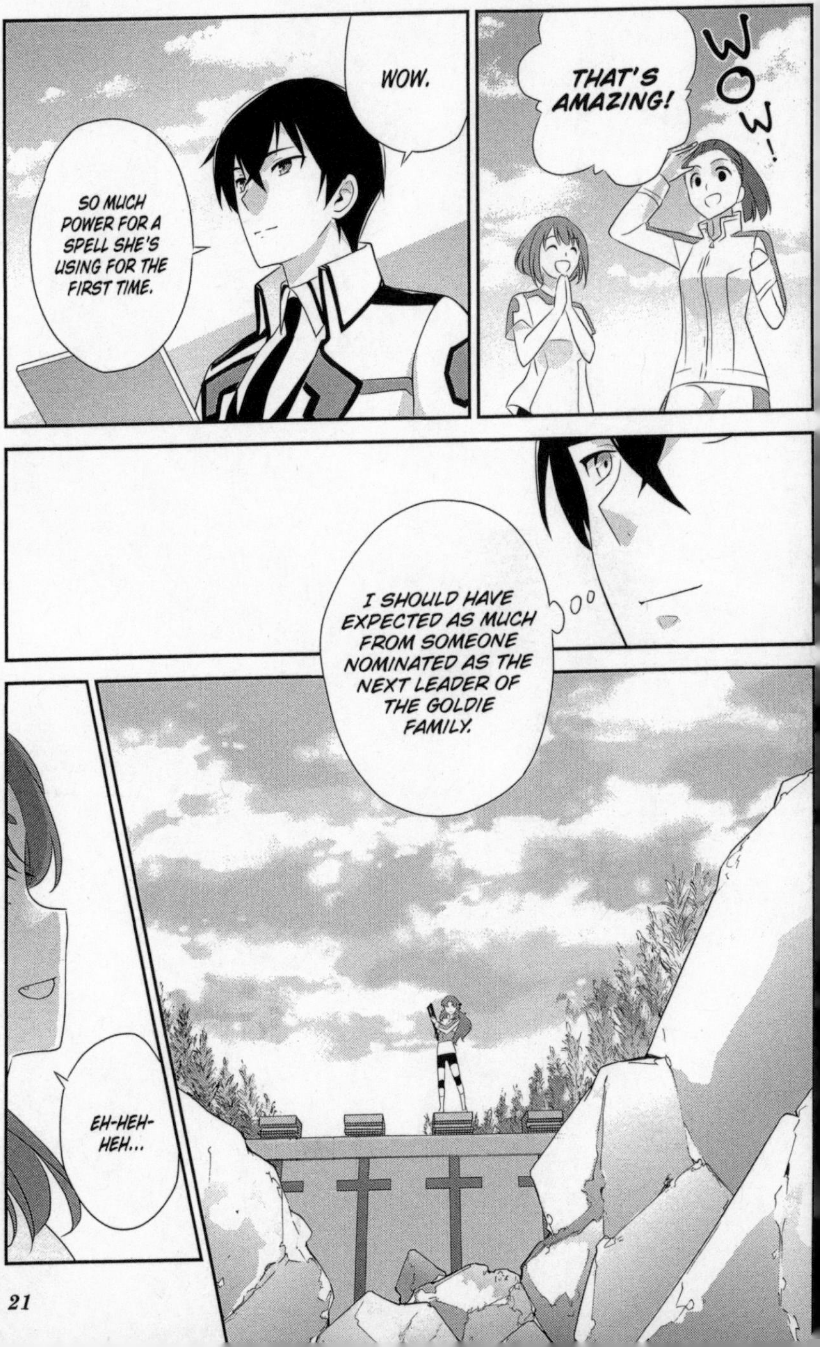
WOW!
THAT'S AMAZING!
WOW.
SO MUCH POWER FOR A SPELL SHE'S USING FOR THE FIRST TIME.
I SHOULD HAVE EXPECTED AS MUCH FROM SOMEONE NOMINATED AS THE NEXT LEADER OF THE GOLDIE FAMILY.
EH-HEH-HEH...

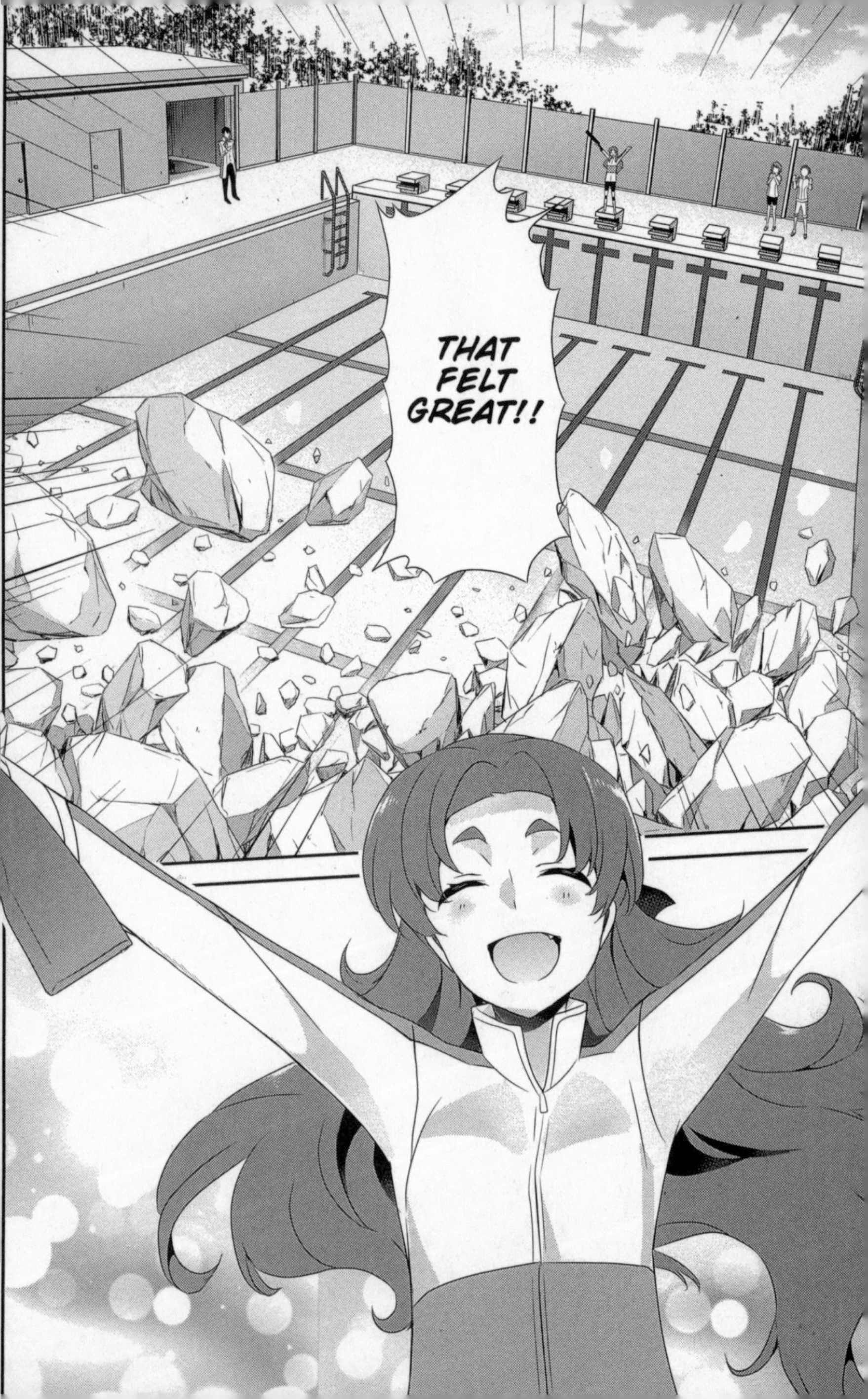
THAT FELT GREAT!!

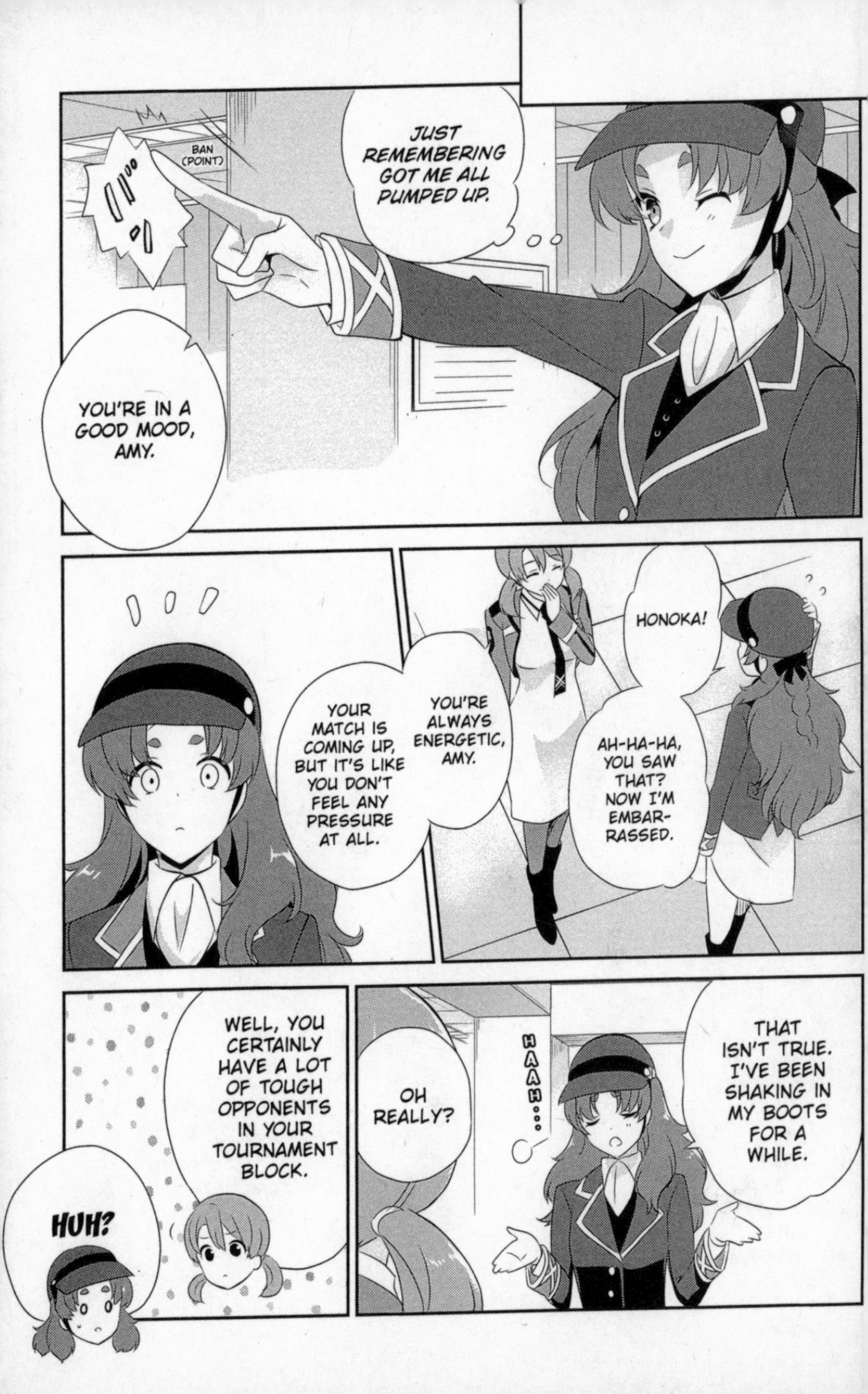
JUST REMEMBERING GOT ME ALL PUMPED UP.
BAN (POINT)
YOU'RE IN A GOOD MOOD, AMY.
HONOKA!
AH-HA-HA, YOU SAW THAT? NOW I'M EMBARRASSED.
YOU'RE ALWAYS ENERGETIC, AMY.
YOUR MATCH IS COMING UP, BUT IT'S LIKE YOU DON'T FEEL ANY PRESSURE AT ALL.
THAT ISN'T TRUE. I'VE BEEN SHAKING IN MY BOOTS FOR A WHILE.
HAAAH...
OH REALLY?
WELL, YOU CERTAINLY HAVE A LOT OF TOUGH OPPONENTS IN YOUR TOURNAMENT BLOCK.
HUH?

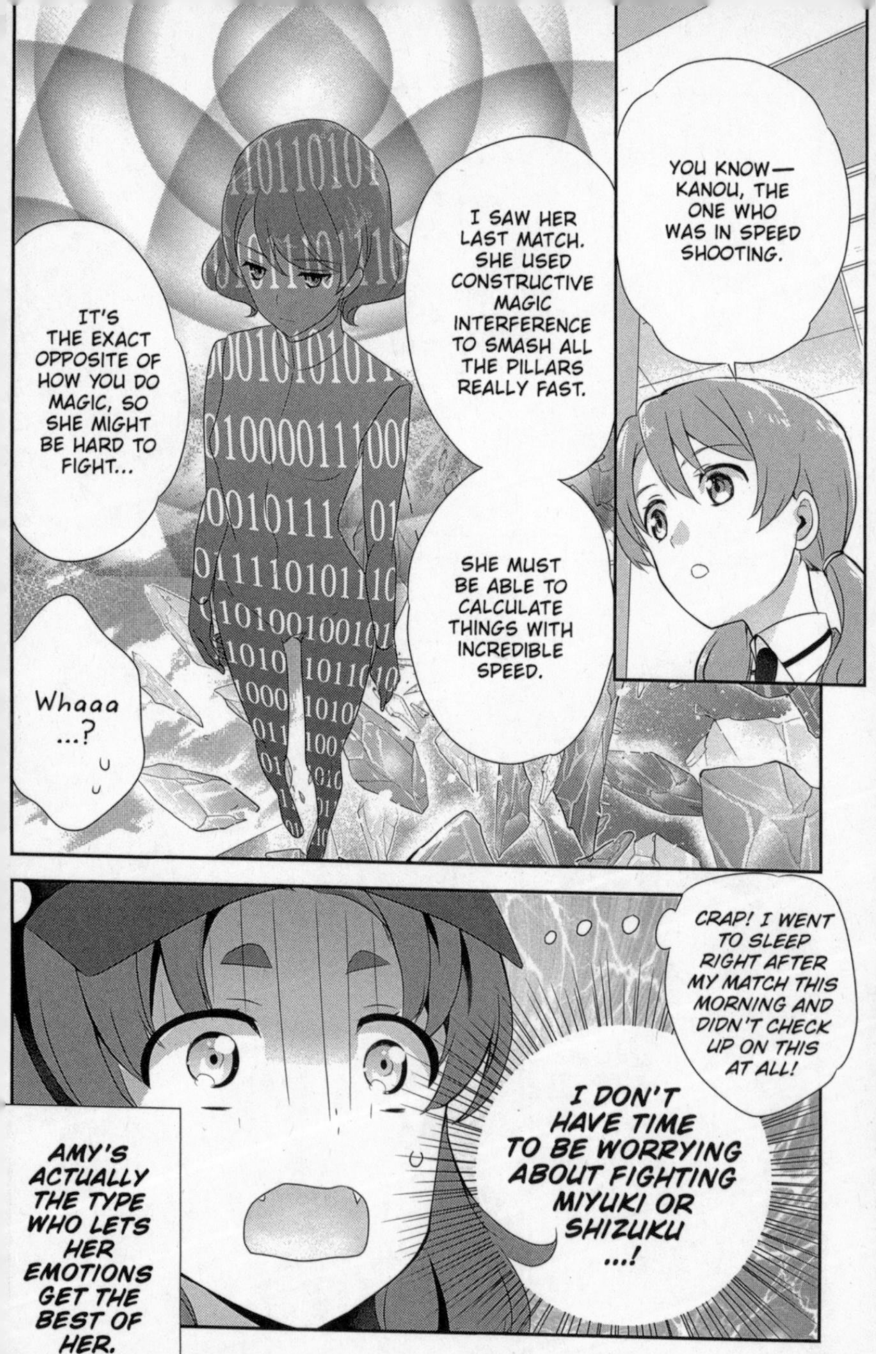
YOU KNOW—KANOU, THE ONE WHO WAS IN SPEED SHOOTING.
I SAW HER LAST MATCH. SHE USED CONSTRUCTIVE MAGIC INTERFERENCE TO SMASH ALL THE PILLARS REALLY FAST.
SHE MUST BE ABLE TO CALCULATE THINGS WITH INCREDIBLE SPEED.
IT'S THE EXACT OPPOSITE OF HOW YOU DO MAGIC, SO SHE MIGHT BE HARD TO FIGHT...
Whaaa ...?
CRAP! I WENT TO SLEEP RIGHT AFTER MY MATCH THIS MORNING AND DIDN'T CHECK UP ON THIS AT ALL!
I DON'T HAVE TIME TO BE WORRYING ABOUT FIGHTING MIYUKI OR SHIZUKU ...!
AMY'S ACTUALLY THE TYPE WHO LETS HER EMOTIONS GET THE BEST OF HER.

THE
HONOR
STUDENT
AT
Magic High
School

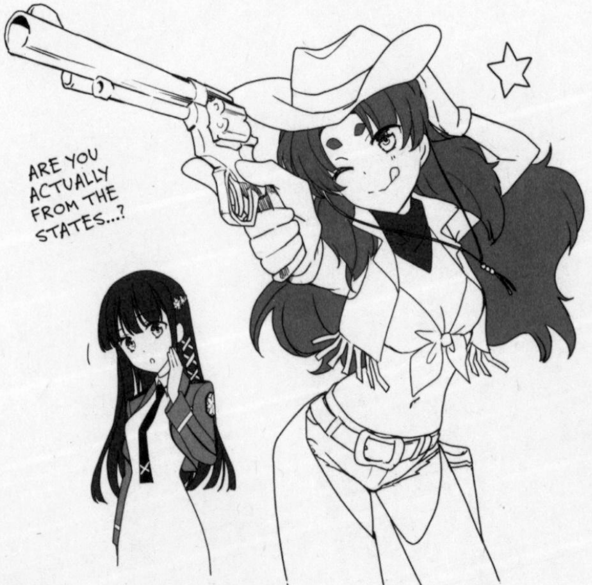
ARE YOU ACTUALLY FROM THE STATES...?

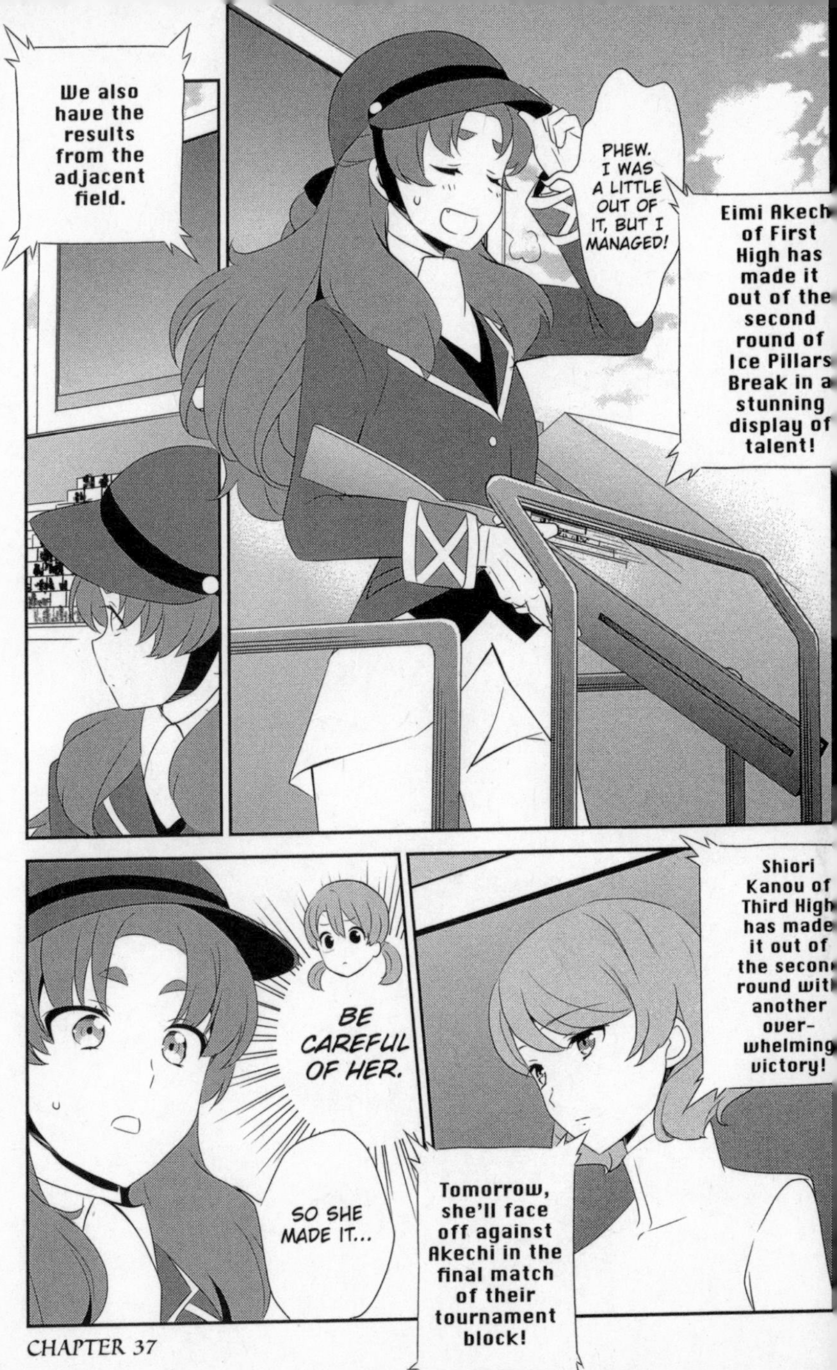
PHEW. I WAS A LITTLE OUT OF IT, BUT I MANAGED!
Eimi Akechi of First High has made it out of the second round of Ice Pillars Break in a stunning display of talent!
We also have the results from the adjacent field.
Shiori Kanou of Third High has made it out of the second round with another over-whelming victory!
Tomorrow, she'll face off against Akechi in the final match of their tournament block!
BE CAREFUL OF HER.
SO SHE MADE IT...

CHAPTER 37

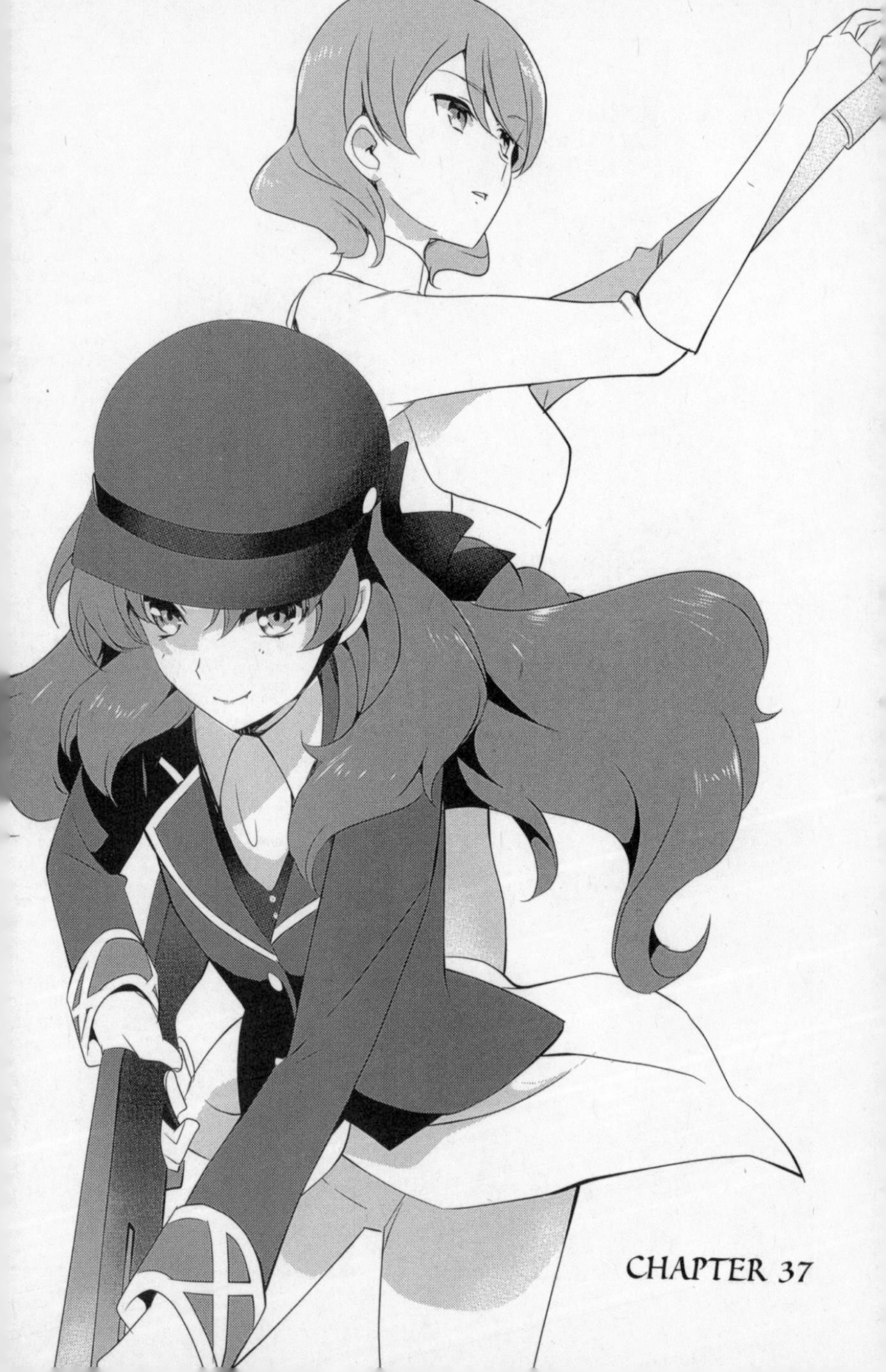

CHAPTER 37

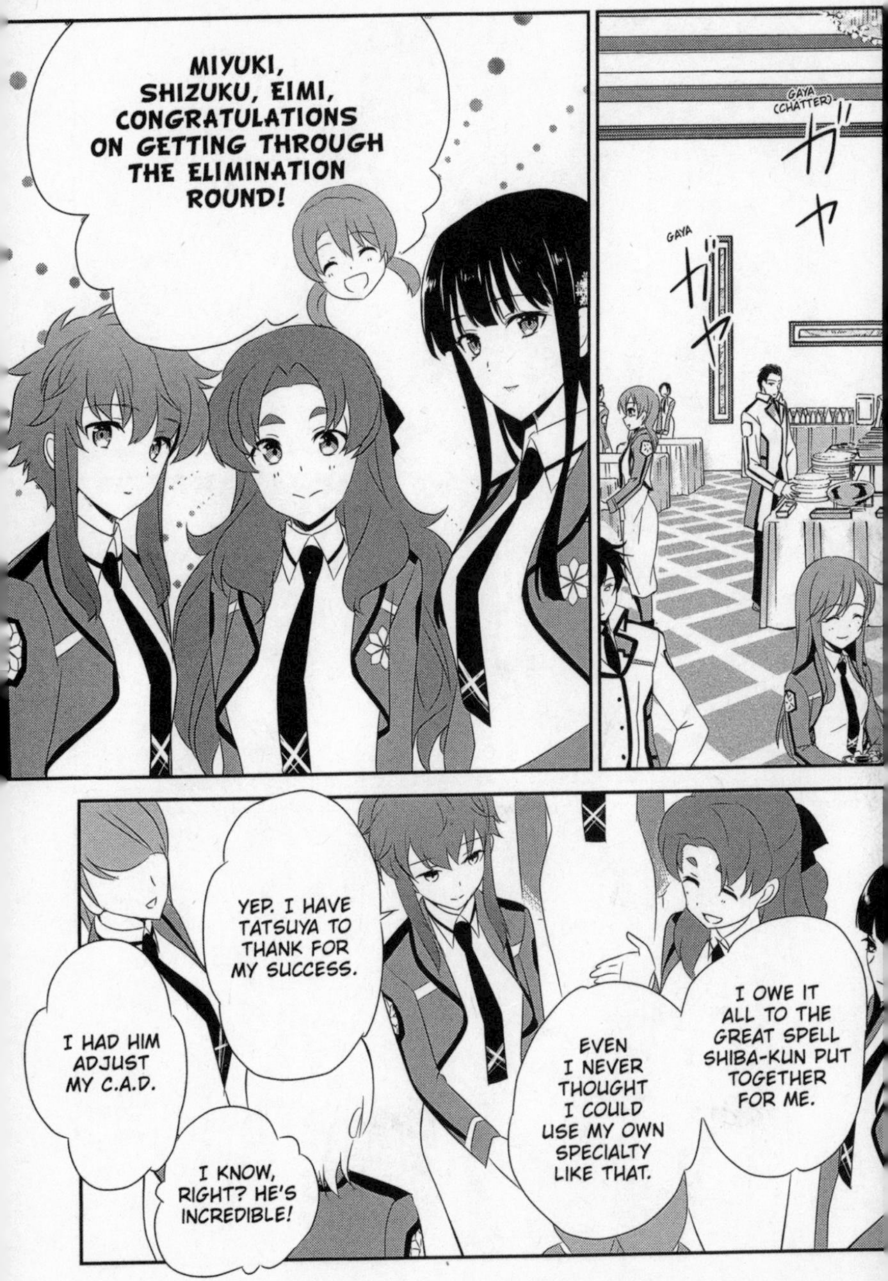
GAYA (CHATTER)
ガヤ
GAYA
ガヤ
MIYUKI, SHIZUKU, EIMI, CONGRATULATIONS ON GETTING THROUGH THE ELIMINATION ROUND!
I OWE IT ALL TO THE GREAT SPELL SHIBA-KUN PUT TOGETHER FOR ME.
EVEN I NEVER THOUGHT I COULD USE MY OWN SPECIALTY LIKE THAT.
YEP. I HAVE TATSUYA TO THANK FOR MY SUCCESS.
I HAD HIM ADJUST MY C.A.D.
I KNOW, RIGHT? HE'S INCREDIBLE!

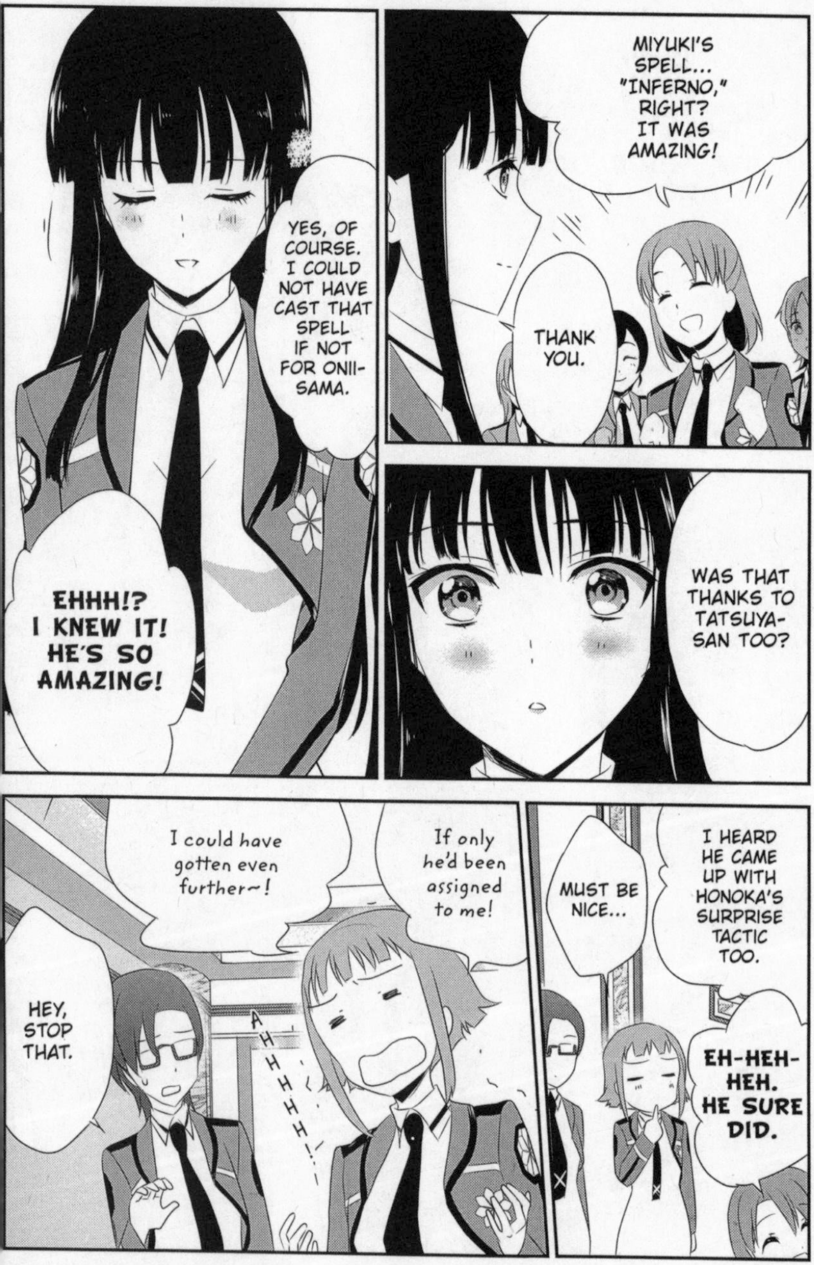
MIYUKI'S SPELL... "INFERNO," RIGHT? IT WAS AMAZING!
THANK YOU.
WAS THAT THANKS TO TATSUYA-SAN TOO?
YES, OF COURSE. I COULD NOT HAVE CAST THAT SPELL IF NOT FOR ONII-SAMA.
EHHH!? I KNEW IT! HE'S SO AMAZING!
I HEARD HE CAME UP WITH HONOKA'S SURPRISE TACTIC TOO.
MUST BE NICE...
EH-HEH-HEH. HE SURE DID.
If only he'd been assigned to me!
I could have gotten even further~!
AHHHHH!
HEY, STOP THAT.

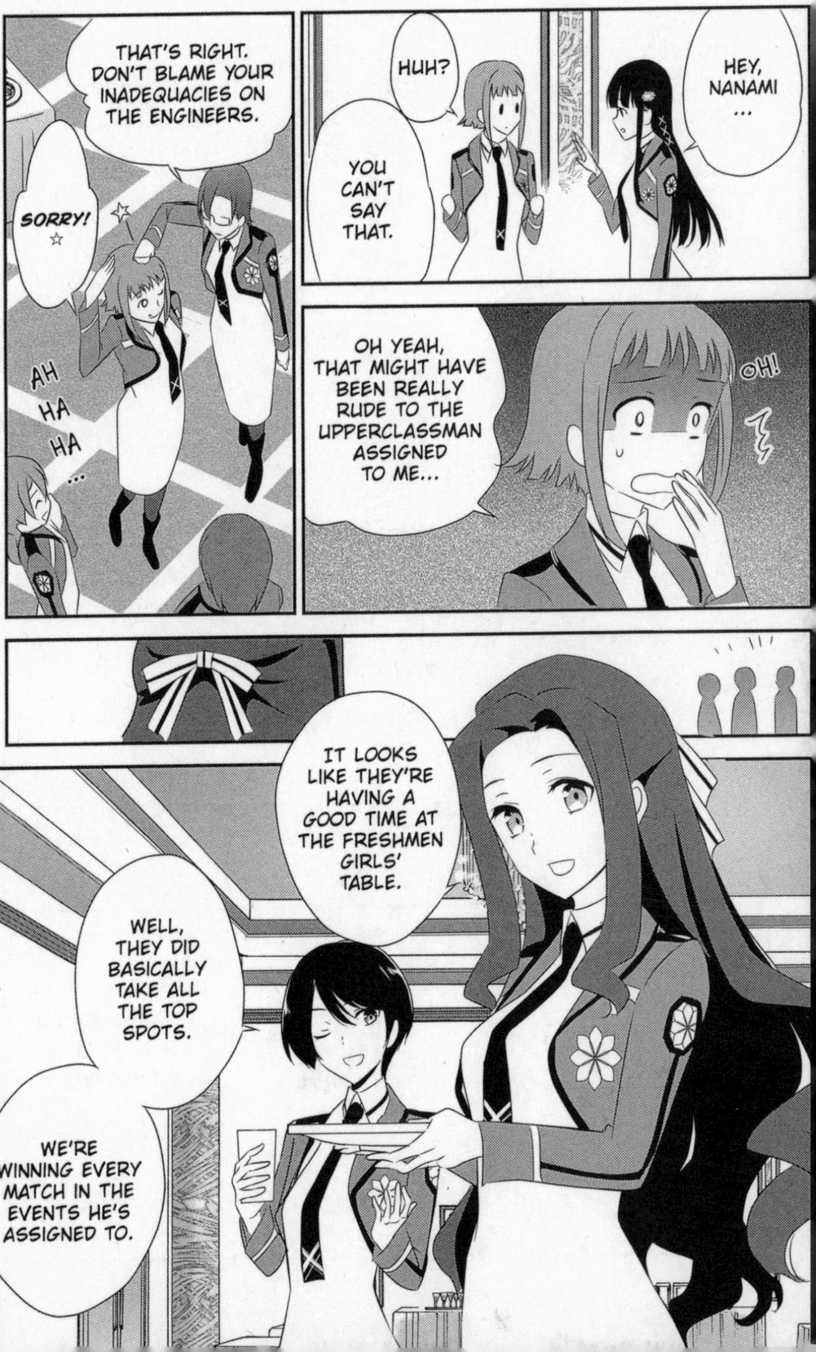
HEY, NANAMI ...
HUH?
YOU CAN'T SAY THAT.
OH!
OH YEAH, THAT MIGHT HAVE BEEN REALLY RUDE TO THE UPPERCLASSMAN ASSIGNED TO ME...
THAT'S RIGHT. DON'T BLAME YOUR INADEQUACIES ON THE ENGINEERS.
SORRY! ☆
AH HA HA ...
IT LOOKS LIKE THEY'RE HAVING A GOOD TIME AT THE FRESHMEN GIRLS' TABLE.
WELL, THEY DID BASICALLY TAKE ALL THE TOP SPOTS.
WE'RE WINNING EVERY MATCH IN THE EVENTS HE'S ASSIGNED TO.

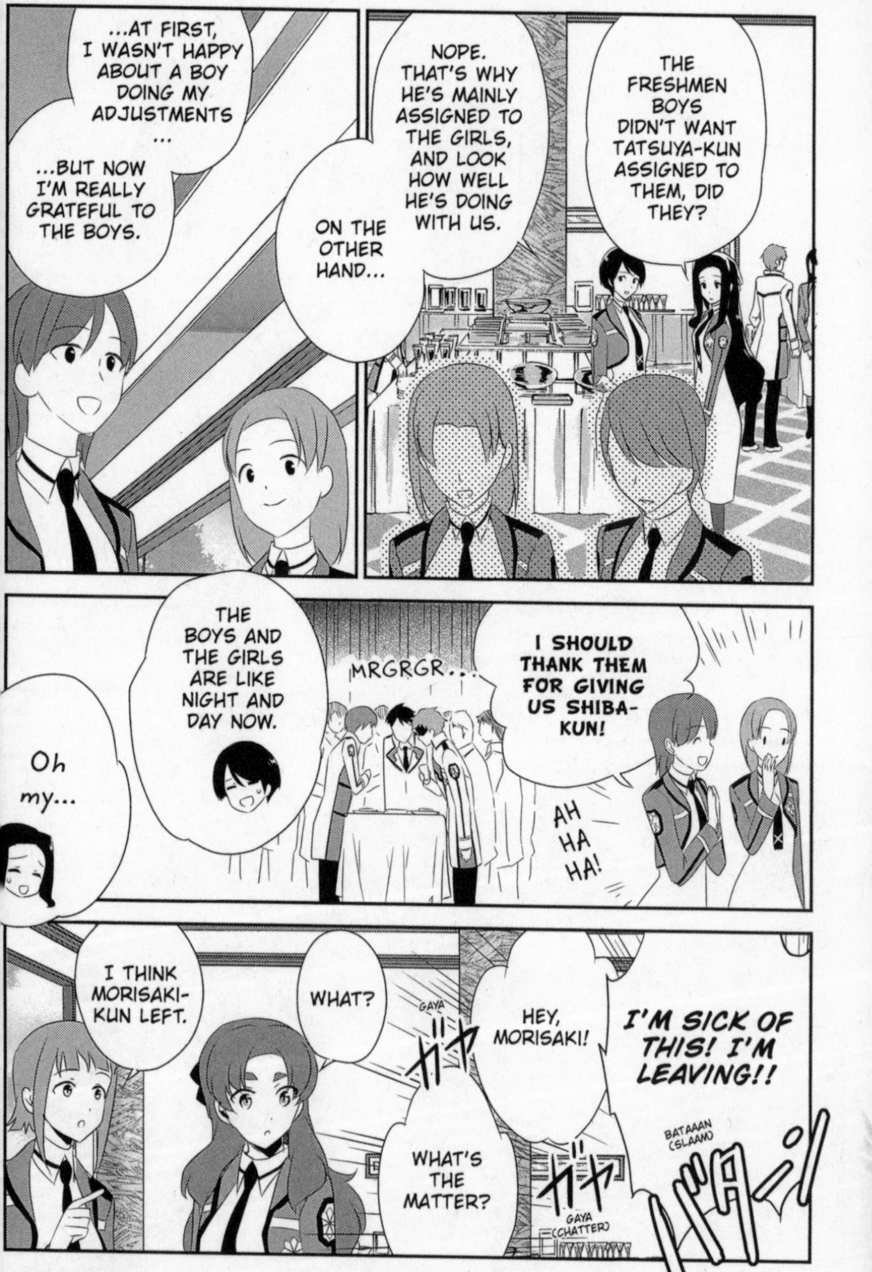
THE FRESHMEN BOYS DIDN'T WANT TATSUYA-KUN ASSIGNED TO THEM, DID THEY?
NOPE. THAT'S WHY HE'S MAINLY ASSIGNED TO THE GIRLS, AND LOOK HOW WELL HE'S DOING WITH US.
ON THE OTHER HAND...
...AT FIRST, I WASN'T HAPPY ABOUT A BOY DOING MY ADJUSTMENTS ...
...BUT NOW I'M REALLY GRATEFUL TO THE BOYS.
I SHOULD THANK THEM FOR GIVING US SHIBA-KUN!
AH HA HA!
MRGRGR...
THE BOYS AND THE GIRLS ARE LIKE NIGHT AND DAY NOW.
Oh my...
BATAAAN (SLAAM)
I'M SICK OF THIS! I'M LEAVING!!
HEY, MORISAKI!
GAYA
WHAT'S THE MATTER?
GAYA (CHATTER)
WHAT?
I THINK MORISAKI-KUN LEFT.

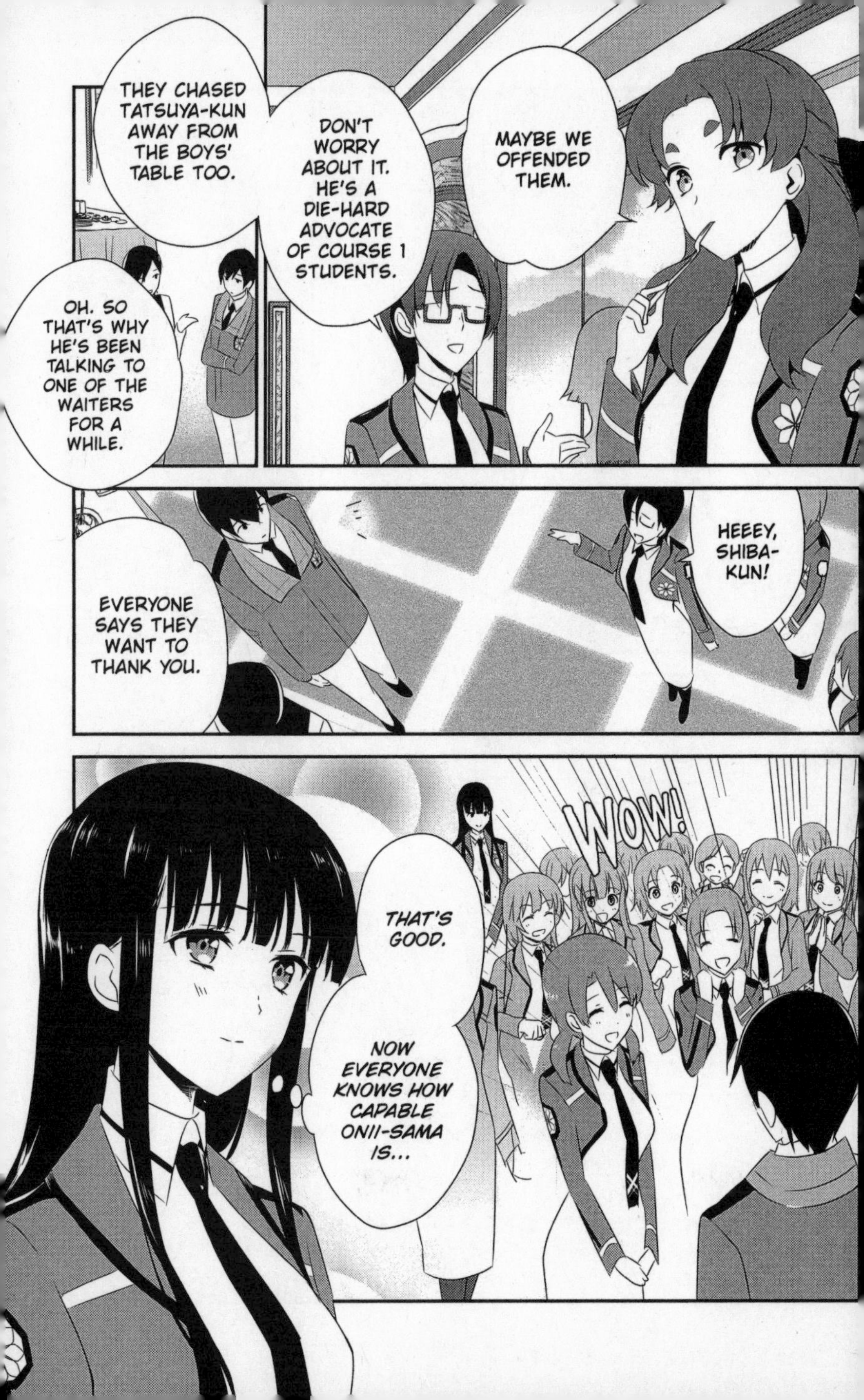
MAYBE WE OFFENDED THEM.
DON'T WORRY ABOUT IT. HE'S A DIE-HARD ADVOCATE OF COURSE 1 STUDENTS.
THEY CHASED TATSUYA-KUN AWAY FROM THE BOYS' TABLE TOO.
OH. SO THAT'S WHY HE'S BEEN TALKING TO ONE OF THE WAITERS FOR A WHILE.
HEEEY, SHIBA-KUN!
EVERYONE SAYS THEY WANT TO THANK YOU.
WOW!
THAT'S GOOD.
NOW EVERYONE KNOWS HOW CAPABLE ONII-SAMA IS...

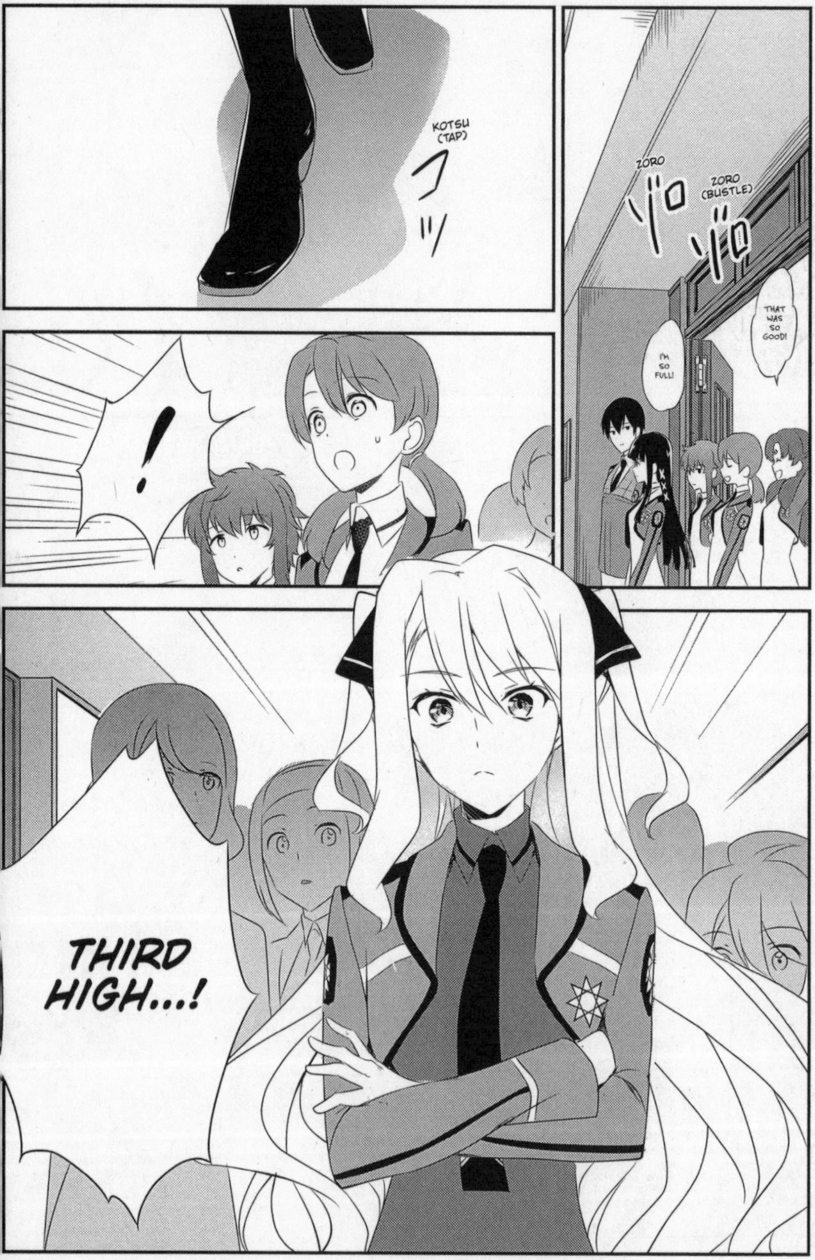
ZORO (BUSTLE)
ZORO
THAT WAS SO GOOD!
I'M SO FULL!
KOTSU (TAP)
!
THIRD HIGH...!

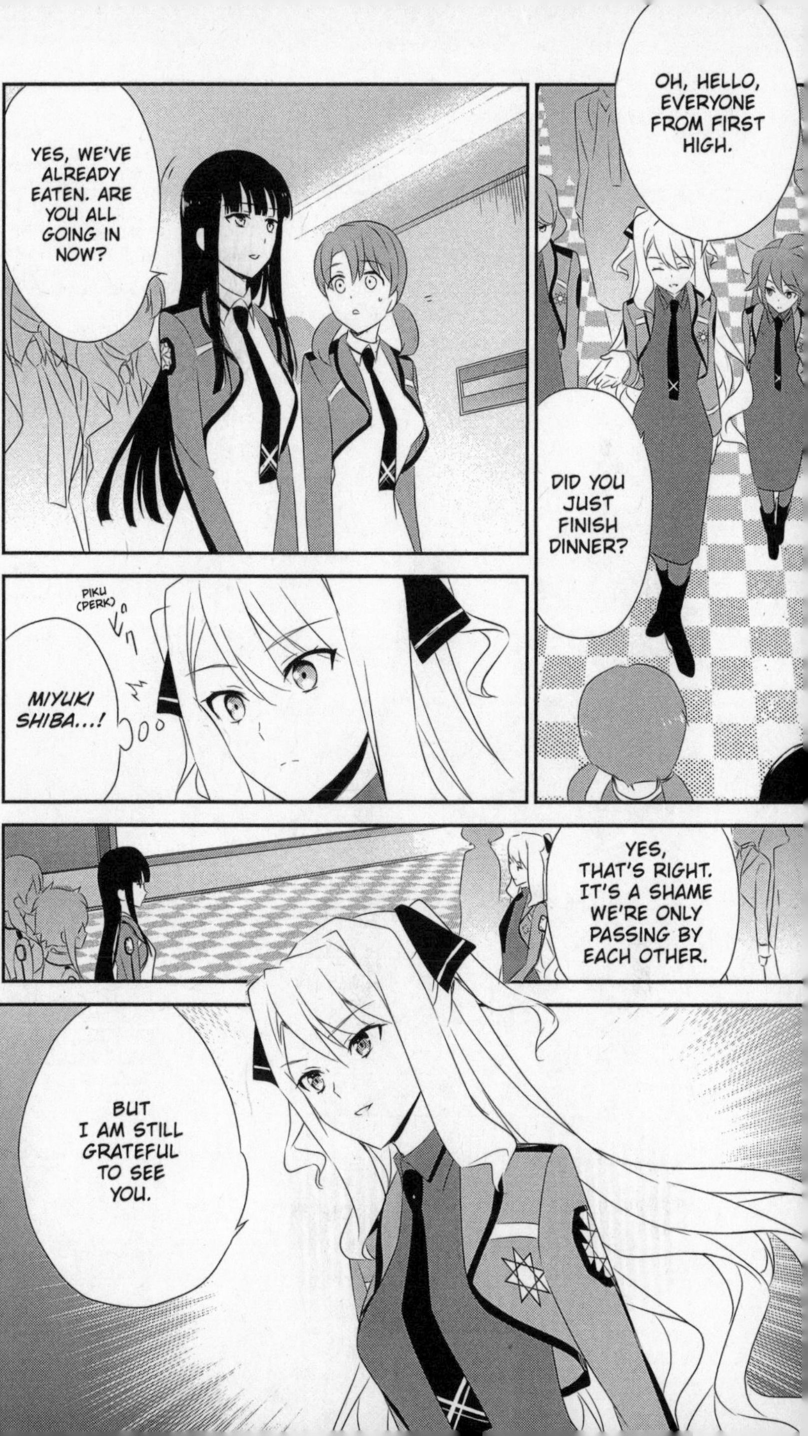
OH, HELLO, EVERYONE FROM FIRST HIGH.
DID YOU JUST FINISH DINNER?
YES, WE'VE ALREADY EATEN. ARE YOU ALL GOING IN NOW?
PIKU (PERK)
MIYUKI SHIBA...!
YES, THAT'S RIGHT. IT'S A SHAME WE'RE ONLY PASSING BY EACH OTHER.
BUT I AM STILL GRATEFUL TO SEE YOU.

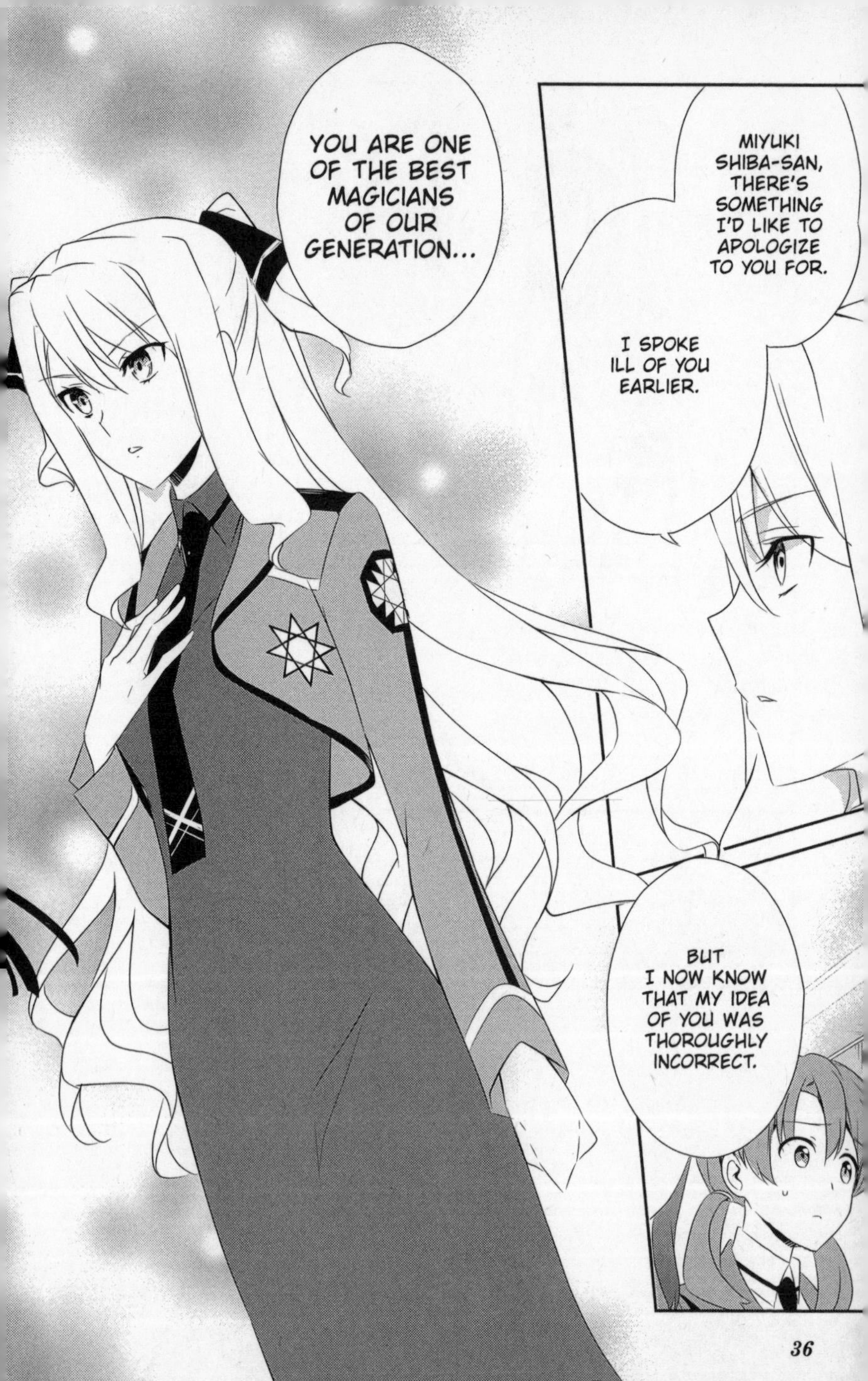
MIYUKI SHIBA-SAN, THERE'S SOMETHING I'D LIKE TO APOLOGIZE TO YOU FOR.
I SPOKE ILL OF YOU EARLIER.
BUT I NOW KNOW THAT MY IDEA OF YOU WAS THOROUGHLY INCORRECT.
YOU ARE ONE OF THE BEST MAGICIANS OF OUR GENERATION...

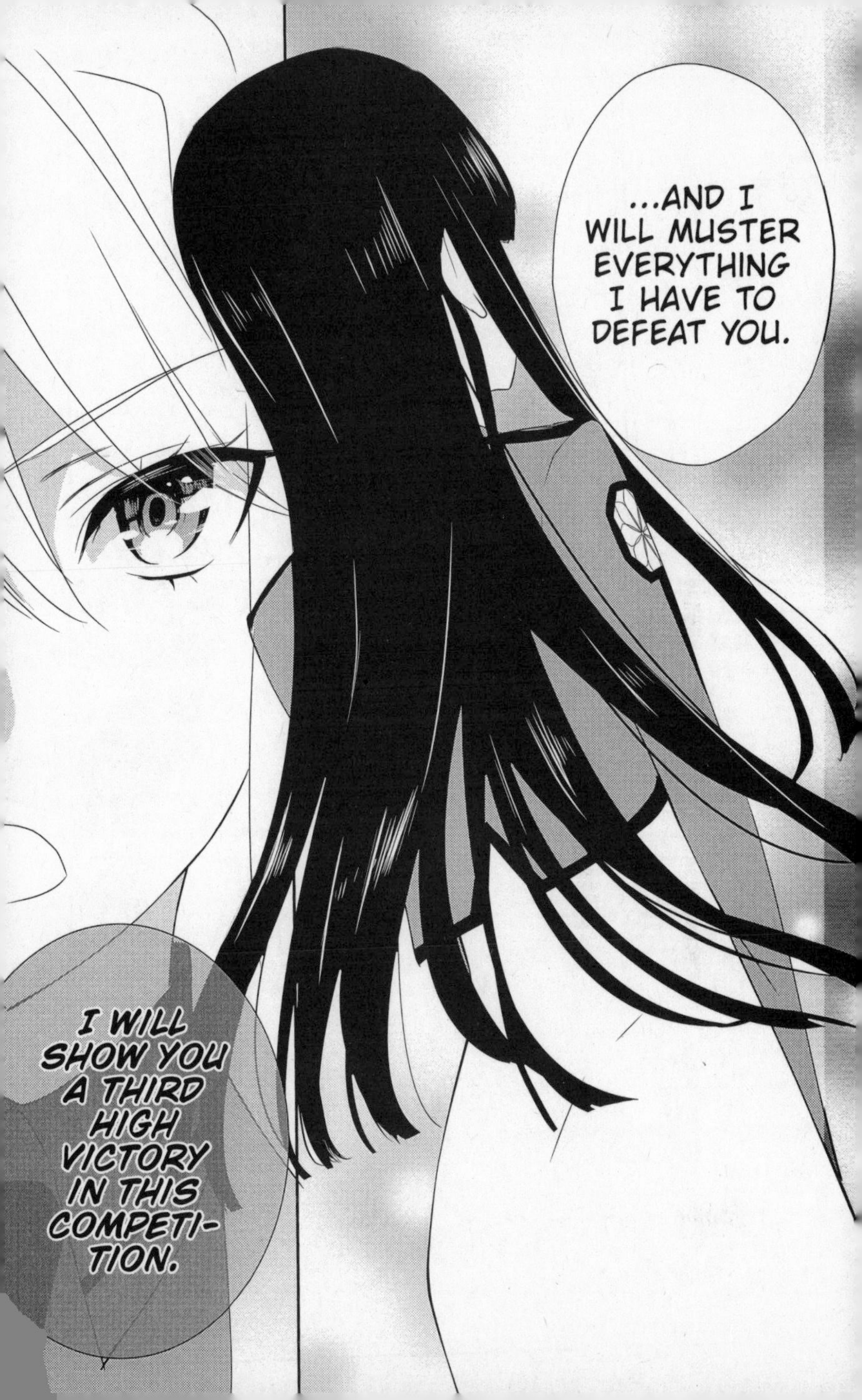
...AND I WILL MUSTER EVERYTHING I HAVE TO DEFEAT YOU.
I WILL SHOW YOU A THIRD HIGH VICTORY IN THIS COMPETI-TION.

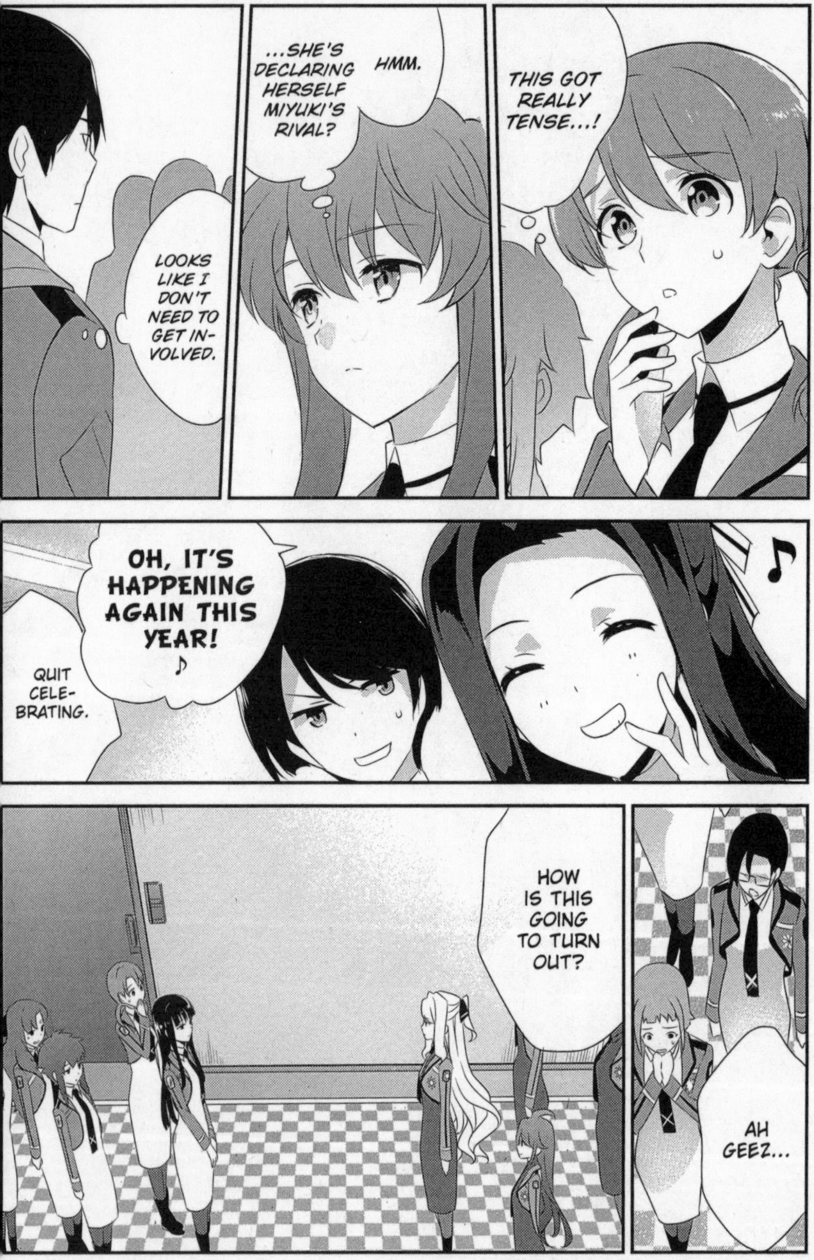
THIS GOT REALLY TENSE...!
HMM.
...SHE'S DECLARING HERSELF MIYUKI'S RIVAL?
LOOKS LIKE I DON'T NEED TO GET INVOLVED.
OH, IT'S HAPPENING AGAIN THIS YEAR! ♪
QUIT CELEBRATING.
AH GEEZ...
HOW IS THIS GOING TO TURN OUT?

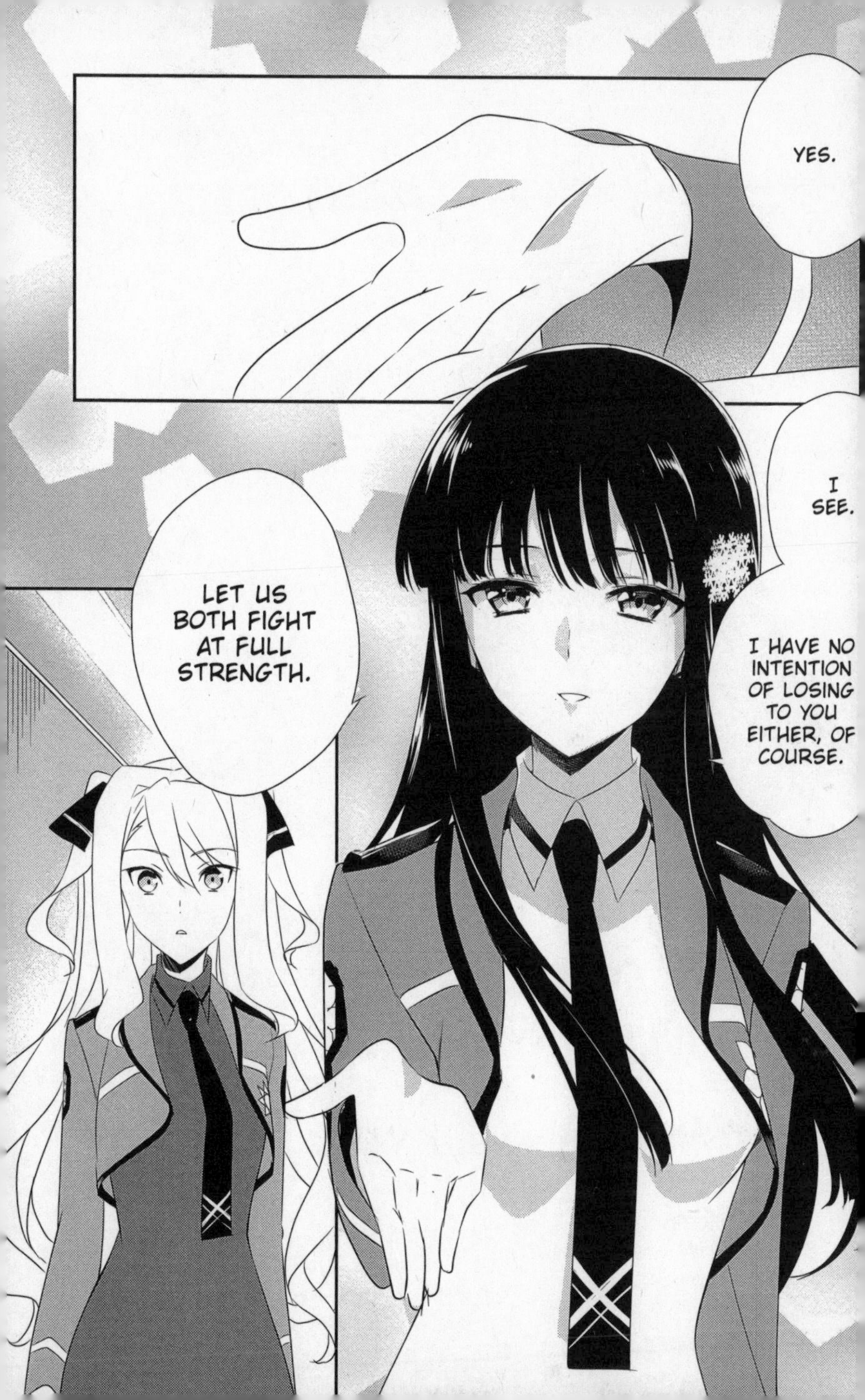
YES.
I SEE.
I HAVE NO INTENTION OF LOSING TO YOU EITHER, OF COURSE.
LET US BOTH FIGHT AT FULL STRENGTH.

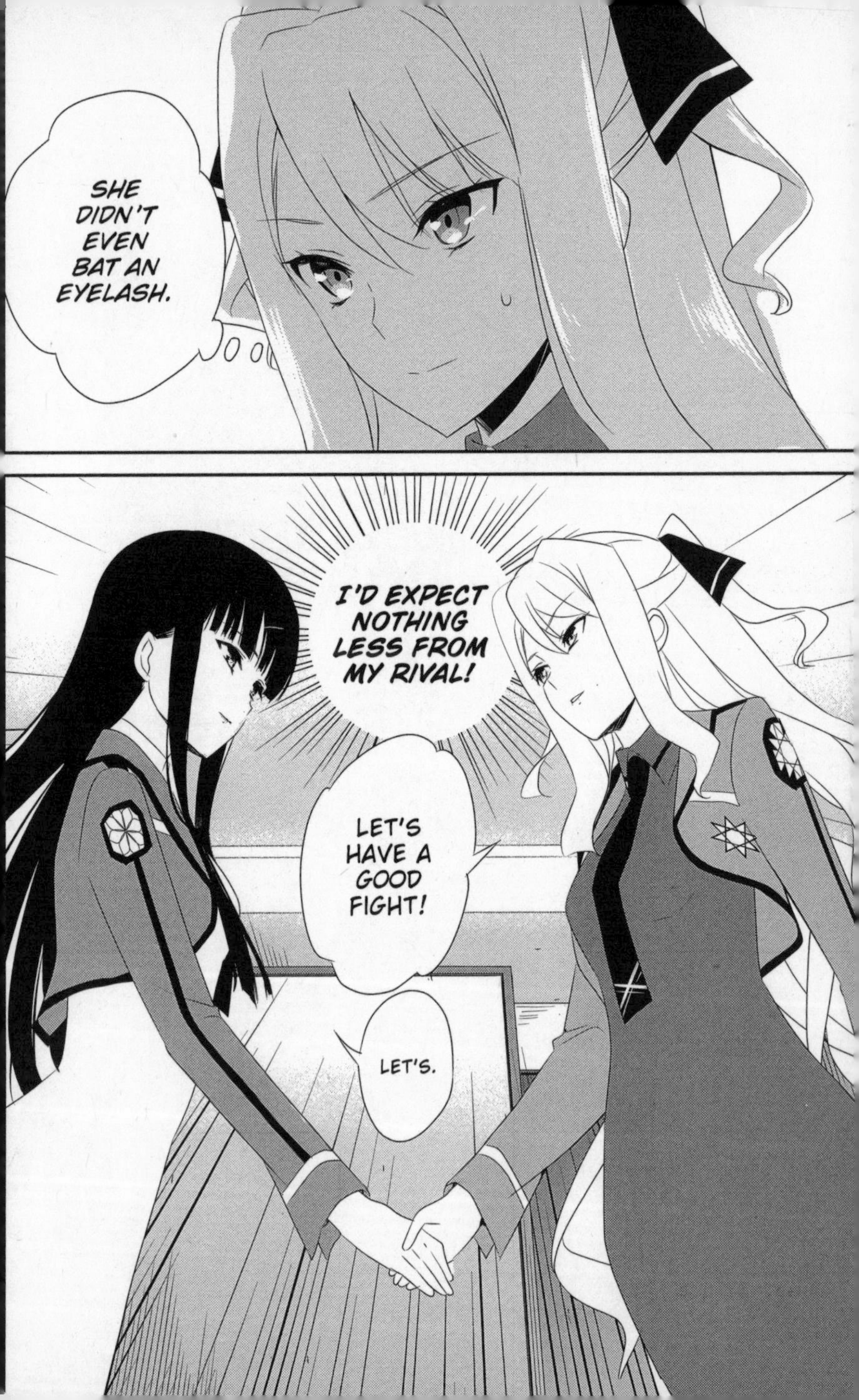
SHE DIDN'T EVEN BAT AN EYELASH.
I'D EXPECT NOTHING LESS FROM MY RIVAL!
LET'S HAVE A GOOD FIGHT!
LET'S.

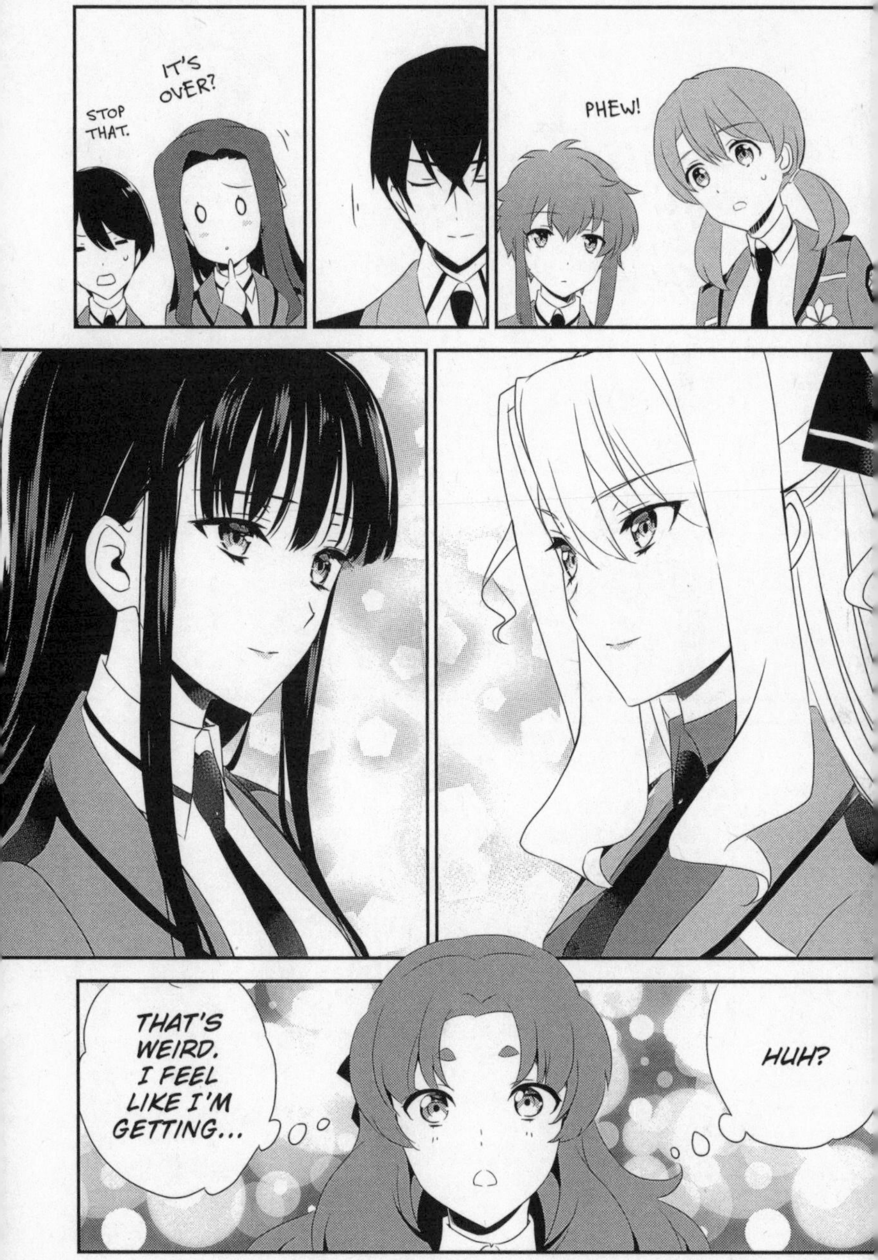
PHEW!
IT'S OVER?
STOP THAT.
HUH?
THAT'S WEIRD. I FEEL LIKE I'M GETTING...

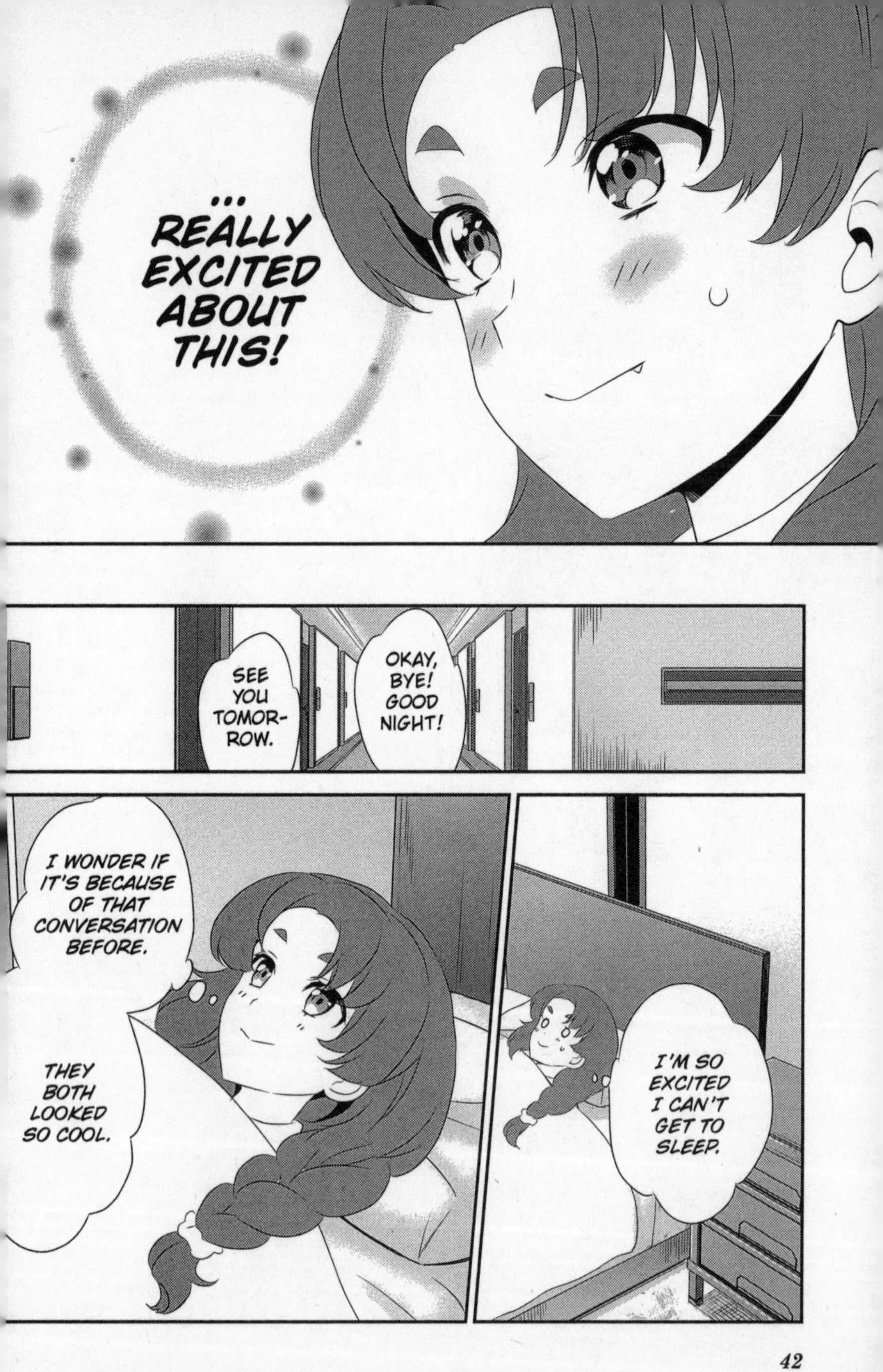
...REALLY EXCITED ABOUT THIS!
OKAY, BYE! GOOD NIGHT!
SEE YOU TOMOR-ROW.
I'M SO EXCITED I CAN'T GET TO SLEEP.
I WONDER IF IT'S BECAUSE OF THAT CONVERSATION BEFORE.
THEY BOTH LOOKED SO COOL.

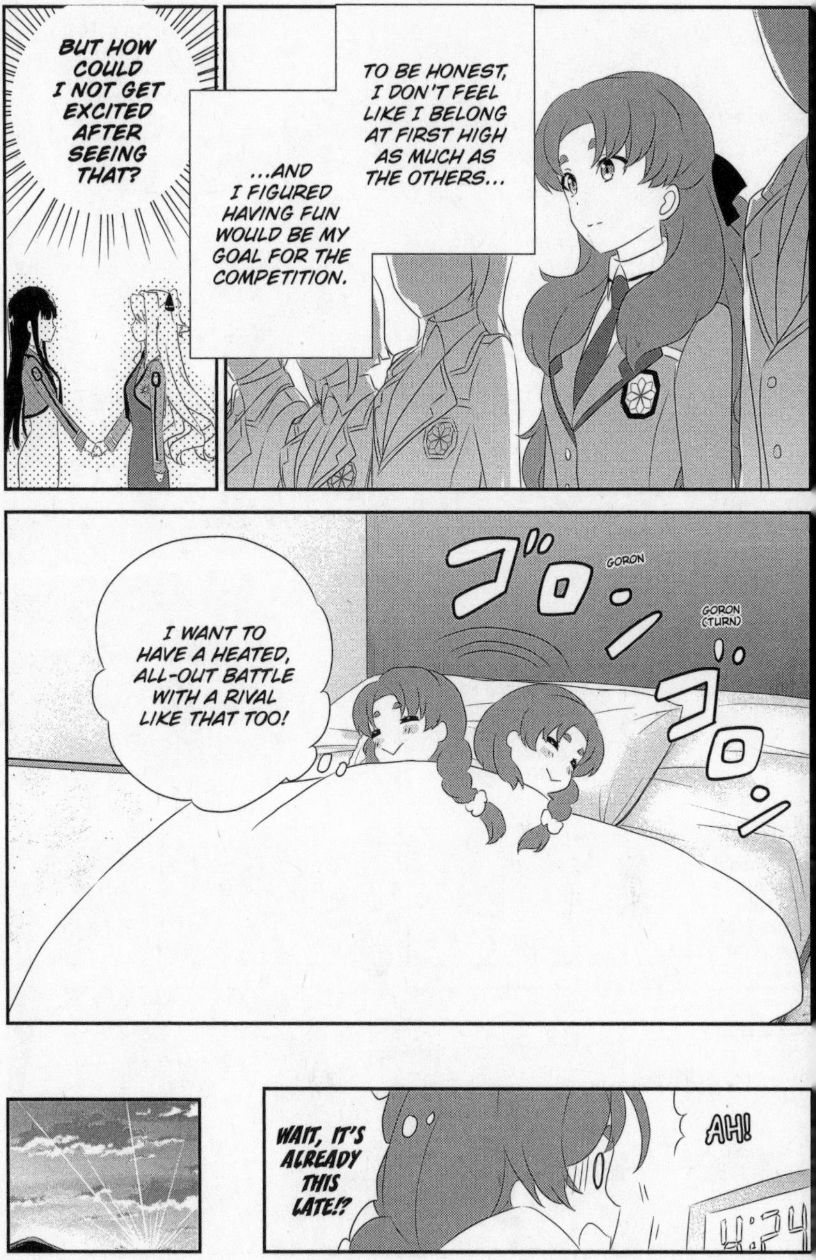
TO BE HONEST, I DON'T FEEL LIKE I BELONG AT FIRST HIGH AS MUCH AS THE OTHERS...
...AND I FIGURED HAVING FUN WOULD BE MY GOAL FOR THE COMPETITION.
BUT HOW COULD I NOT GET EXCITED AFTER SEEING THAT?
ゴロン
GORON
ゴロン
GORON (TURN)
I WANT TO HAVE A HEATED, ALL-OUT BATTLE WITH A RIVAL LIKE THAT TOO!
AH!
WAIT, IT'S ALREADY THIS LATE!?
4:24

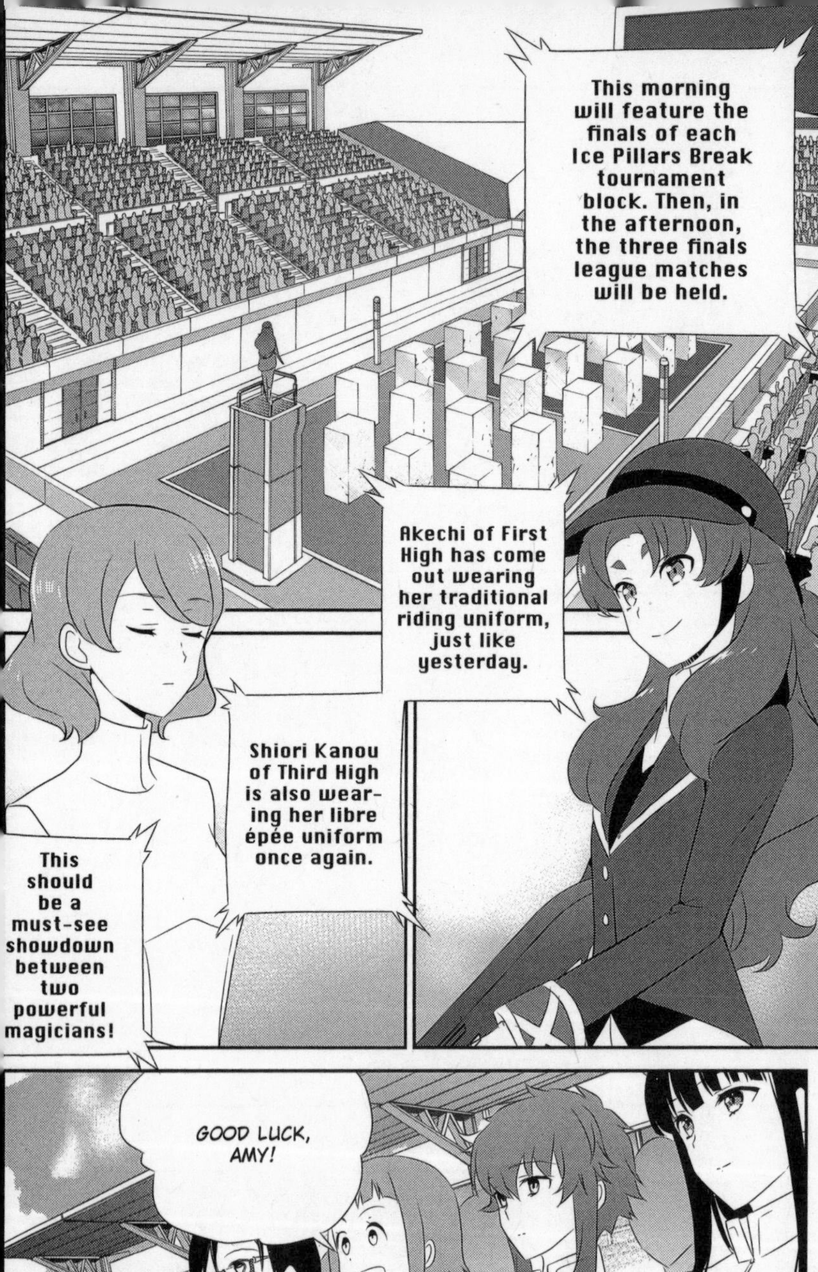
This morning will feature the finals of each Ice Pillars Break tournament block. Then, in the afternoon, the three finals league matches will be held.
Akechi of First High has come out wearing her traditional riding uniform, just like yesterday.
Shiori Kanou of Third High is also wear-ing her libre épée uniform once again.
This should be a must-see showdown between two powerful magicians!
GOOD LUCK, AMY!

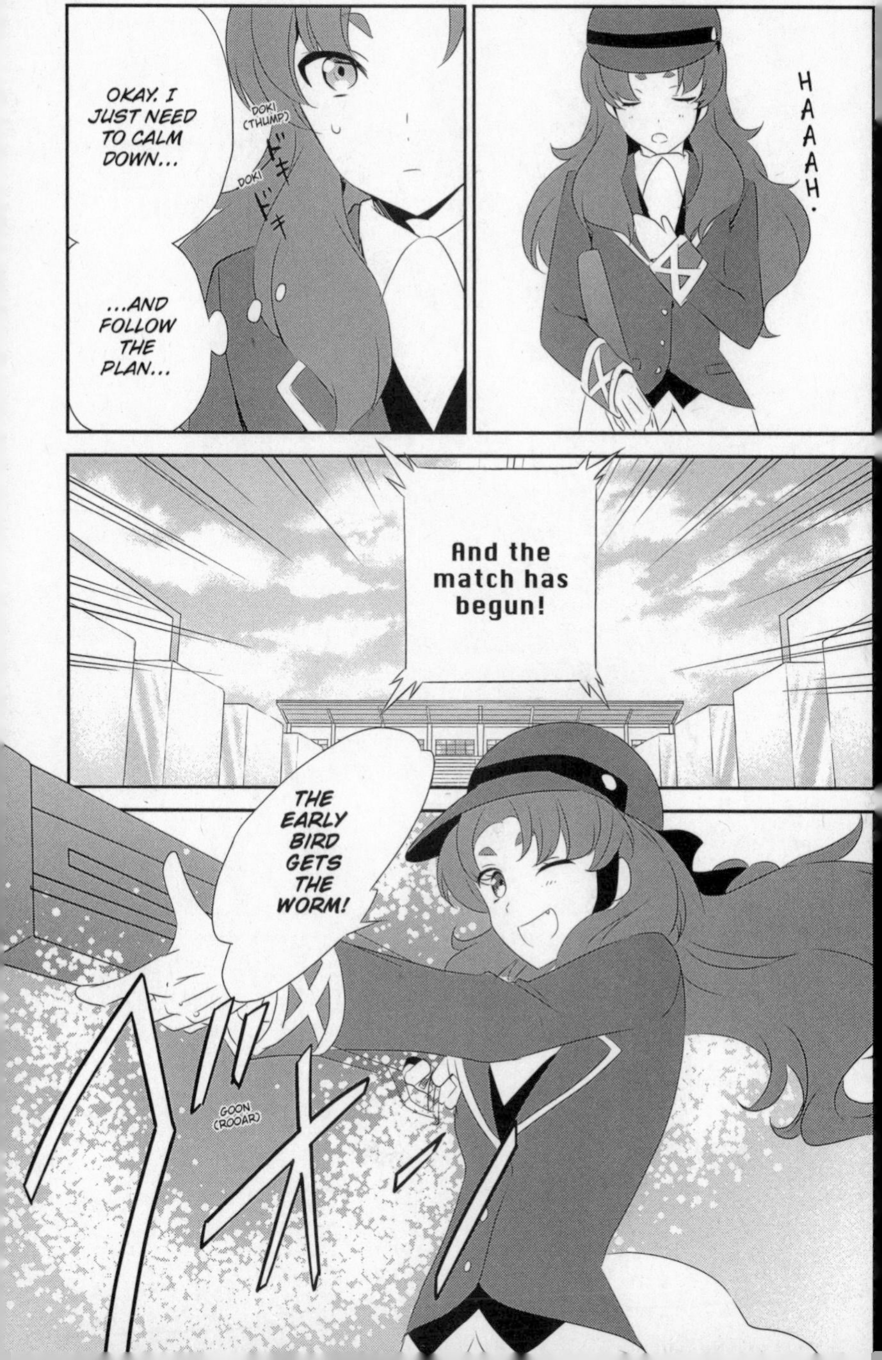
HAAAAH.
OKAY. I JUST NEED TO CALM DOWN...
DOKI (THUMP)
DOKI
...AND FOLLOW THE PLAN...
And the match has begun!
THE EARLY BIRD GETS THE WORM!
GOON (ROOAR)

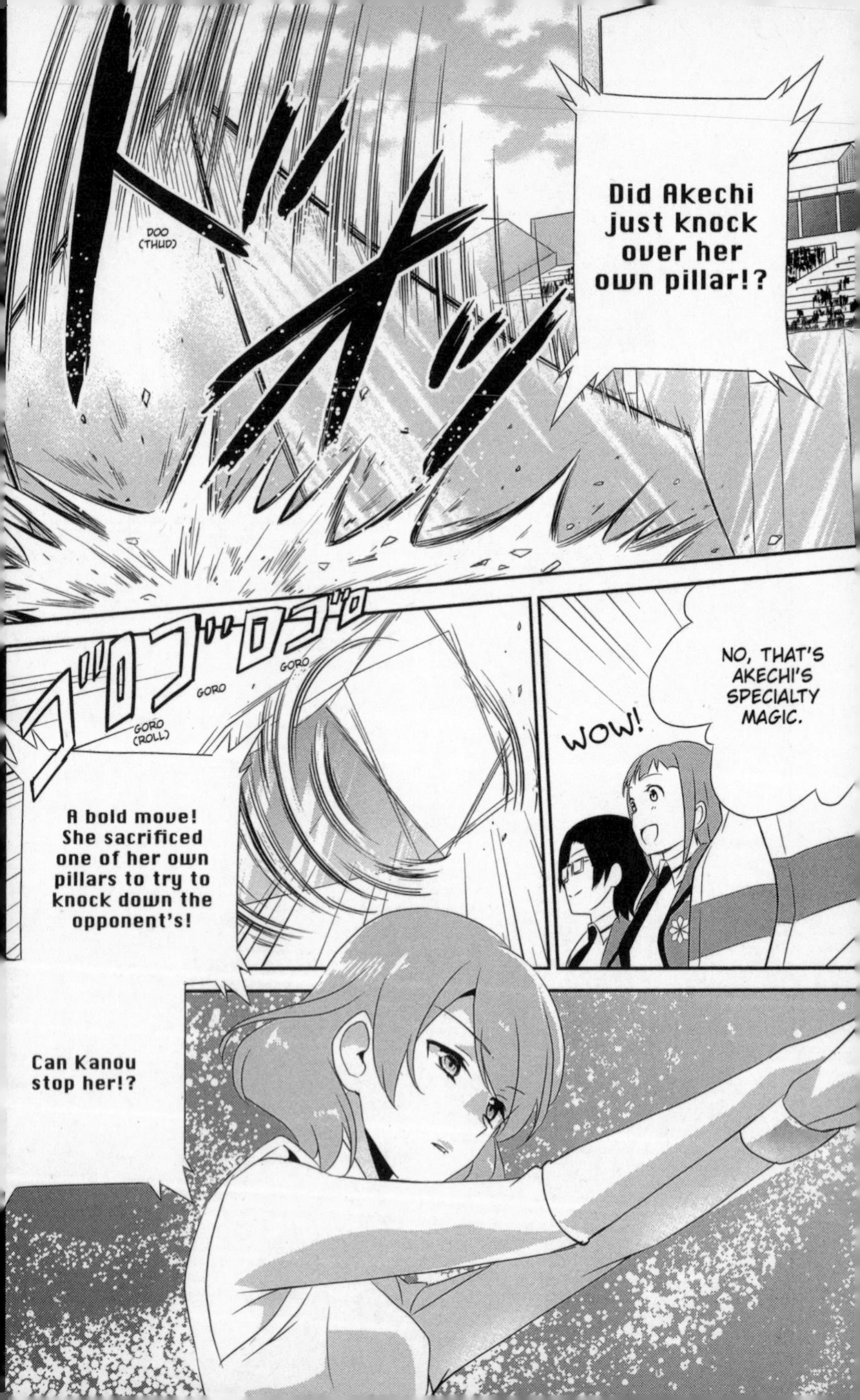
Did Akechi just knock over her own pillar!?
DOO (THUD)
NO, THAT'S AKECHI'S SPECIALTY MAGIC.
WOW!
GORO
GORO
GORO (ROLL)
A bold move! She sacrificed one of her own pillars to try to knock down the opponent's!
Can Kanou stop her!?

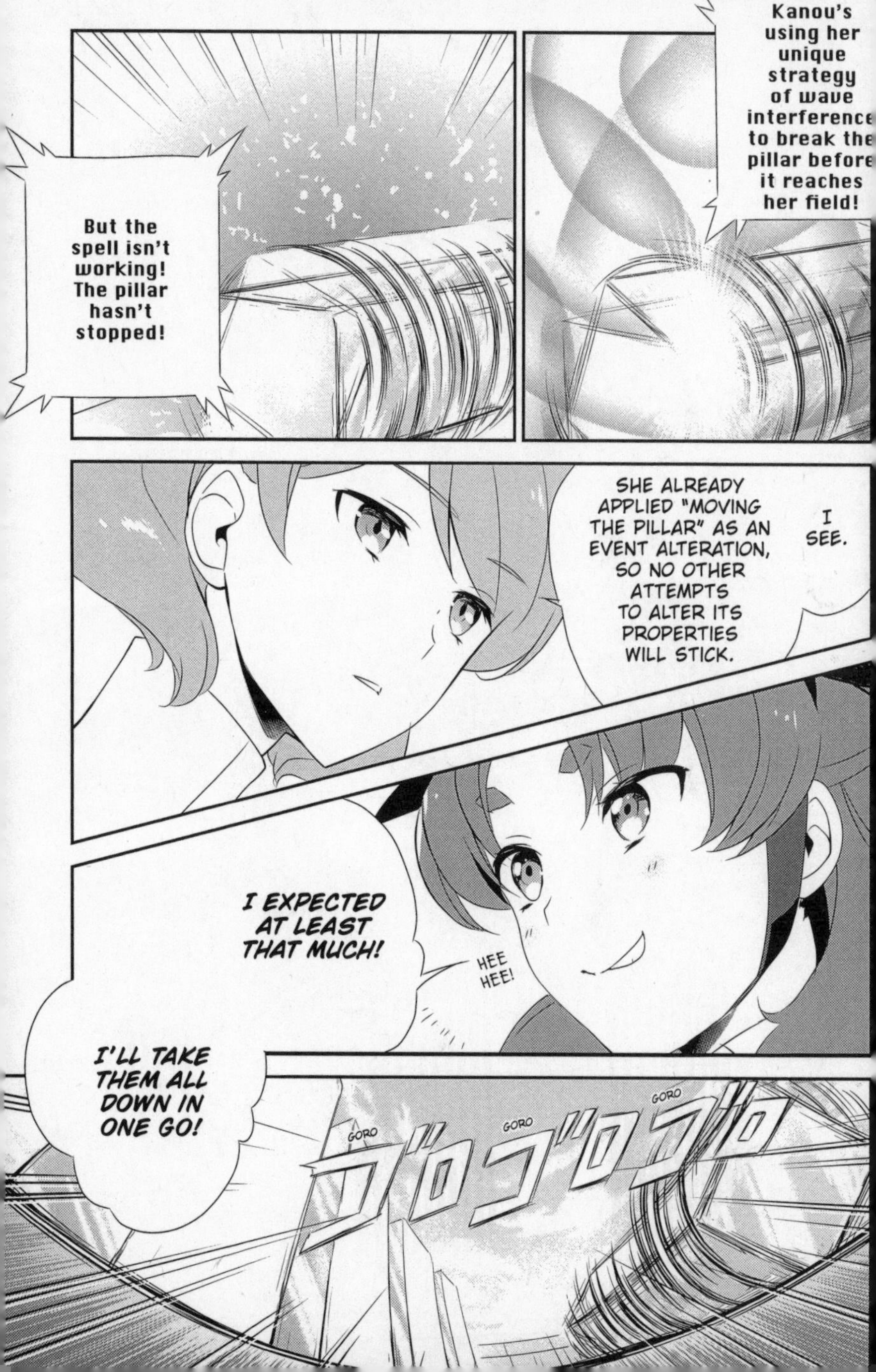
Kanou's using her unique strategy of wave interference to break the pillar before it reaches her field!
But the spell isn't working! The pillar hasn't stopped!
I SEE.
SHE ALREADY APPLIED "MOVING THE PILLAR" AS AN EVENT ALTERATION, SO NO OTHER ATTEMPTS TO ALTER ITS PROPERTIES WILL STICK.
I EXPECTED AT LEAST THAT MUCH!
HEE HEE!
I'LL TAKE THEM ALL DOWN IN ONE GO!
ゴロゴロゴロ
GORO GORO GORO

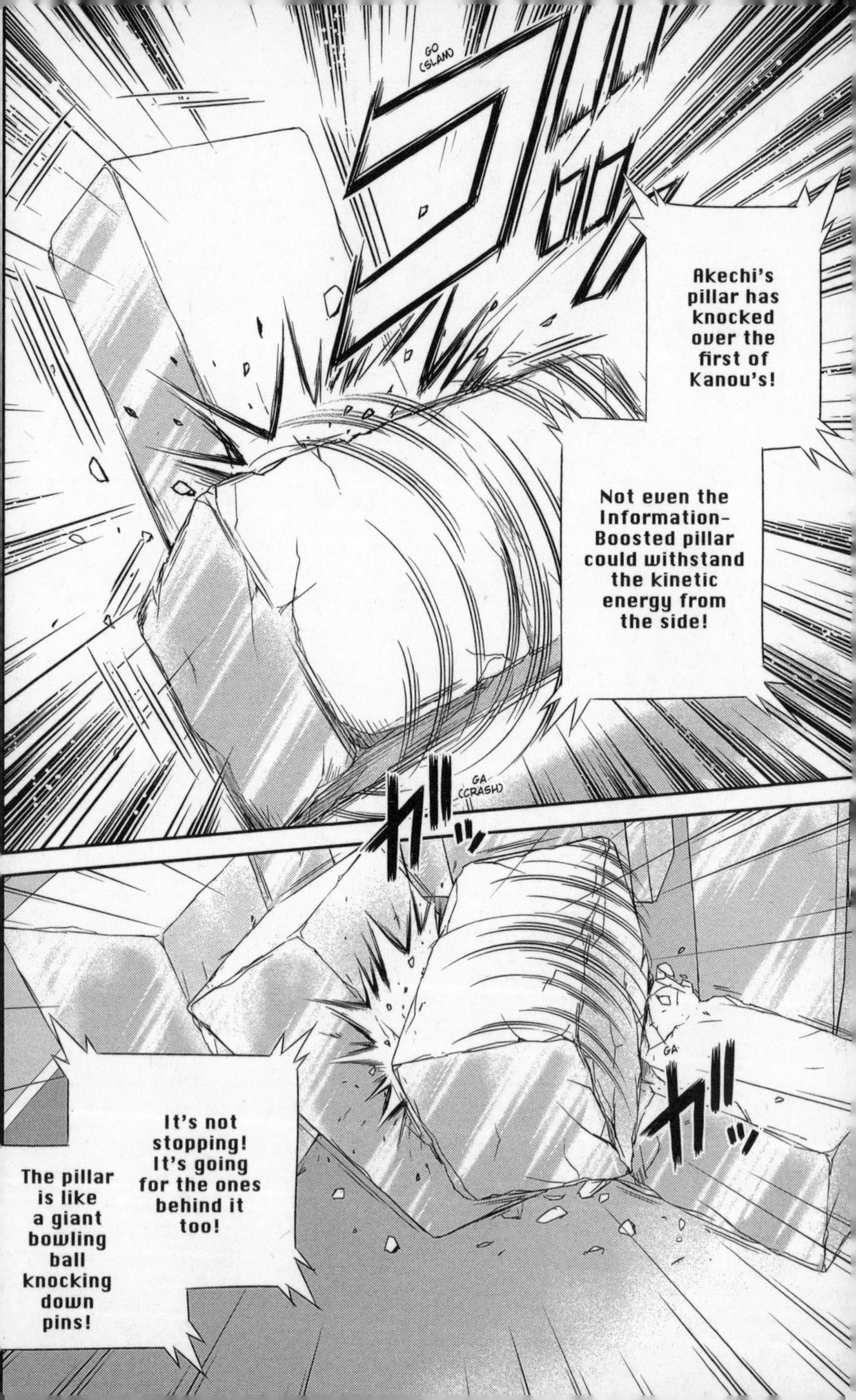
GO (SLAM)
Akechi's pillar has knocked over the first of Kanou's!
Not even the Information-Boosted pillar could withstand the kinetic energy from the side!
GA (CRASH)
GA
It's not stopping! It's going for the ones behind it too!
The pillar is like a giant bowling ball knocking down pins!

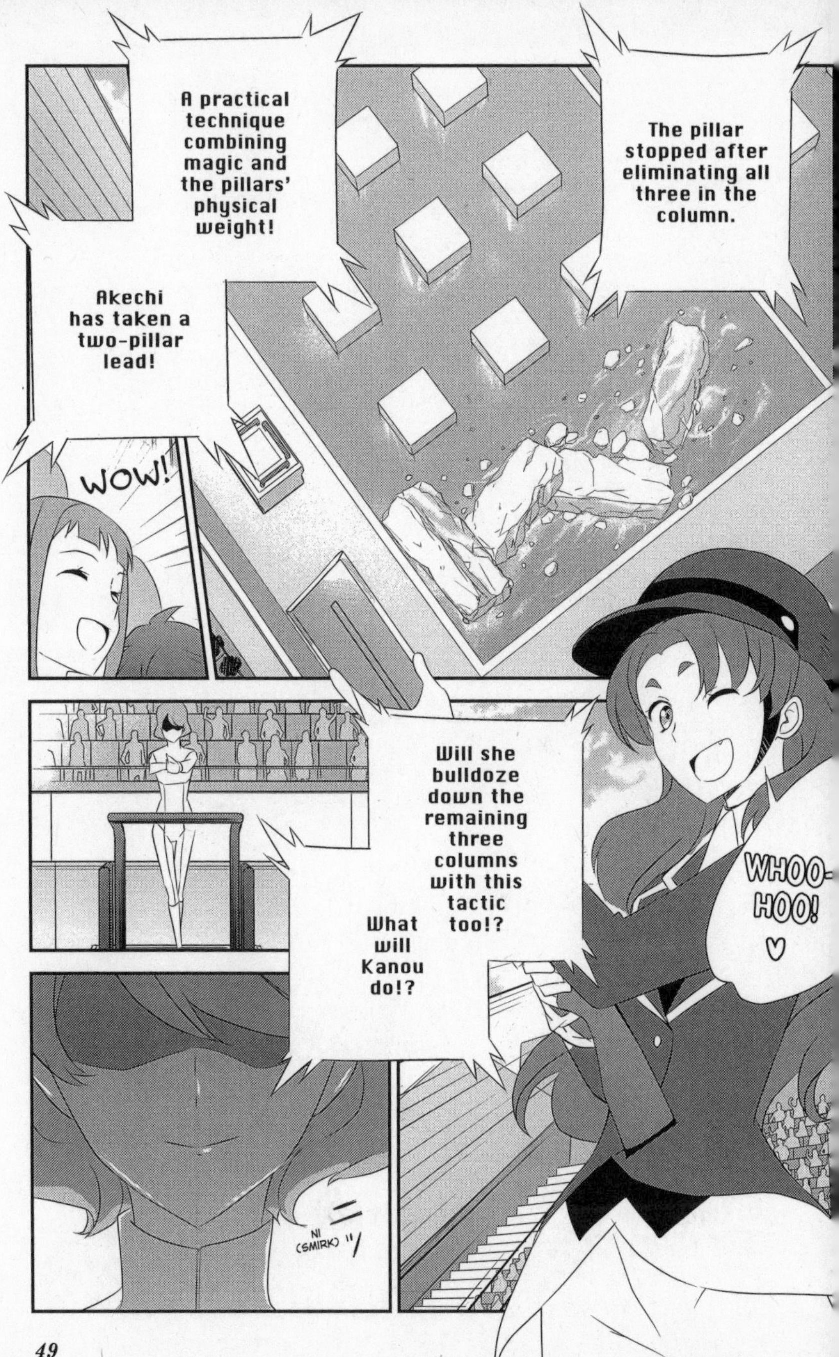
The pillar stopped after eliminating all three in the column.
A practical technique combining magic and the pillars' physical weight!
Akechi has taken a two-pillar lead!
WOW!
WHOO-HOO! ♥
Will she bulldoze down the remaining three columns with this tactic too!?
What will Kanou do!?
NI (SMIRK)

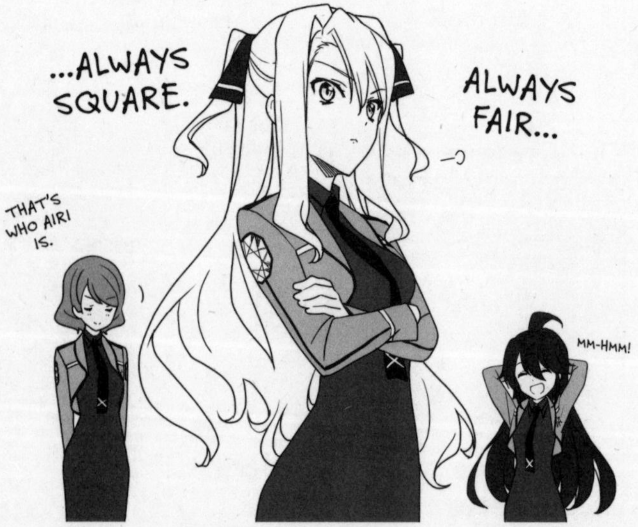
ALWAYS FAIR...
...ALWAYS SQUARE.
THAT'S WHO AIRI IS.
MM-HMM!

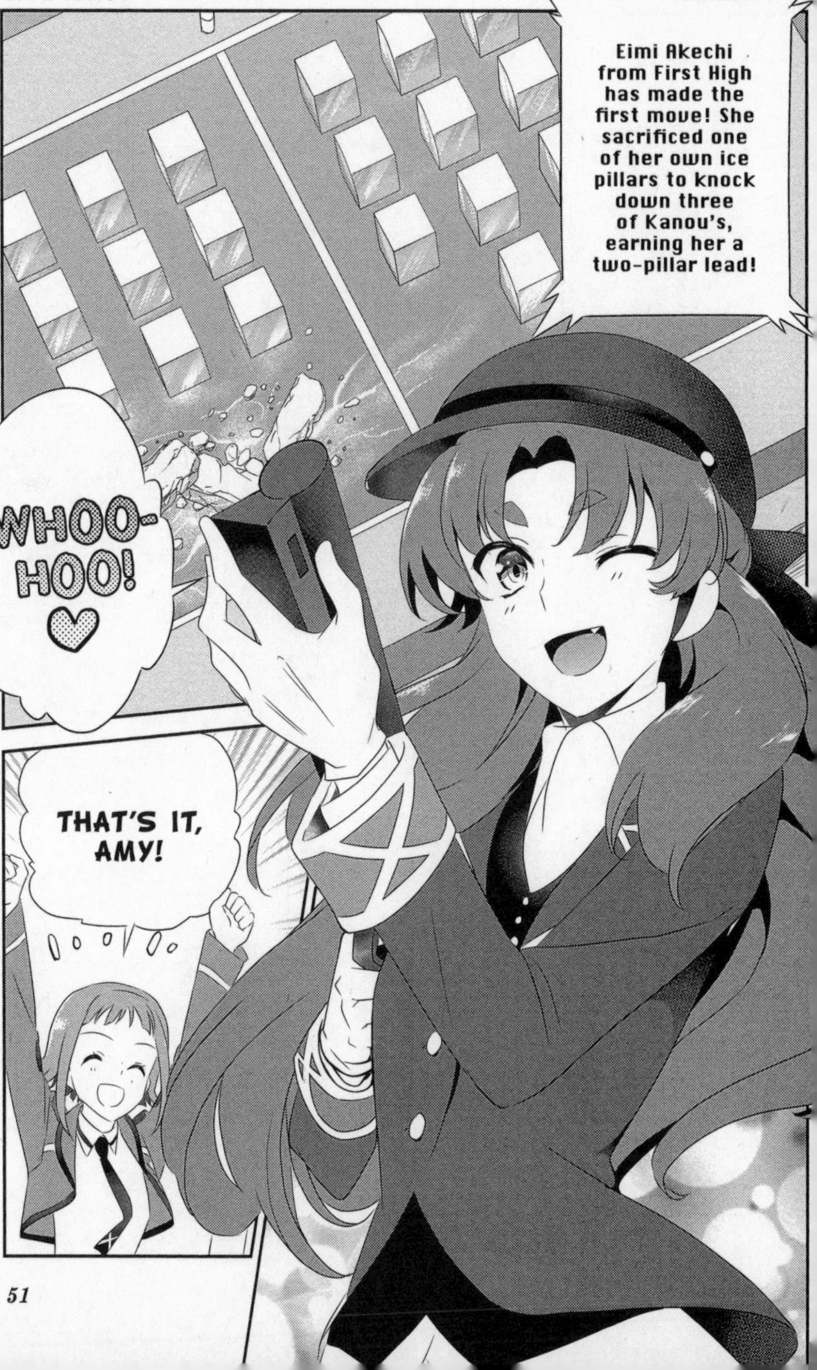
Eimi Akechi from First High has made the first move! She sacrificed one of her own ice pillars to knock down three of Kanou's, earning her a two-pillar lead!
WHOO-HOO! ♥
THAT'S IT, AMY!

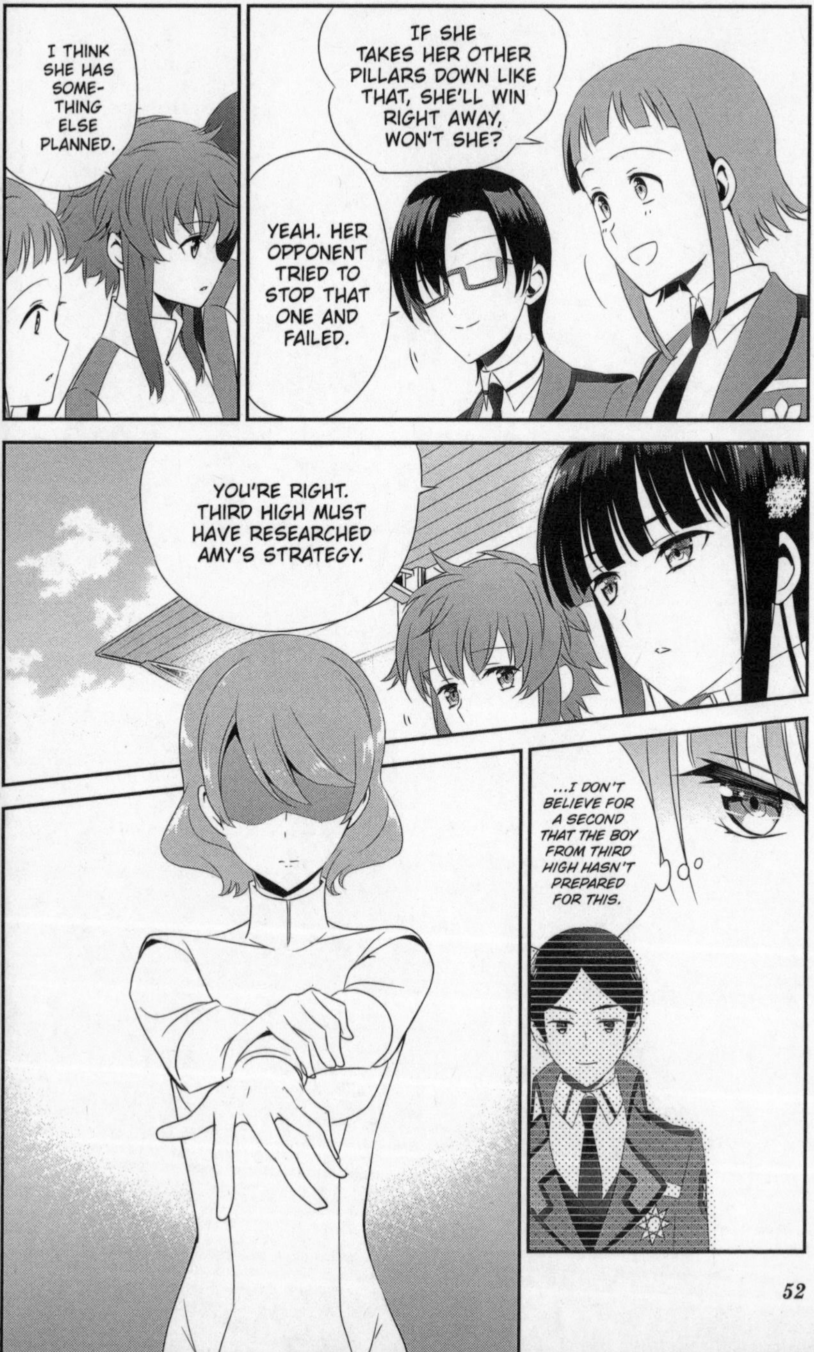
IF SHE TAKES HER OTHER PILLARS DOWN LIKE THAT, SHE'LL WIN RIGHT AWAY, WON'T SHE?
YEAH. HER OPPONENT TRIED TO STOP THAT ONE AND FAILED.
I THINK SHE HAS SOME-THING ELSE PLANNED.
YOU'RE RIGHT. THIRD HIGH MUST HAVE RESEARCHED AMY'S STRATEGY.
...I DON'T BELIEVE FOR A SECOND THAT THE BOY FROM THIRD HIGH HASN'T PREPARED FOR THIS.

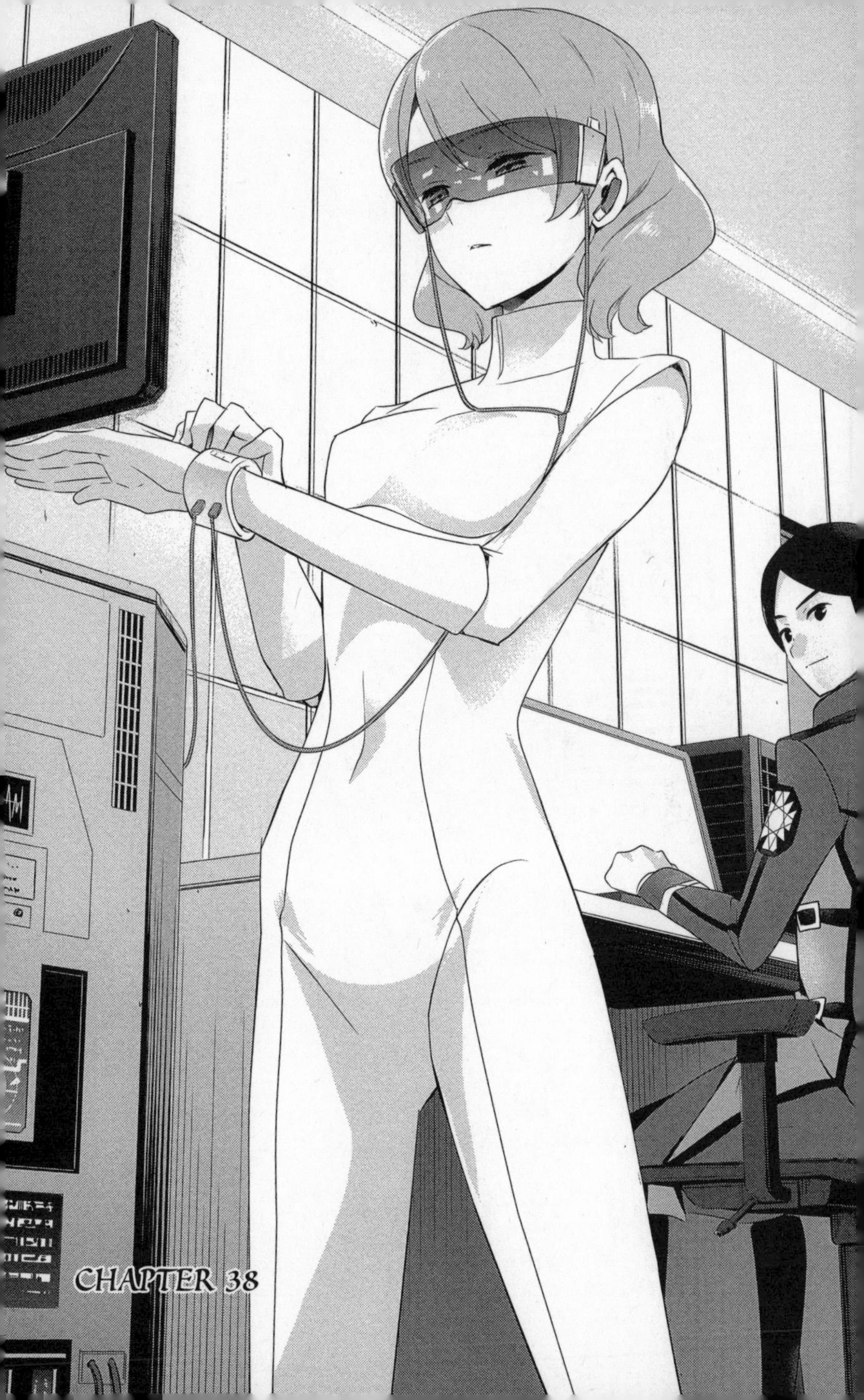
CHAPTER 38

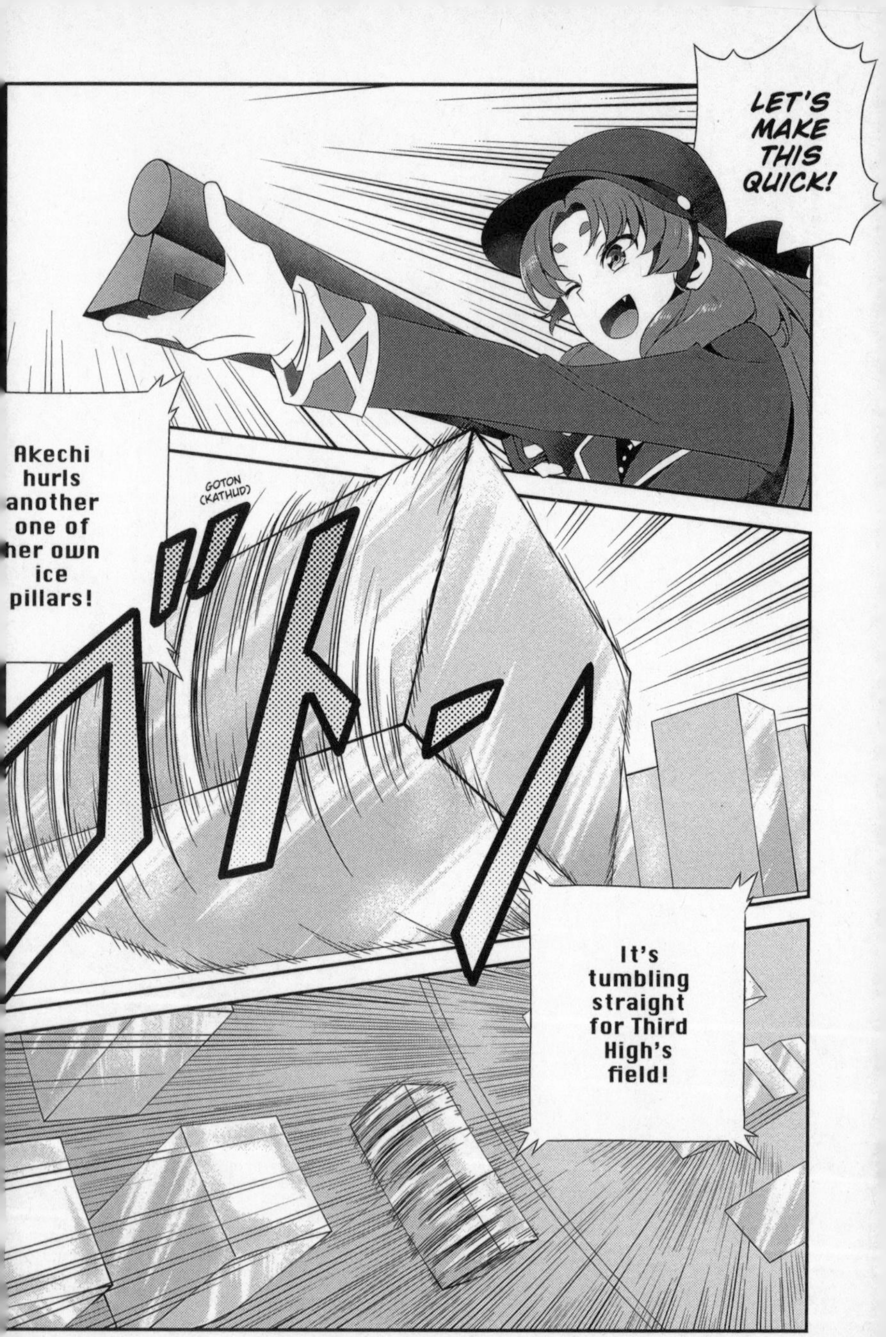
LET'S MAKE THIS QUICK!
Akechi hurls another one of her own ice pillars!
GOTON (KATHUD)
It's tumbling straight for Third High's field!

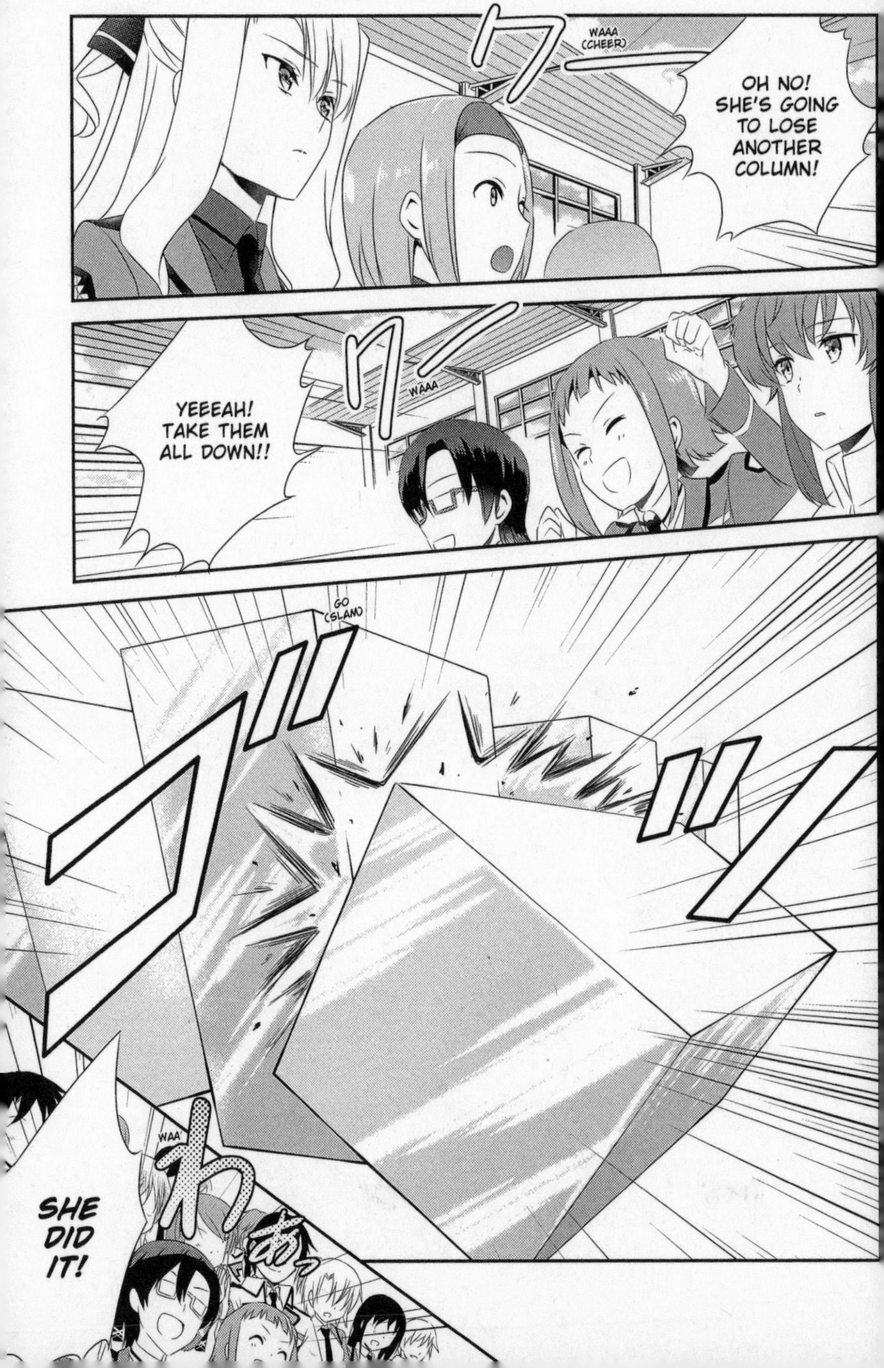
WAAA (CHEER)
OH NO! SHE'S GOING TO LOSE ANOTHER COLUMN!
WAAA
YEEEAH! TAKE THEM ALL DOWN!!
GO (SLAM)
WAA
SHE DID IT!

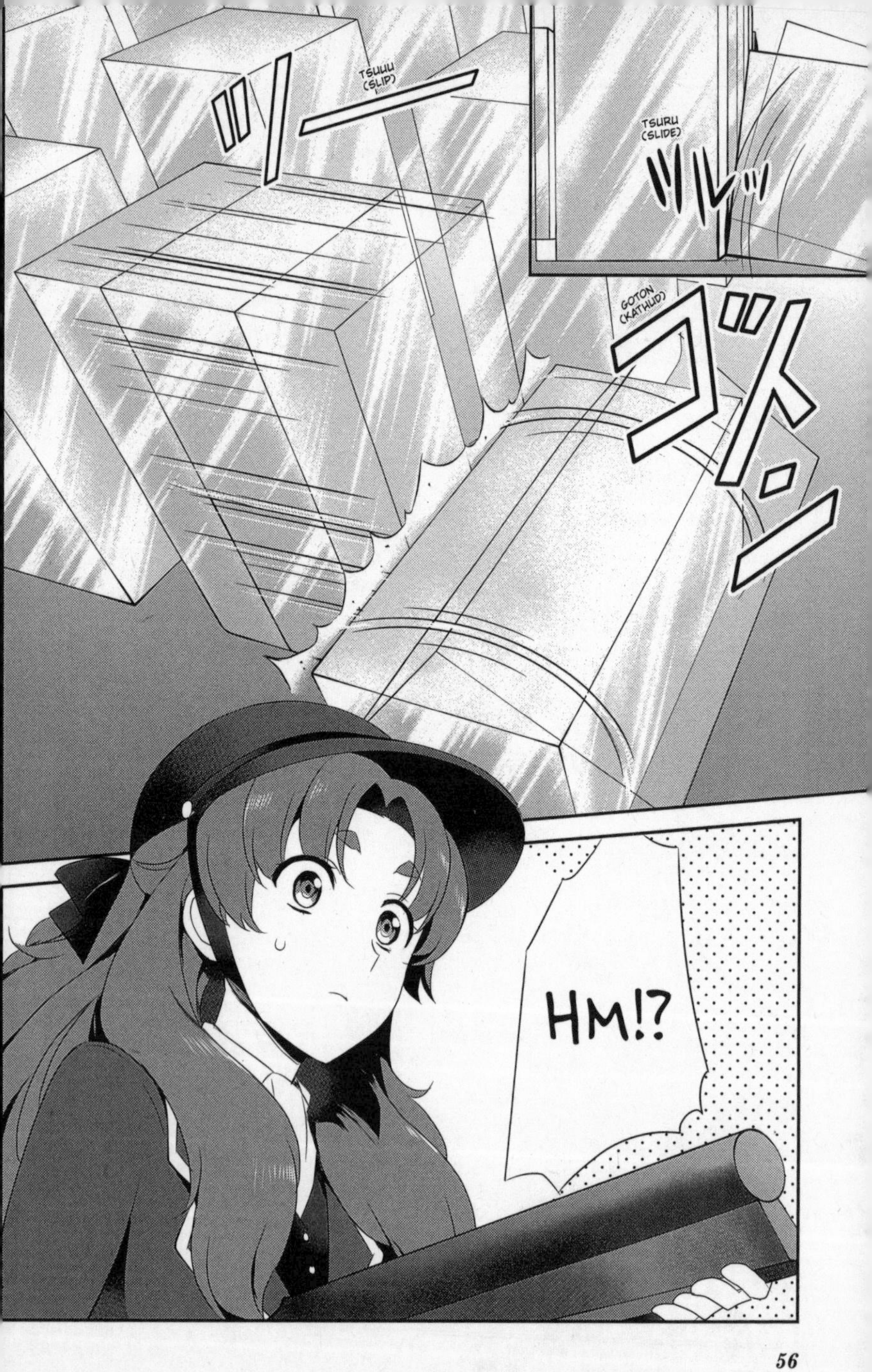

TSURU (SLIDE)
TSUUU (SLIP)
GOTON (KATHUD)
HM!?

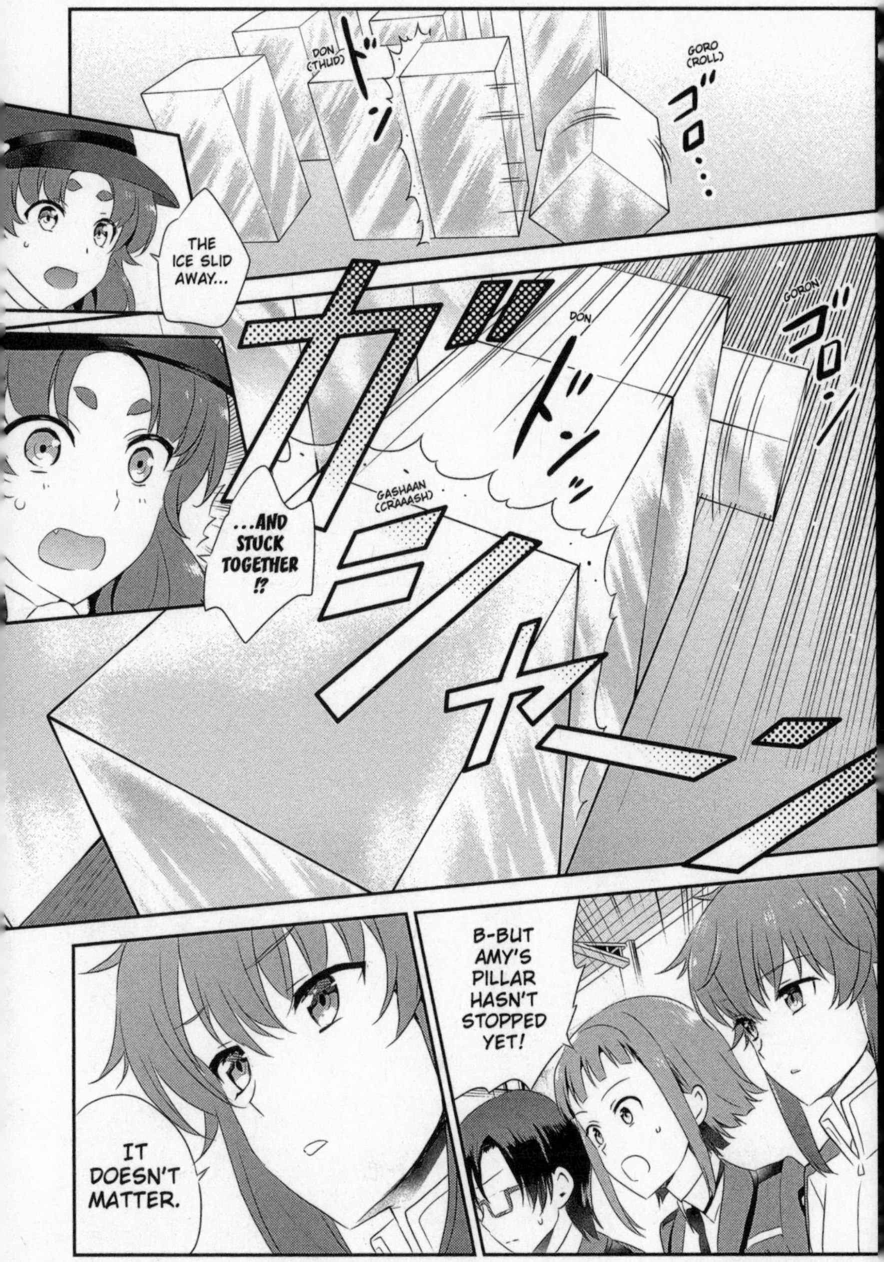

GORO (ROLL)
ゴロ…
DON (THUD)
ドン
THE ICE SLID AWAY…
GORON
ゴロン
DON
ドンッ
GASHAAN (CRAAASH)
ガシャーン
…AND STUCK TOGETHER!?
B-BUT AMY'S PILLAR HASN'T STOPPED YET!
IT DOESN'T MATTER.

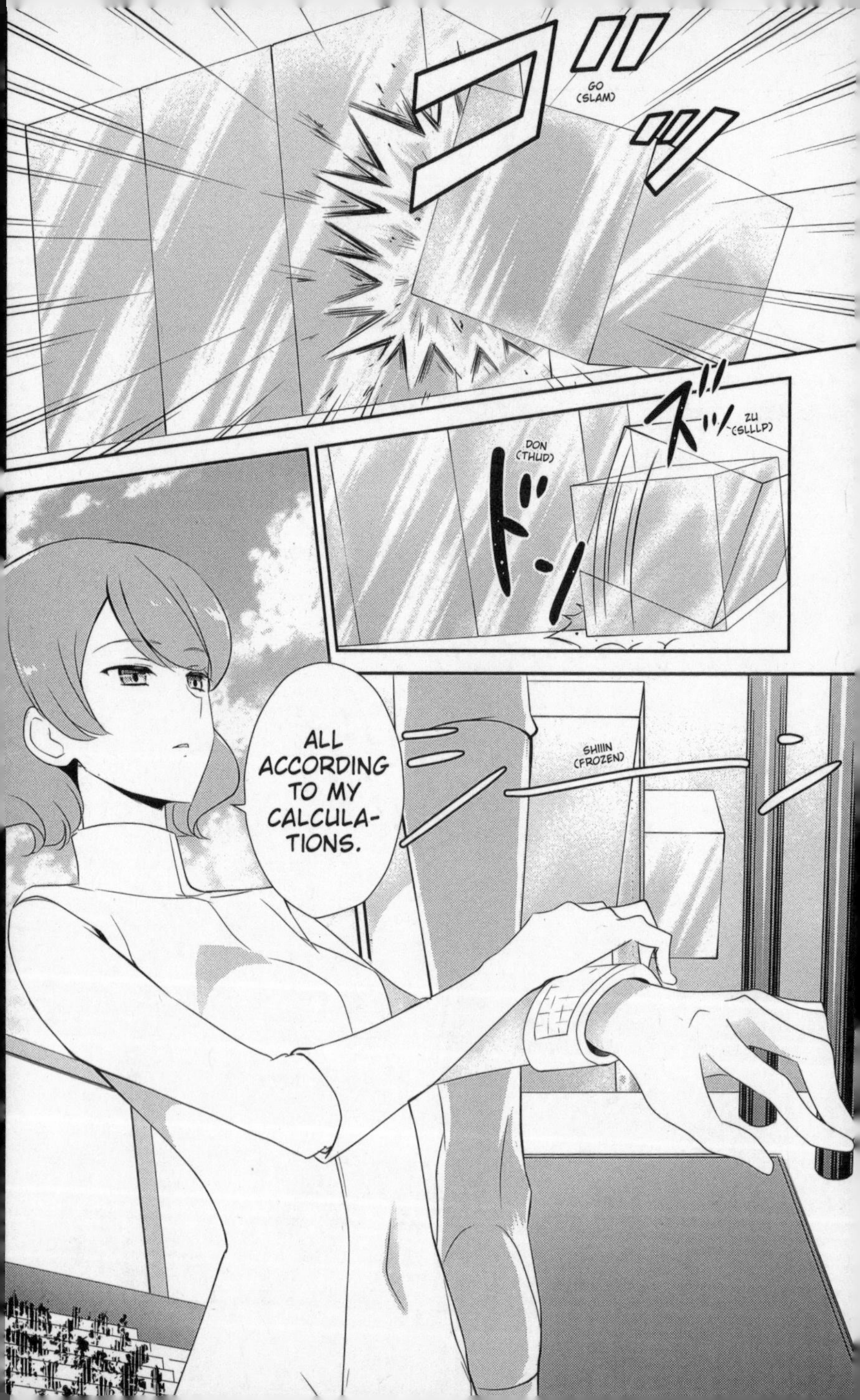
GO
(SLAM)
ZU
(SLLLP)
DON
(THUD)
SHIIIN
(FROZEN)
ALL ACCORDING TO MY CALCULATIONS.

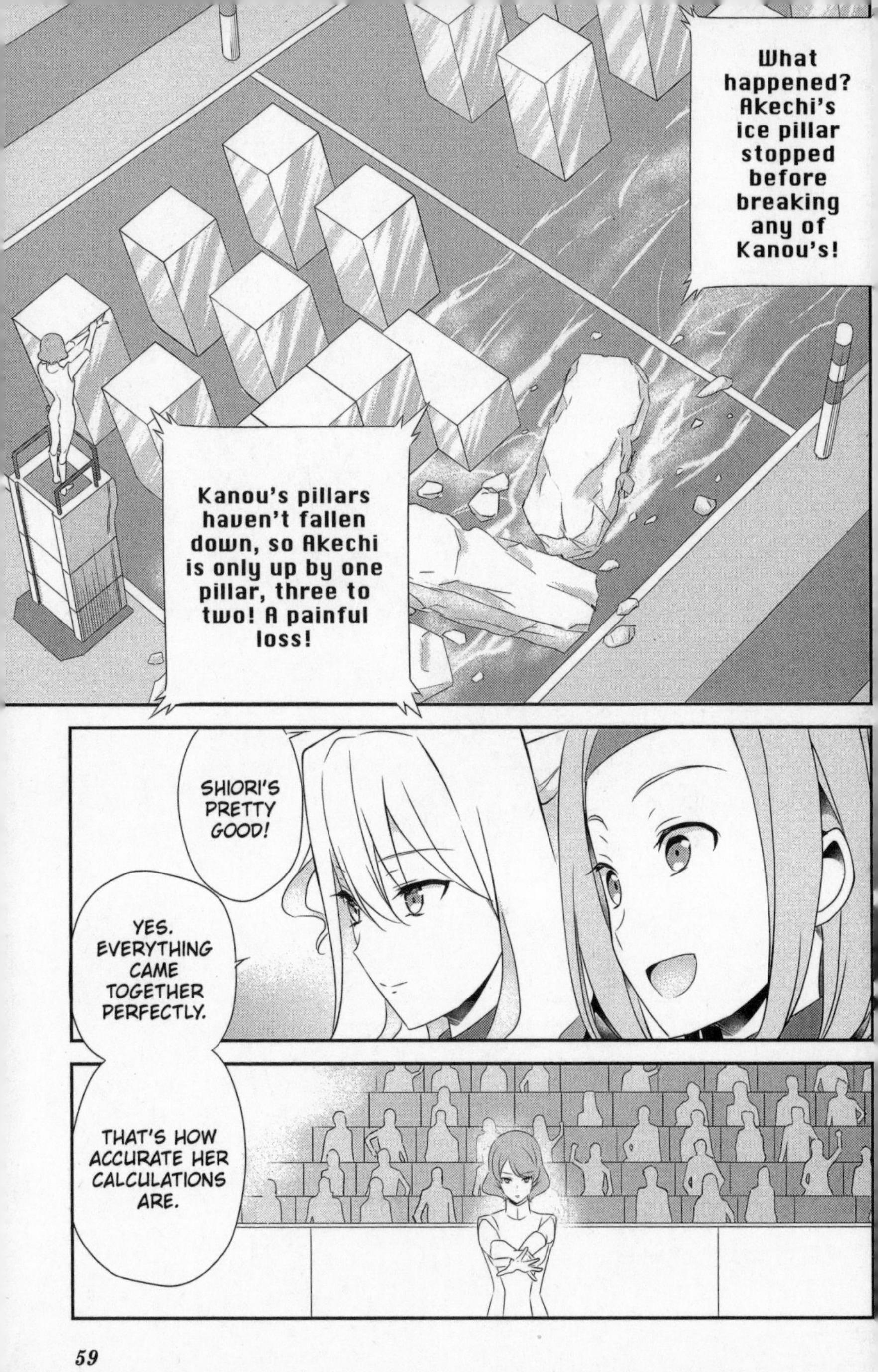
What happened? Akechi's ice pillar stopped before breaking any of Kanou's!
Kanou's pillars haven't fallen down, so Akechi is only up by one pillar, three to two! A painful loss!
SHIORI'S PRETTY GOOD!
YES. EVERYTHING CAME TOGETHER PERFECTLY.
THAT'S HOW ACCURATE HER CALCULATIONS ARE.

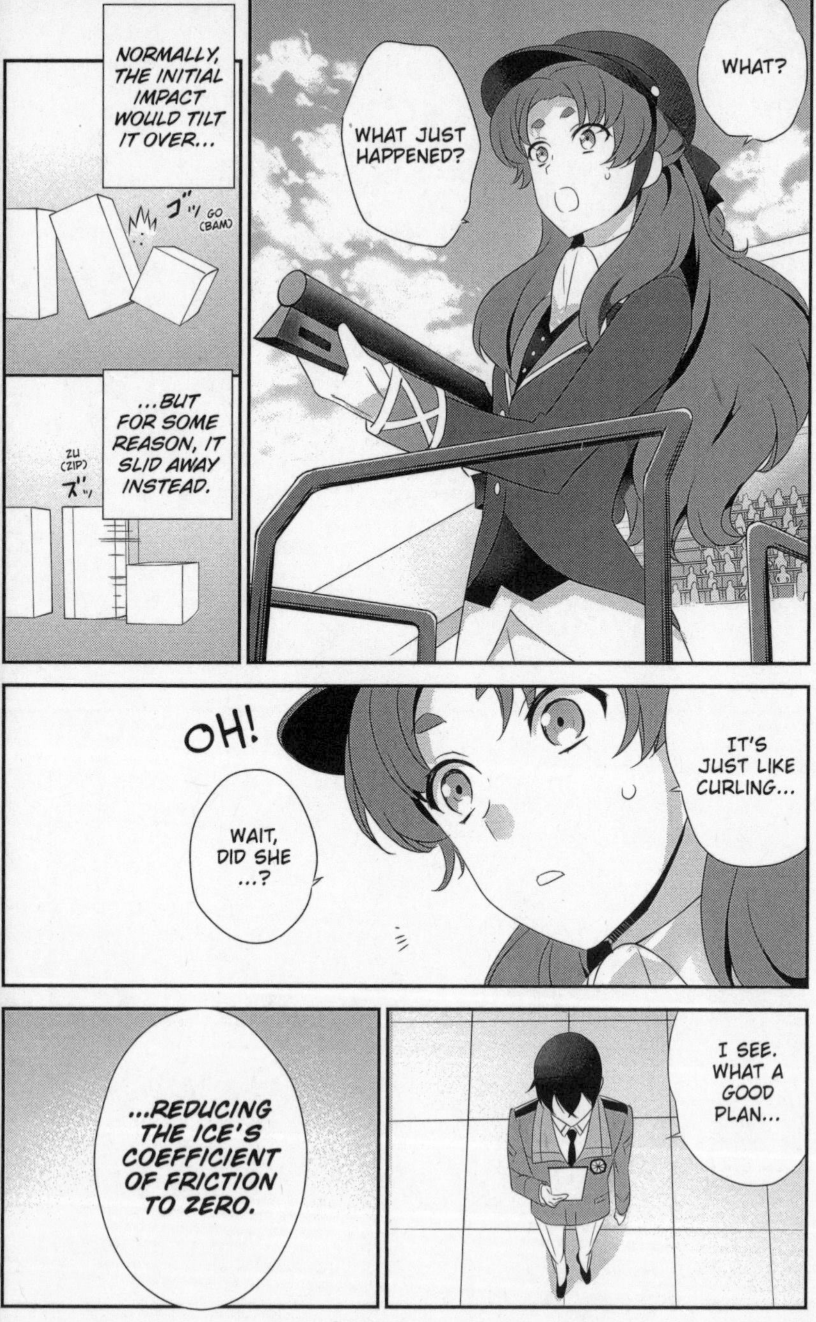
WHAT?
WHAT JUST HAPPENED?
NORMALLY, THE INITIAL IMPACT WOULD TILT IT OVER...
ゴッ GO (BAM)
...BUT FOR SOME REASON, IT SLID AWAY INSTEAD.
ズッ ZU (ZIP)
IT'S JUST LIKE CURLING...
WAIT, DID SHE ...?
OH!
I SEE. WHAT A GOOD PLAN...
...REDUCING THE ICE'S COEFFICIENT OF FRICTION TO ZERO.

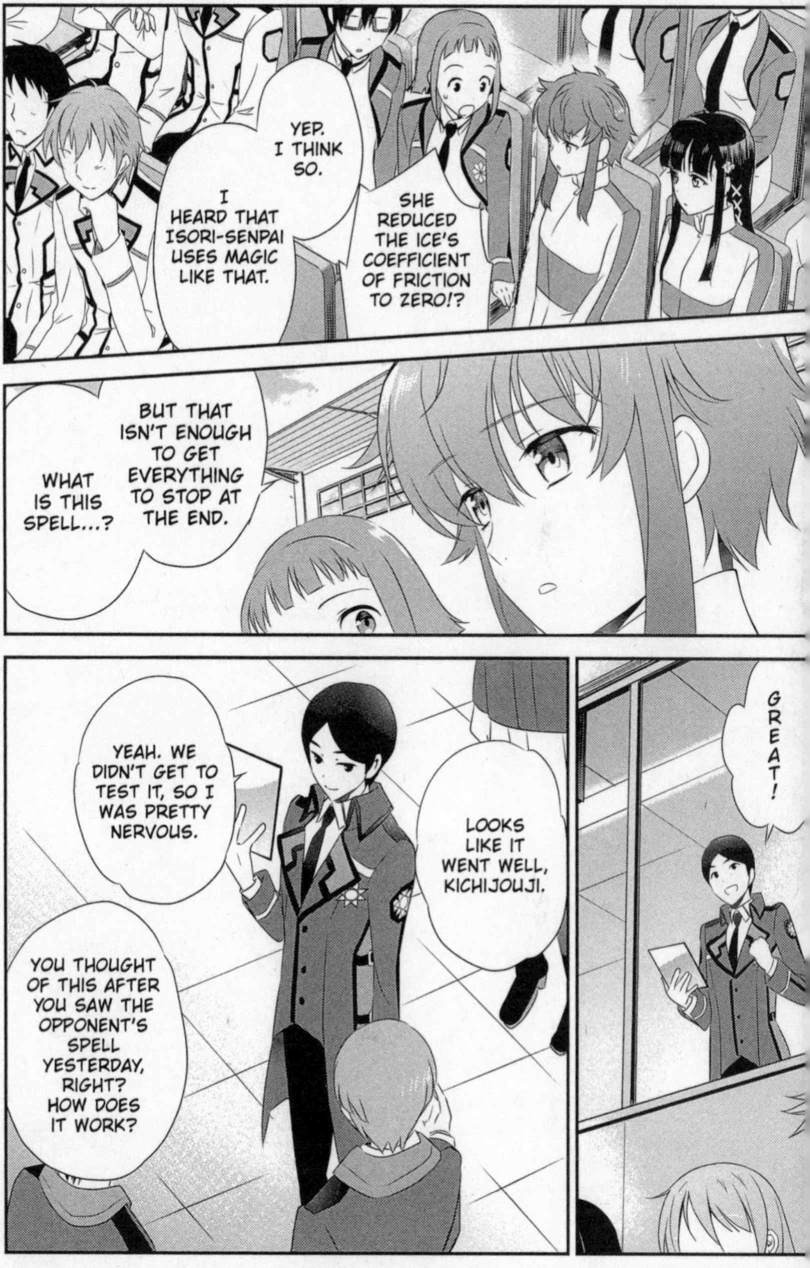
SHE REDUCED THE ICE'S COEFFICIENT OF FRICTION TO ZERO!?
YEP. I THINK SO.
I HEARD THAT ISORI-SENPAI USES MAGIC LIKE THAT.
BUT THAT ISN'T ENOUGH TO GET EVERYTHING TO STOP AT THE END.
WHAT IS THIS SPELL...?
GREAT!
LOOKS LIKE IT WENT WELL, KICHIJOUJI.
YEAH. WE DIDN'T GET TO TEST IT, SO I WAS PRETTY NERVOUS.
YOU THOUGHT OF THIS AFTER YOU SAW THE OPPONENT'S SPELL YESTERDAY, RIGHT? HOW DOES IT WORK?

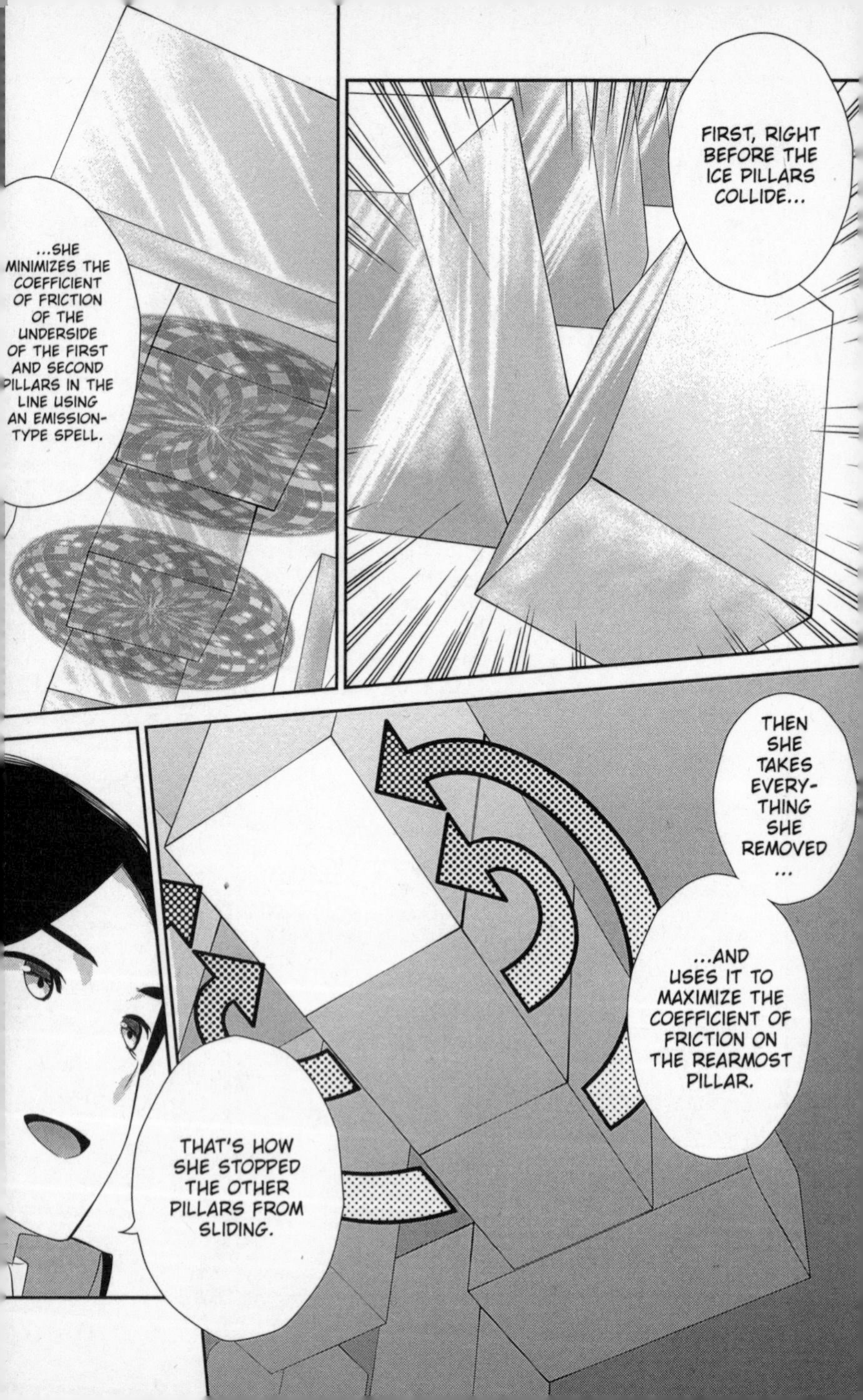
FIRST, RIGHT BEFORE THE ICE PILLARS COLLIDE...
...SHE MINIMIZES THE COEFFICIENT OF FRICTION OF THE UNDERSIDE OF THE FIRST AND SECOND PILLARS IN THE LINE USING AN EMISSION-TYPE SPELL.
THEN SHE TAKES EVERY-THING SHE REMOVED ...
...AND USES IT TO MAXIMIZE THE COEFFICIENT OF FRICTION ON THE REARMOST PILLAR.
THAT'S HOW SHE STOPPED THE OTHER PILLARS FROM SLIDING.

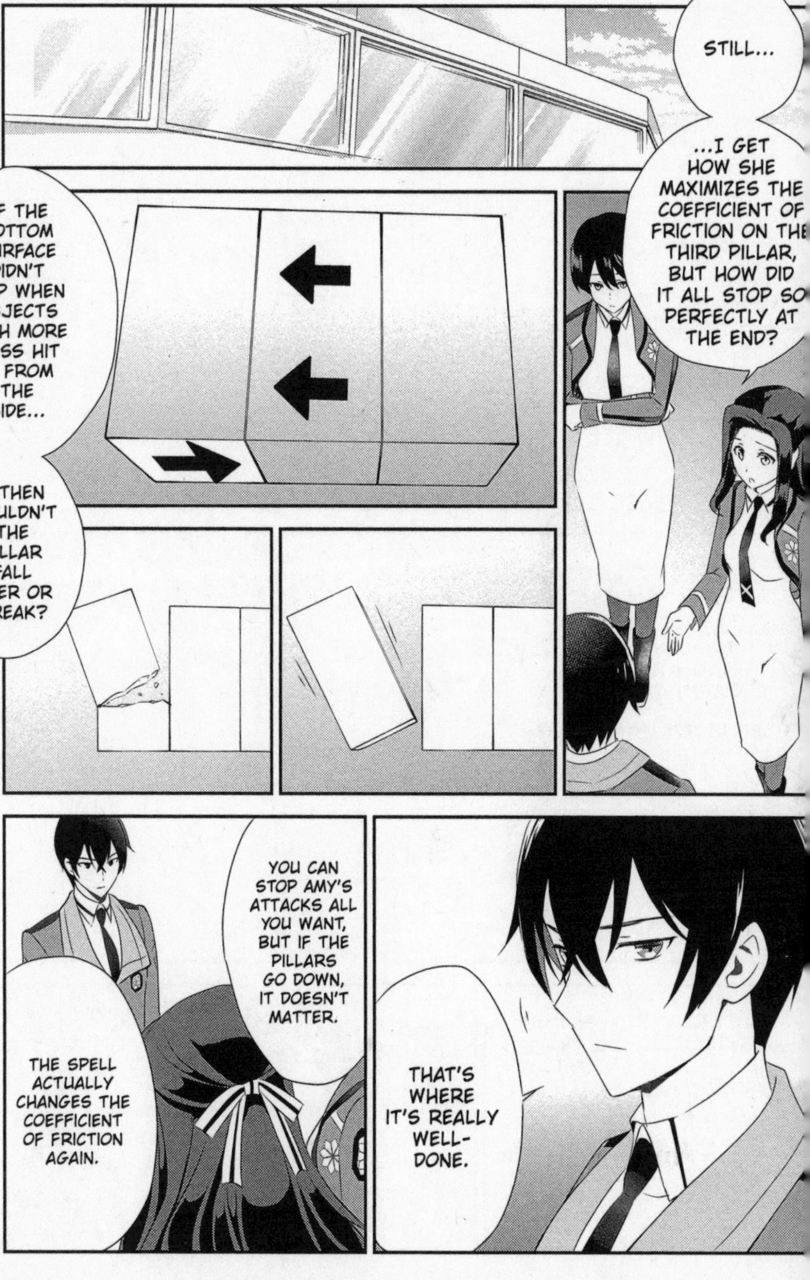
STILL...
...I GET HOW SHE MAXIMIZES THE COEFFICIENT OF FRICTION ON THE THIRD PILLAR, BUT HOW DID IT ALL STOP SO PERFECTLY AT THE END?
IF THE BOTTOM SURFACE DIDN'T SLIP WHEN OBJECTS WITH MORE MASS HIT IT FROM THE SIDE...
...THEN WOULDN'T THE PILLAR FALL OVER OR BREAK?
THAT'S WHERE IT'S REALLY WELL-DONE.
YOU CAN STOP AMY'S ATTACKS ALL YOU WANT, BUT IF THE PILLARS GO DOWN, IT DOESN'T MATTER.
THE SPELL ACTUALLY CHANGES THE COEFFICIENT OF FRICTION AGAIN.

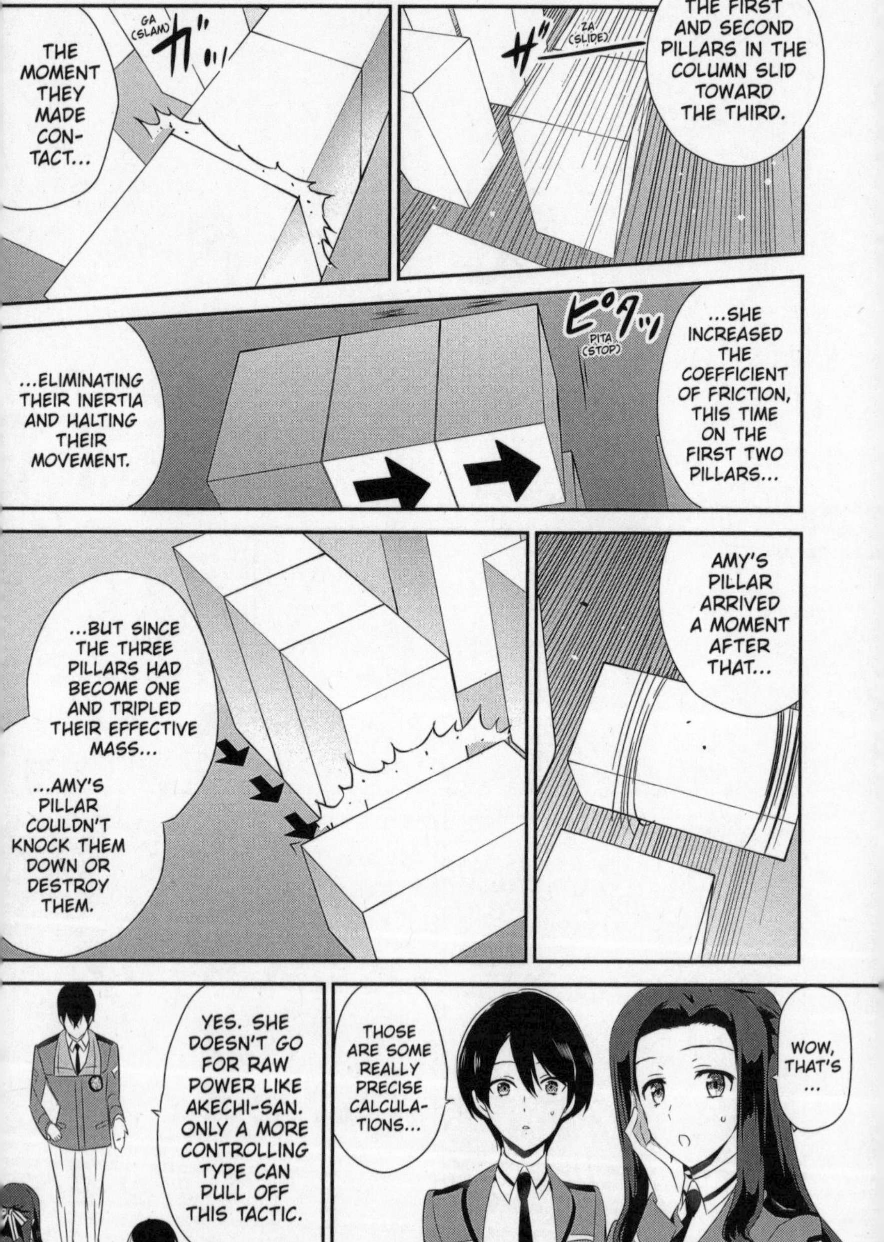
ZA (SLIDE)
THE FIRST AND SECOND PILLARS IN THE COLUMN SLID TOWARD THE THIRD.
GA (SLAM)
THE MOMENT THEY MADE CONTACT...
PITA (STOP)
...SHE INCREASED THE COEFFICIENT OF FRICTION, THIS TIME ON THE FIRST TWO PILLARS...
...ELIMINATING THEIR INERTIA AND HALTING THEIR MOVEMENT.
AMY'S PILLAR ARRIVED A MOMENT AFTER THAT...
...BUT SINCE THE THREE PILLARS HAD BECOME ONE AND TRIPLED THEIR EFFECTIVE MASS...
...AMY'S PILLAR COULDN'T KNOCK THEM DOWN OR DESTROY THEM.
WOW, THAT'S ...
THOSE ARE SOME REALLY PRECISE CALCULATIONS...
YES. SHE DOESN'T GO FOR RAW POWER LIKE AKECHI-SAN. ONLY A MORE CONTROLLING TYPE CAN PULL OFF THIS TACTIC.

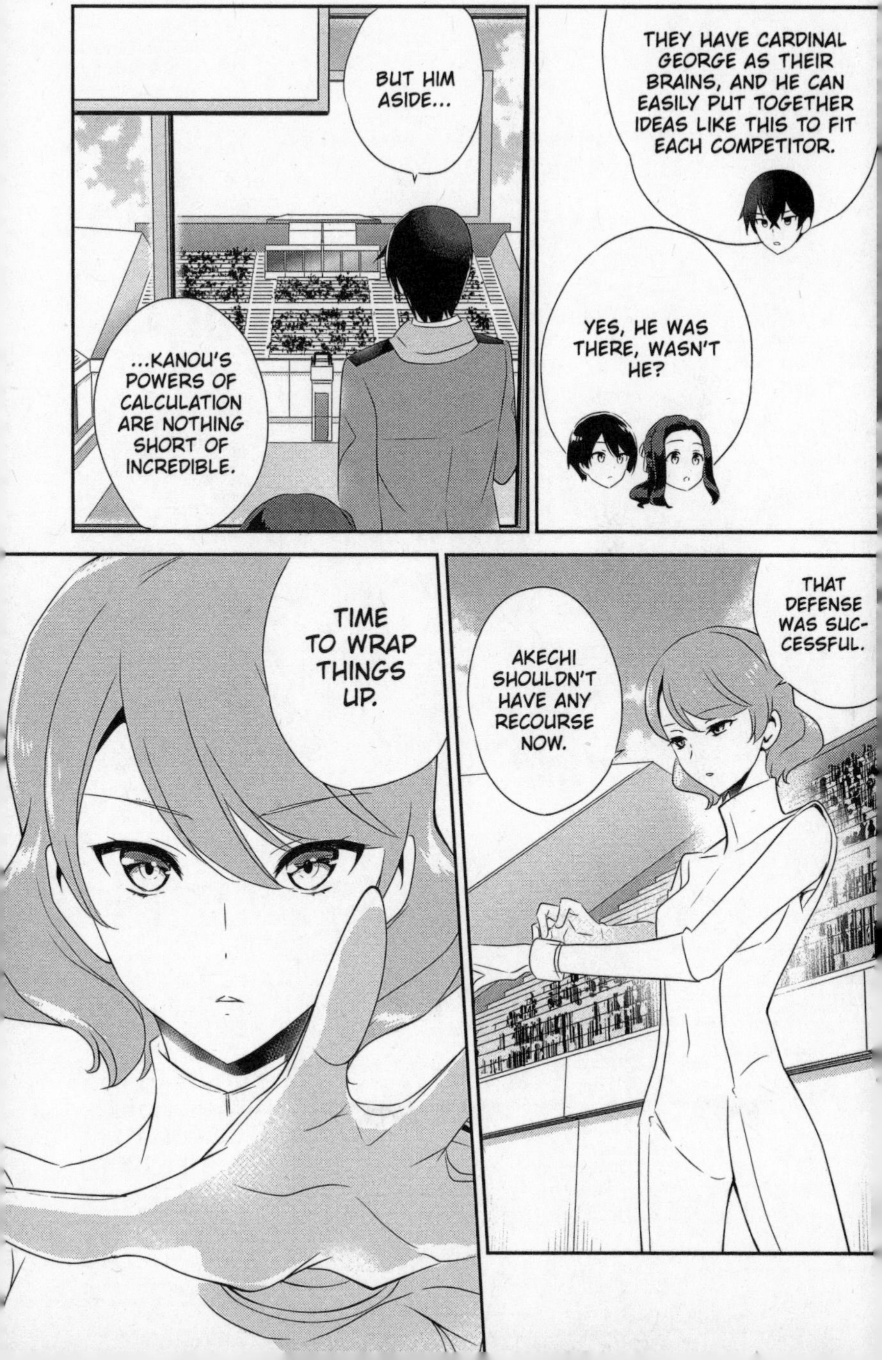
THEY HAVE CARDINAL GEORGE AS THEIR BRAINS, AND HE CAN EASILY PUT TOGETHER IDEAS LIKE THIS TO FIT EACH COMPETITOR.
YES, HE WAS THERE, WASN'T HE?
BUT HIM ASIDE...
...KANOU'S POWERS OF CALCULATION ARE NOTHING SHORT OF INCREDIBLE.
THAT DEFENSE WAS SUC-CESSFUL.
AKECHI SHOULDN'T HAVE ANY RECOURSE NOW.
TIME TO WRAP THINGS UP.

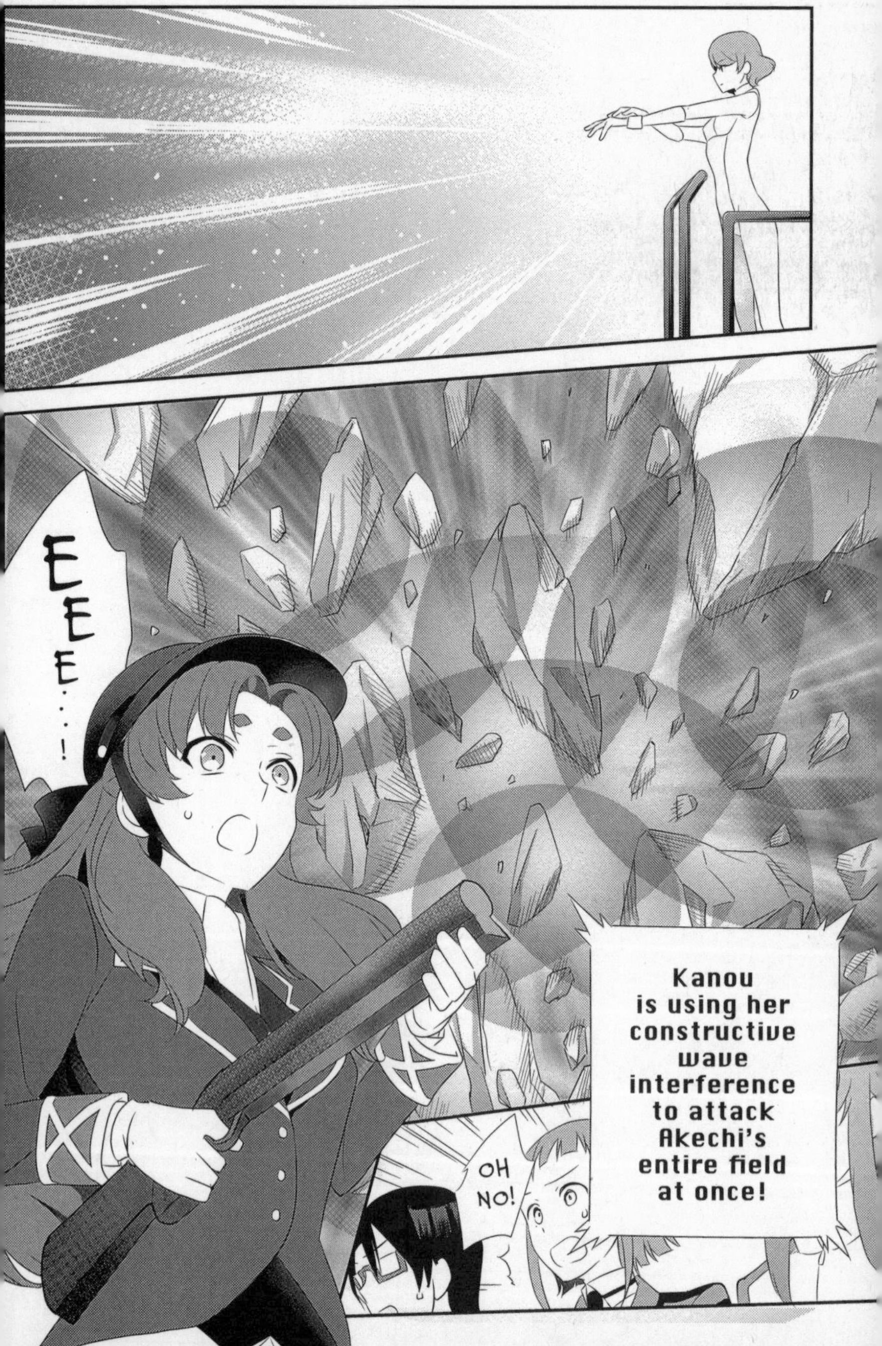
Kanou is using her constructive wave interference to attack Akechi's entire field at once!
OH NO!
EEE...!

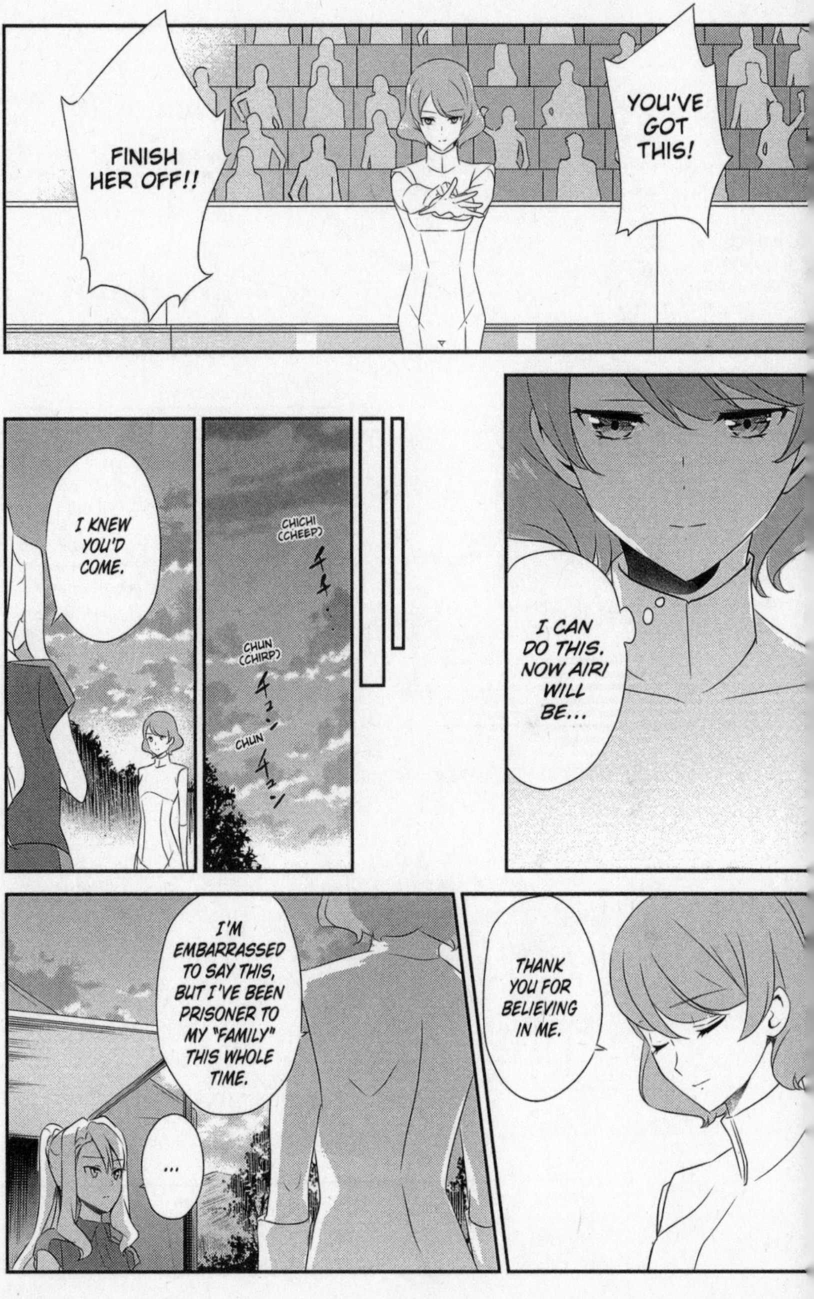
YOU'VE GOT THIS!
FINISH HER OFF!!
I CAN DO THIS. NOW AIRI WILL BE...
CHICHI (CHEEP)
CHUN (CHIRP)
CHUN
I KNEW YOU'D COME.
THANK YOU FOR BELIEVING IN ME.
I'M EMBARRASSED TO SAY THIS, BUT I'VE BEEN PRISONER TO MY "FAMILY" THIS WHOLE TIME.
...

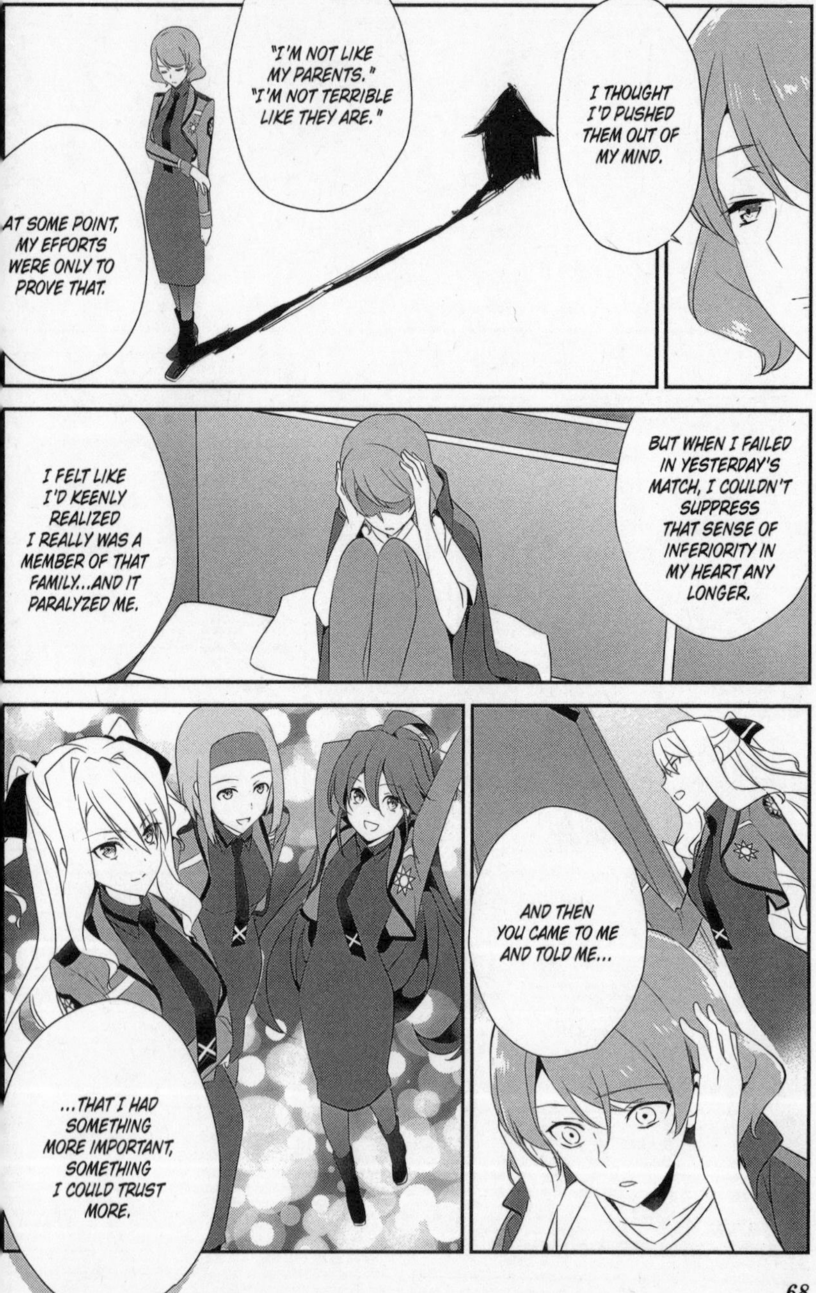
I THOUGHT I'D PUSHED THEM OUT OF MY MIND.
"I'M NOT LIKE MY PARENTS." "I'M NOT TERRIBLE LIKE THEY ARE."
AT SOME POINT, MY EFFORTS WERE ONLY TO PROVE THAT.
BUT WHEN I FAILED IN YESTERDAY'S MATCH, I COULDN'T SUPPRESS THAT SENSE OF INFERIORITY IN MY HEART ANY LONGER.
I FELT LIKE I'D KEENLY REALIZED I REALLY WAS A MEMBER OF THAT FAMILY...AND IT PARALYZED ME.
AND THEN YOU CAME TO ME AND TOLD ME...
...THAT I HAD SOMETHING MORE IMPORTANT, SOMETHING I COULD TRUST MORE.

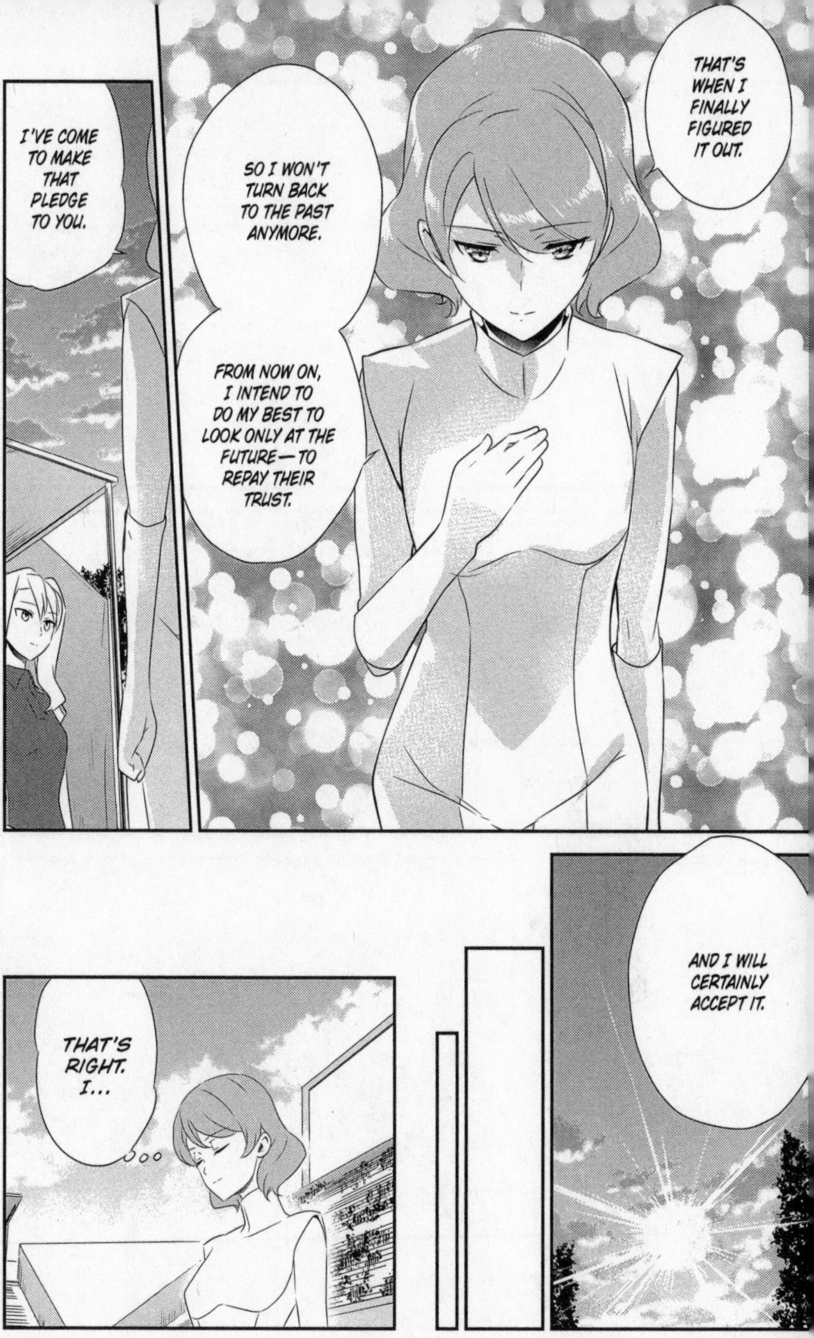
THAT'S WHEN I FINALLY FIGURED IT OUT.
SO I WON'T TURN BACK TO THE PAST ANYMORE.
FROM NOW ON, I INTEND TO DO MY BEST TO LOOK ONLY AT THE FUTURE—TO REPAY THEIR TRUST.
I'VE COME TO MAKE THAT PLEDGE TO YOU.
AND I WILL CERTAINLY ACCEPT IT.
THAT'S RIGHT. I...

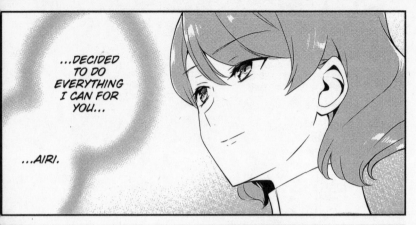

...DECIDED TO DO EVERYTHING I CAN FOR YOU...
...AIRI.
WAY TO GO, SHIORI!
......
I'M HAPPY SHE SEEMS TO BE DOING WELL.
? WHAT'S WRONG?
WHAT? OH, NOTHING.

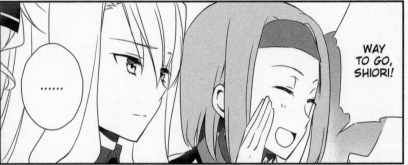

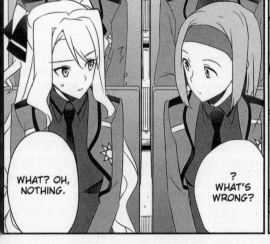

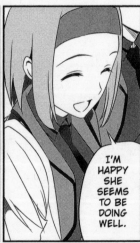

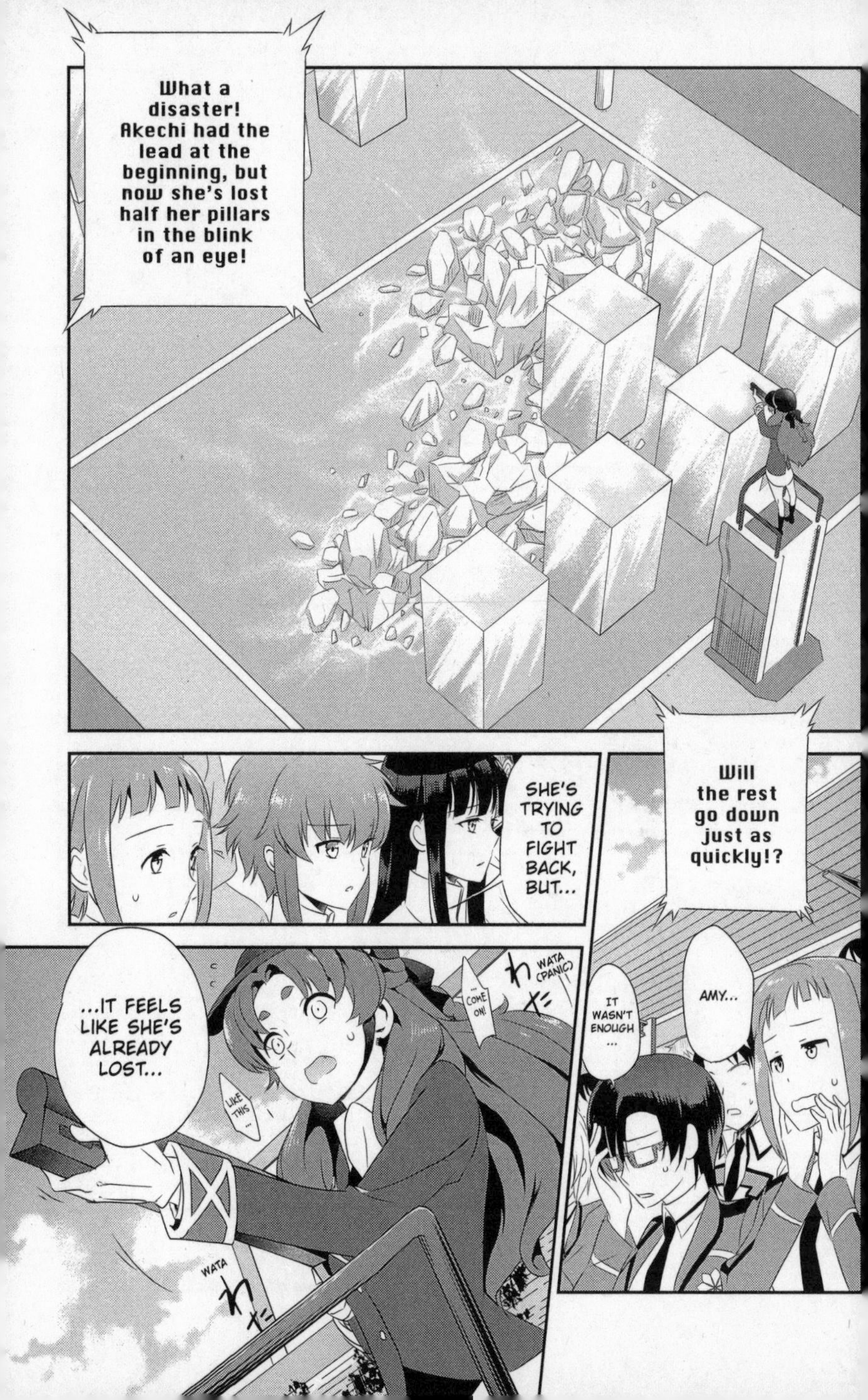
What a disaster! Akechi had the lead at the beginning, but now she's lost half her pillars in the blink of an eye!
Will the rest go down just as quickly!?
SHE'S TRYING TO FIGHT BACK, BUT...
AMY...
IT WASN'T ENOUGH...
WATA (PANIC)
...COME ON!
...IT FEELS LIKE SHE'S ALREADY LOST...
LIKE THIS...
WATA

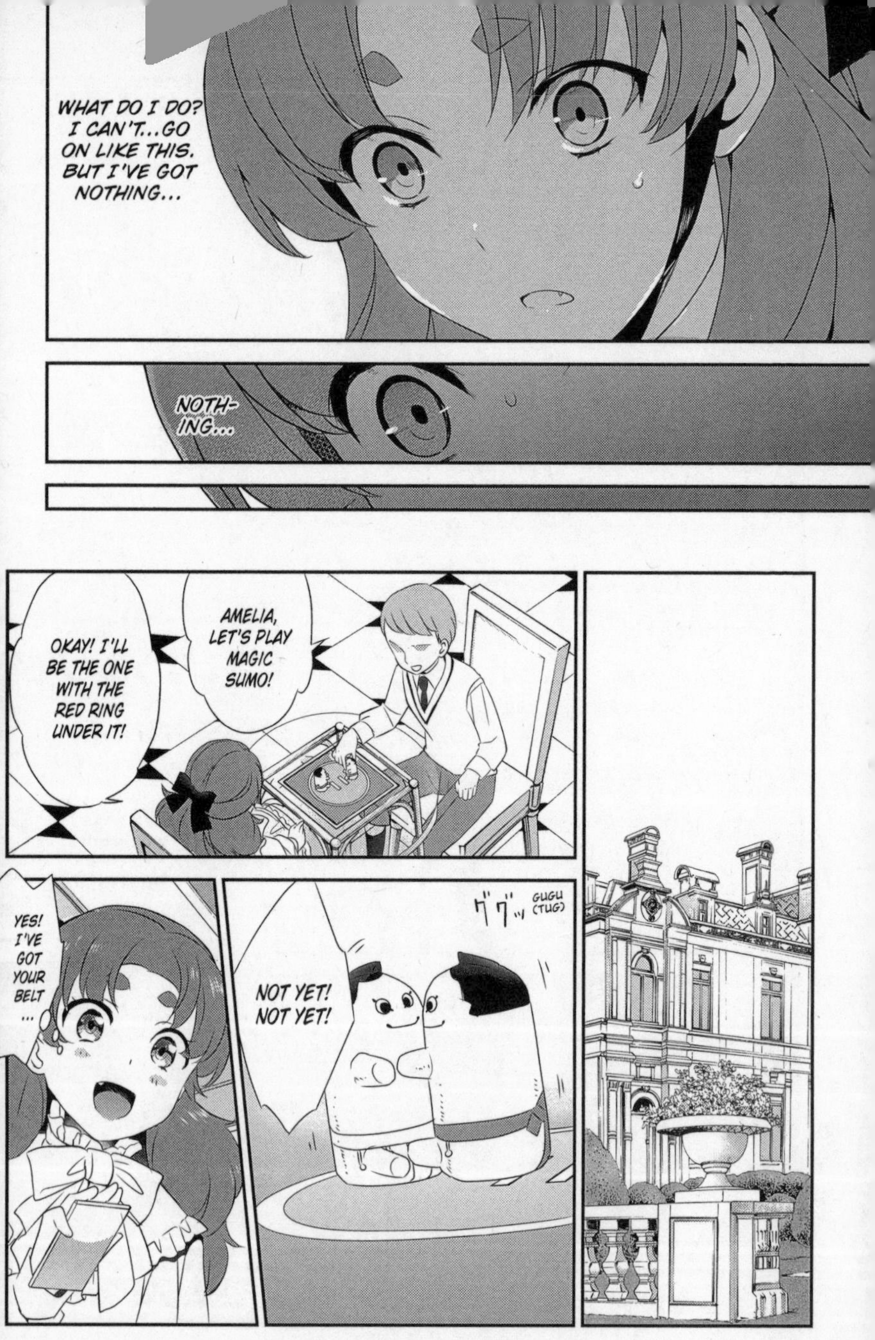
WHAT DO I DO? I CAN'T...GO ON LIKE THIS. BUT I'VE GOT NOTHING...
NOTH-ING...
AMELIA, LET'S PLAY MAGIC SUMO!
OKAY! I'LL BE THE ONE WITH THE RED RING UNDER IT!
ググッ GUGU (TUG)
NOT YET! NOT YET!
YES! I'VE GOT YOUR BELT ...

LAUNCHER! CRAP. MOVE! COME ON, MOVE!!

...

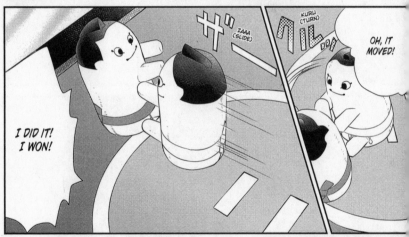

ザー ZAAA (SLIDE)

クル KURU (TURN)

OH, IT MOVED!

I DID IT! I WON!

EH-HEH-HEH. I GUESS I LOST.

YAAAY!

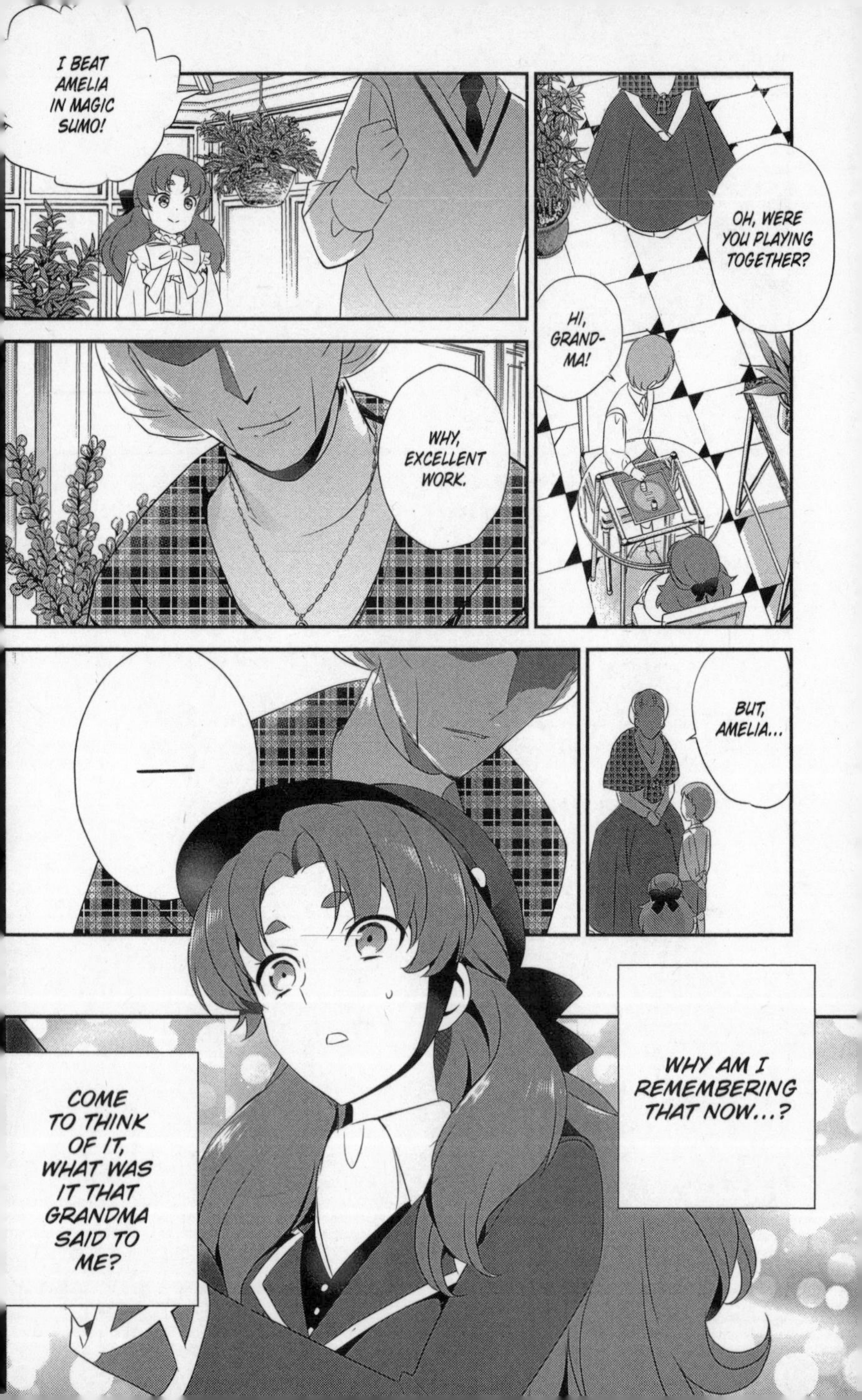
OH, WERE YOU PLAYING TOGETHER?
HI, GRAND-MA!
I BEAT AMELIA IN MAGIC SUMO!
WHY, EXCELLENT WORK.
BUT, AMELIA...
—
WHY AM I REMEMBERING THAT NOW...?
COME TO THINK OF IT, WHAT WAS IT THAT GRANDMA SAID TO ME?

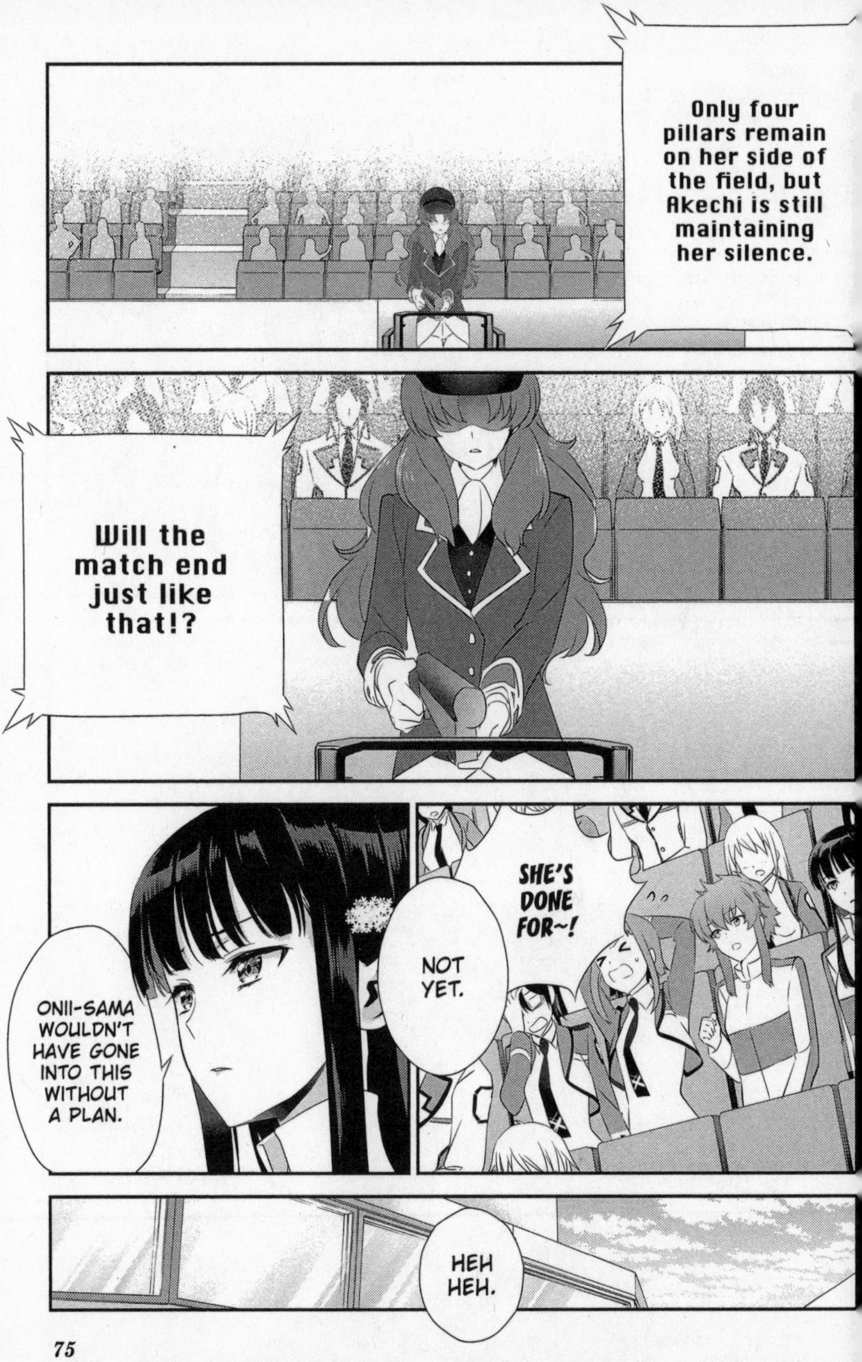
Only four pillars remain on her side of the field, but Akechi is still maintaining her silence.
Will the match end just like that!?
SHE'S DONE FOR~!
NOT YET.
ONII-SAMA WOULDN'T HAVE GONE INTO THIS WITHOUT A PLAN.
HEH HEH.

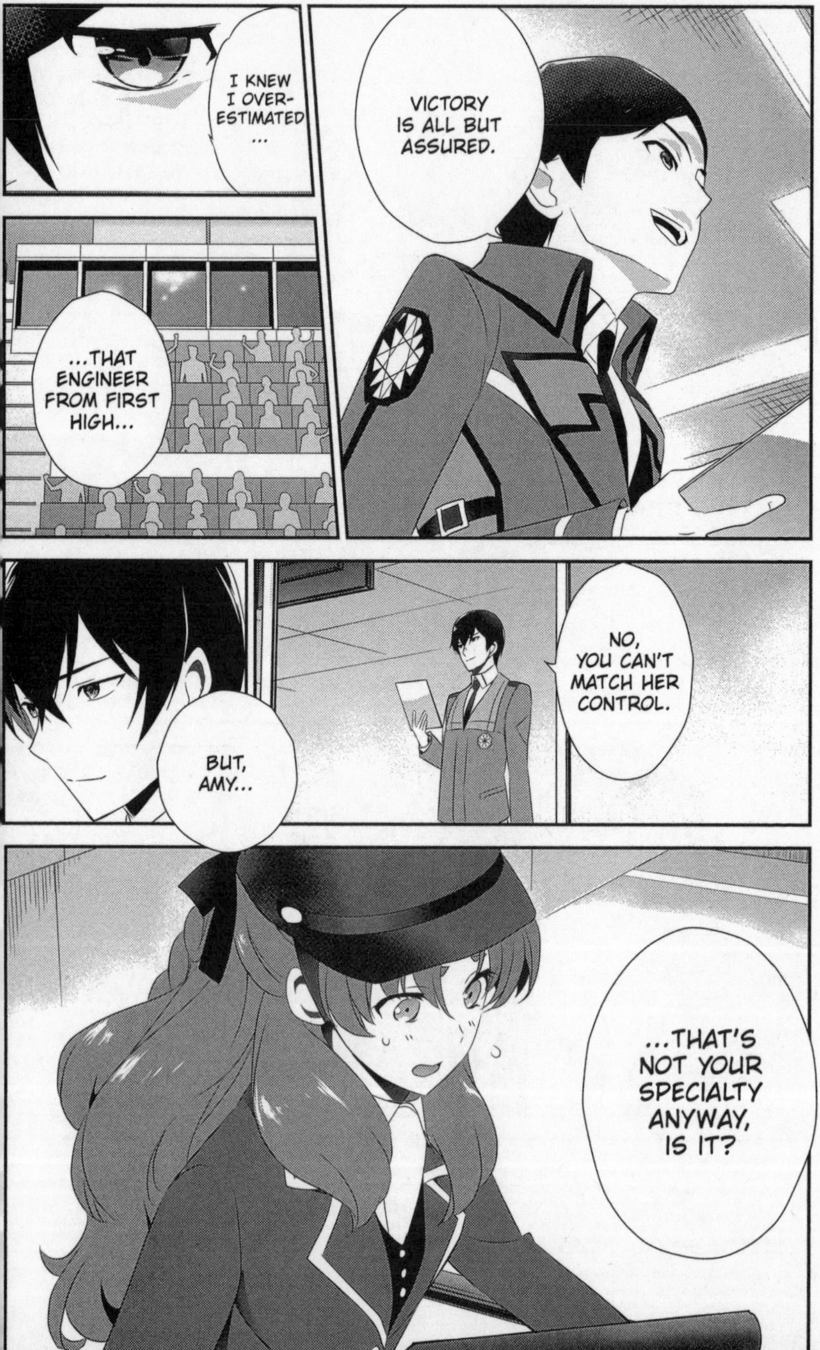
VICTORY IS ALL BUT ASSURED.
I KNEW I OVER-ESTIMATED...
...THAT ENGINEER FROM FIRST HIGH...
NO, YOU CAN'T MATCH HER CONTROL.
BUT, AMY...
...THAT'S NOT YOUR SPECIALTY ANYWAY, IS IT?

THE
HONOR
STUDENT
STUDENT
AT
Magic High
School

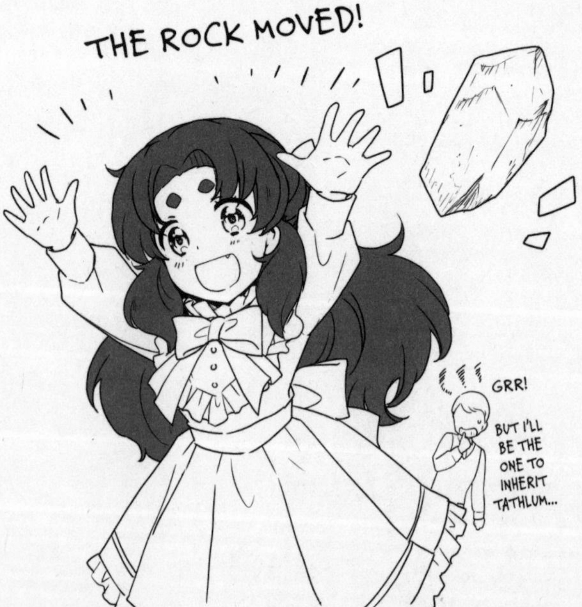
THE ROCK MOVED!
GRR!
BUT I'LL BE THE ONE TO INHERIT TATHLUM...

CHAPTER 39

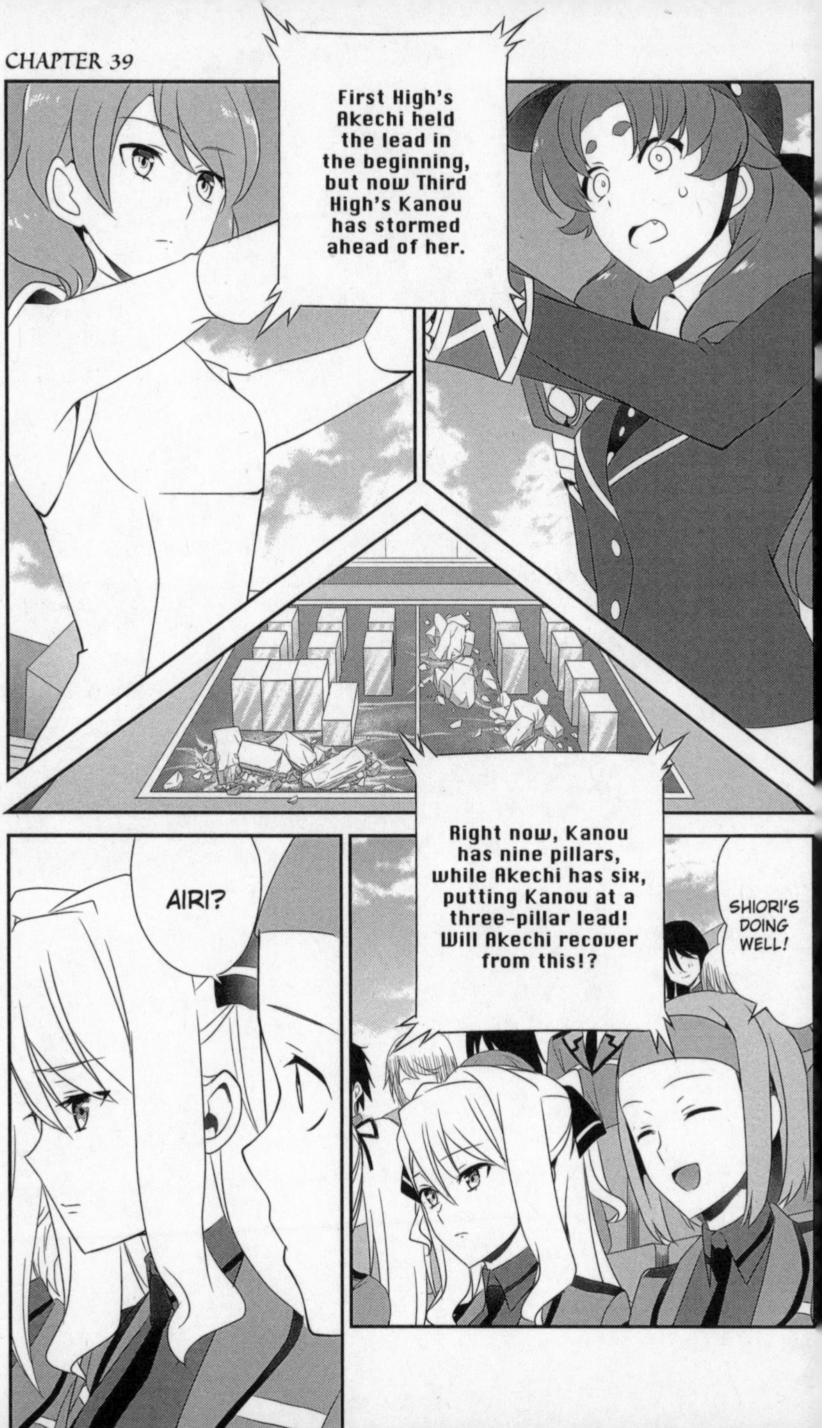
First High's Akechi held the lead in the beginning, but now Third High's Kanou has stormed ahead of her.
Right now, Kanou has nine pillars, while Akechi has six, putting Kanou at a three-pillar lead! Will Akechi recover from this!?
SHIORI'S DOING WELL!
AIRI?

CHAPTER 39

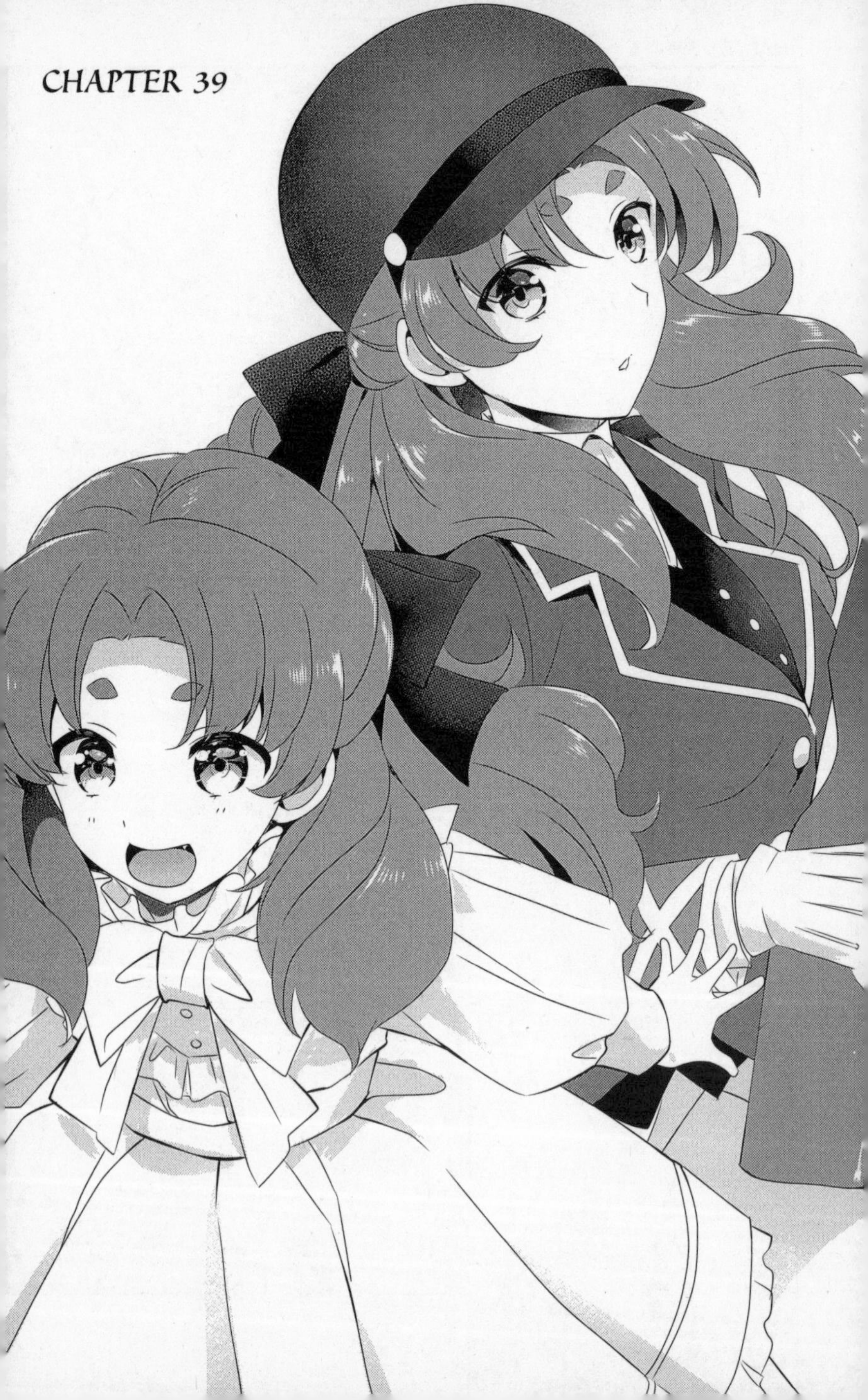

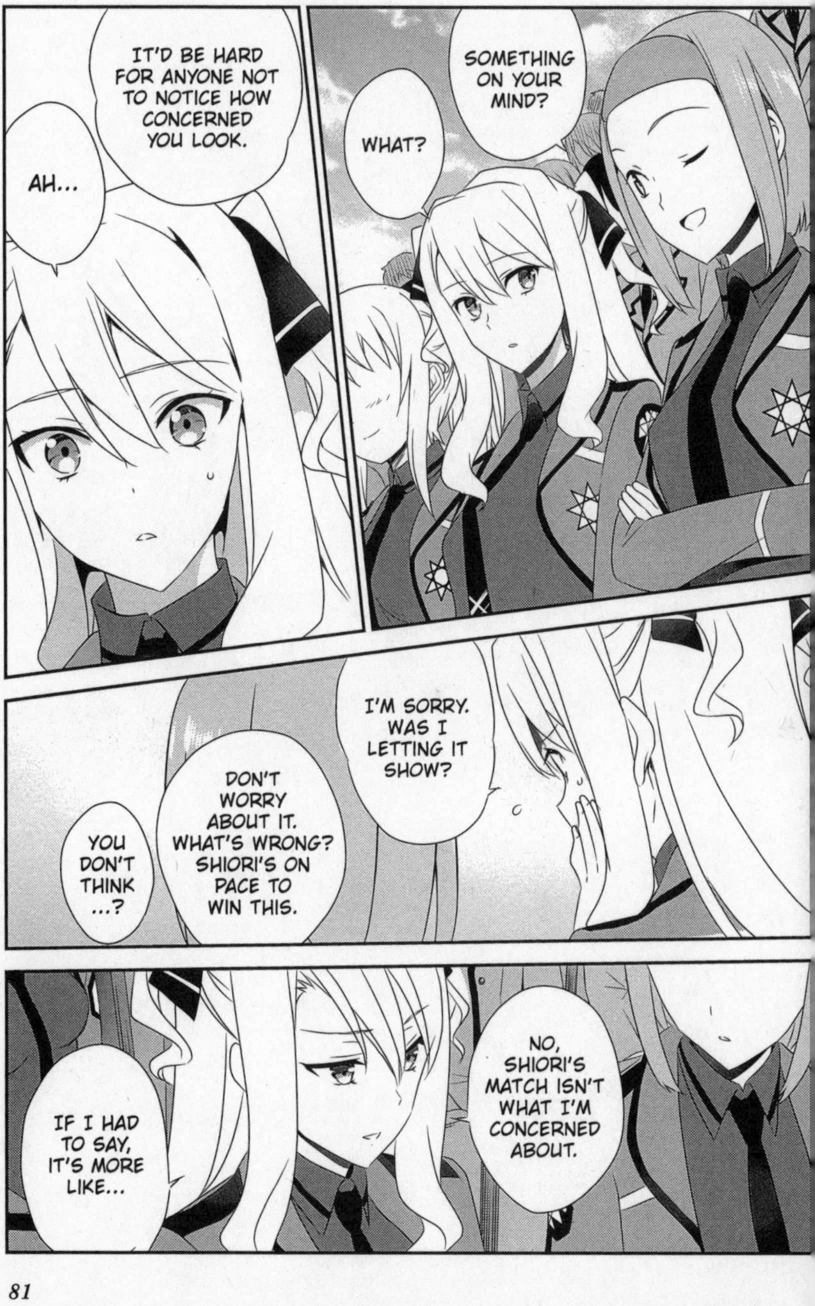
SOMETHING ON YOUR MIND?
WHAT?
IT'D BE HARD FOR ANYONE NOT TO NOTICE HOW CONCERNED YOU LOOK.
AH...
I'M SORRY. WAS I LETTING IT SHOW?
DON'T WORRY ABOUT IT. WHAT'S WRONG? SHIORI'S ON PACE TO WIN THIS.
YOU DON'T THINK ...?
NO, SHIORI'S MATCH ISN'T WHAT I'M CONCERNED ABOUT.
IF I HAD TO SAY, IT'S MORE LIKE...

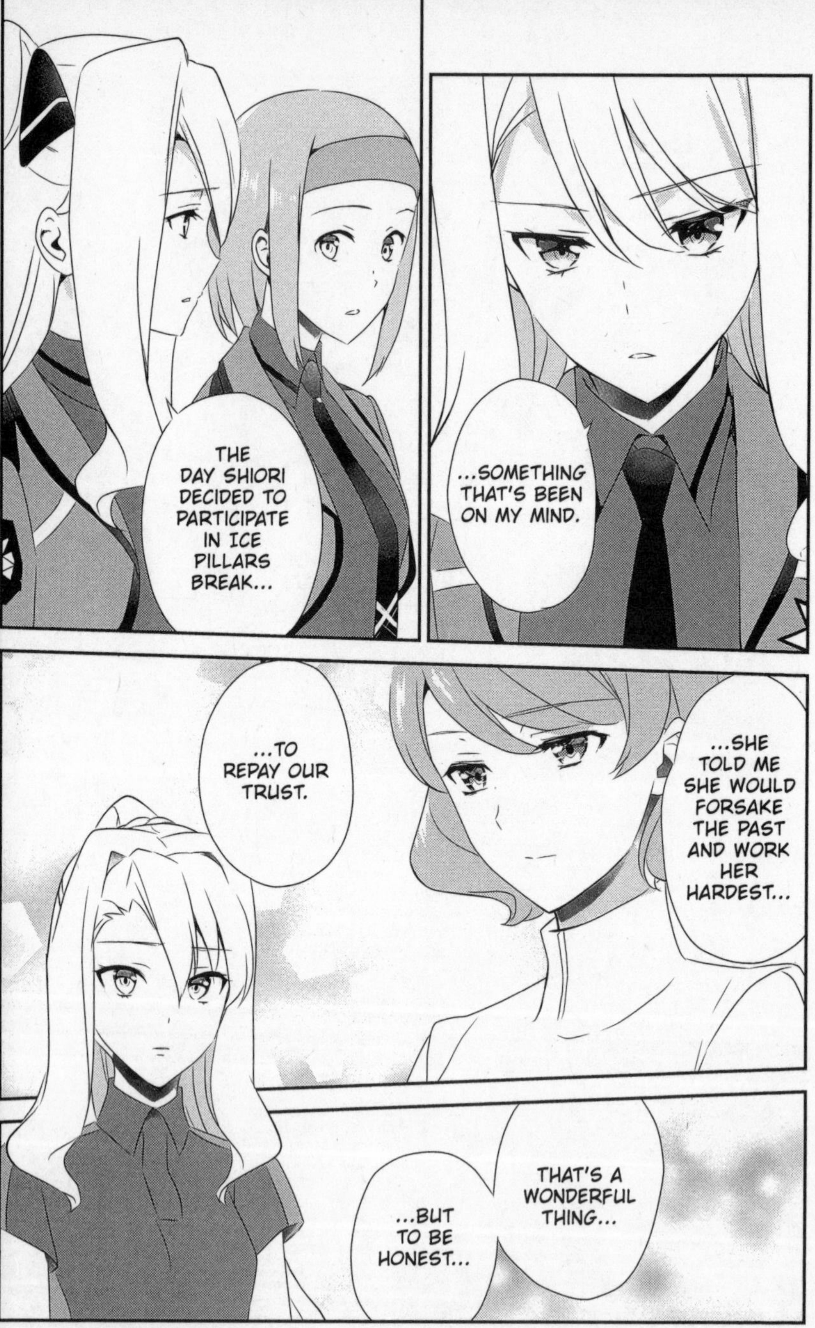
...SOMETHING THAT'S BEEN ON MY MIND.
THE DAY SHIORI DECIDED TO PARTICIPATE IN ICE PILLARS BREAK...
...SHE TOLD ME SHE WOULD FORSAKE THE PAST AND WORK HER HARDEST...
...TO REPAY OUR TRUST.
THAT'S A WONDERFUL THING...
...BUT TO BE HONEST...

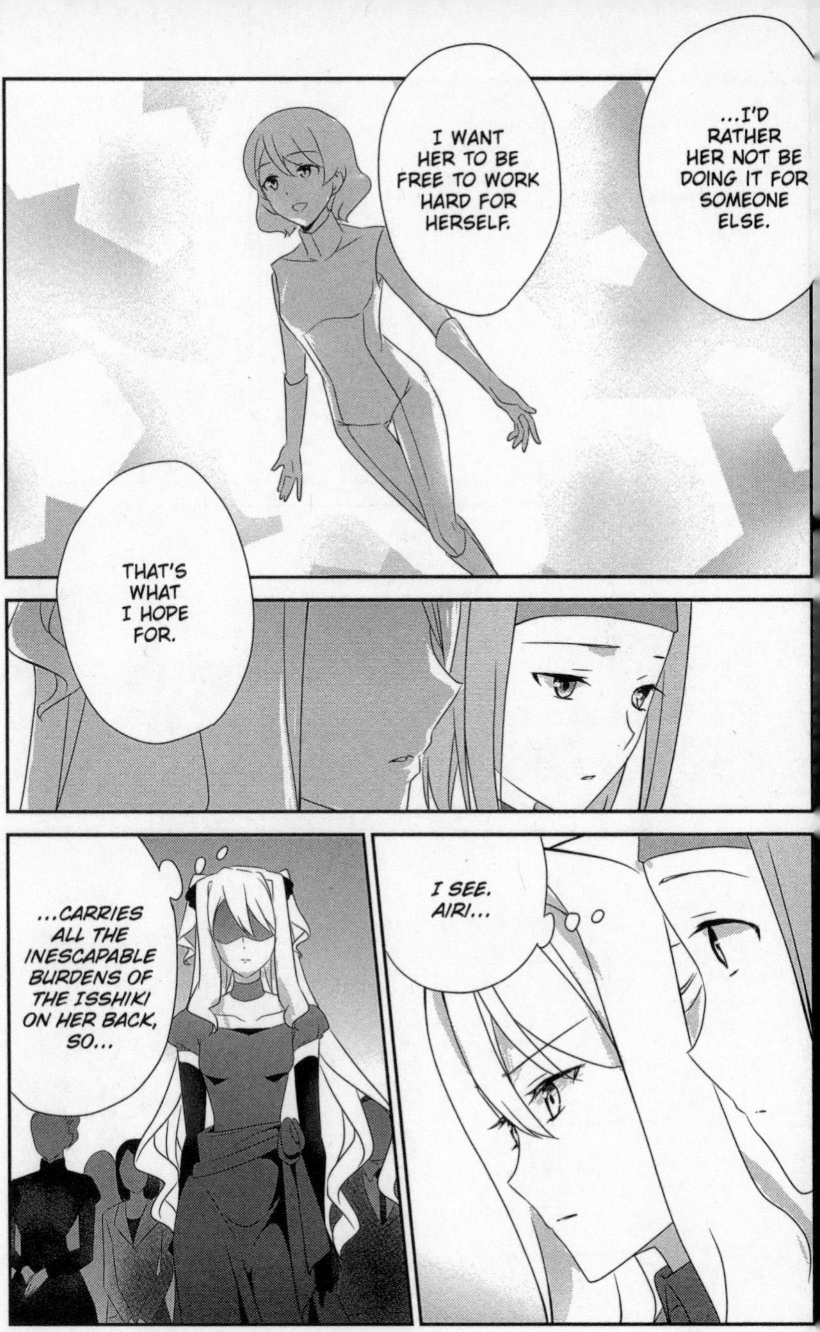
...I'D RATHER HER NOT BE DOING IT FOR SOMEONE ELSE.
I WANT HER TO BE FREE TO WORK HARD FOR HERSELF.
THAT'S WHAT I HOPE FOR.
I SEE. AIRI...
...CARRIES ALL THE INESCAPABLE BURDENS OF THE ISSHIKI ON HER BACK, SO...

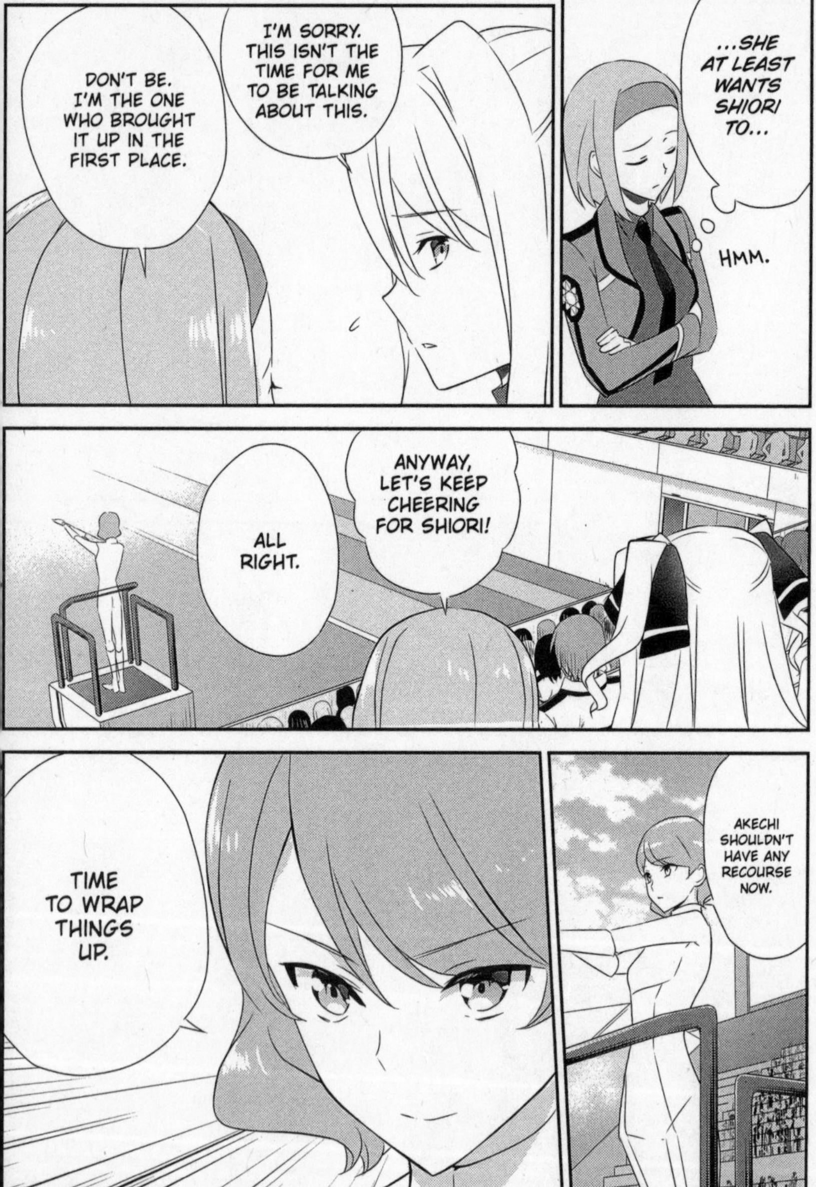
...SHE AT LEAST WANTS SHIORI TO...
HMM.
I'M SORRY. THIS ISN'T THE TIME FOR ME TO BE TALKING ABOUT THIS.
DON'T BE. I'M THE ONE WHO BROUGHT IT UP IN THE FIRST PLACE.
ANYWAY, LET'S KEEP CHEERING FOR SHIORI!
ALL RIGHT.
AKECHI SHOULDN'T HAVE ANY RECOURSE NOW.
TIME TO WRAP THINGS UP.

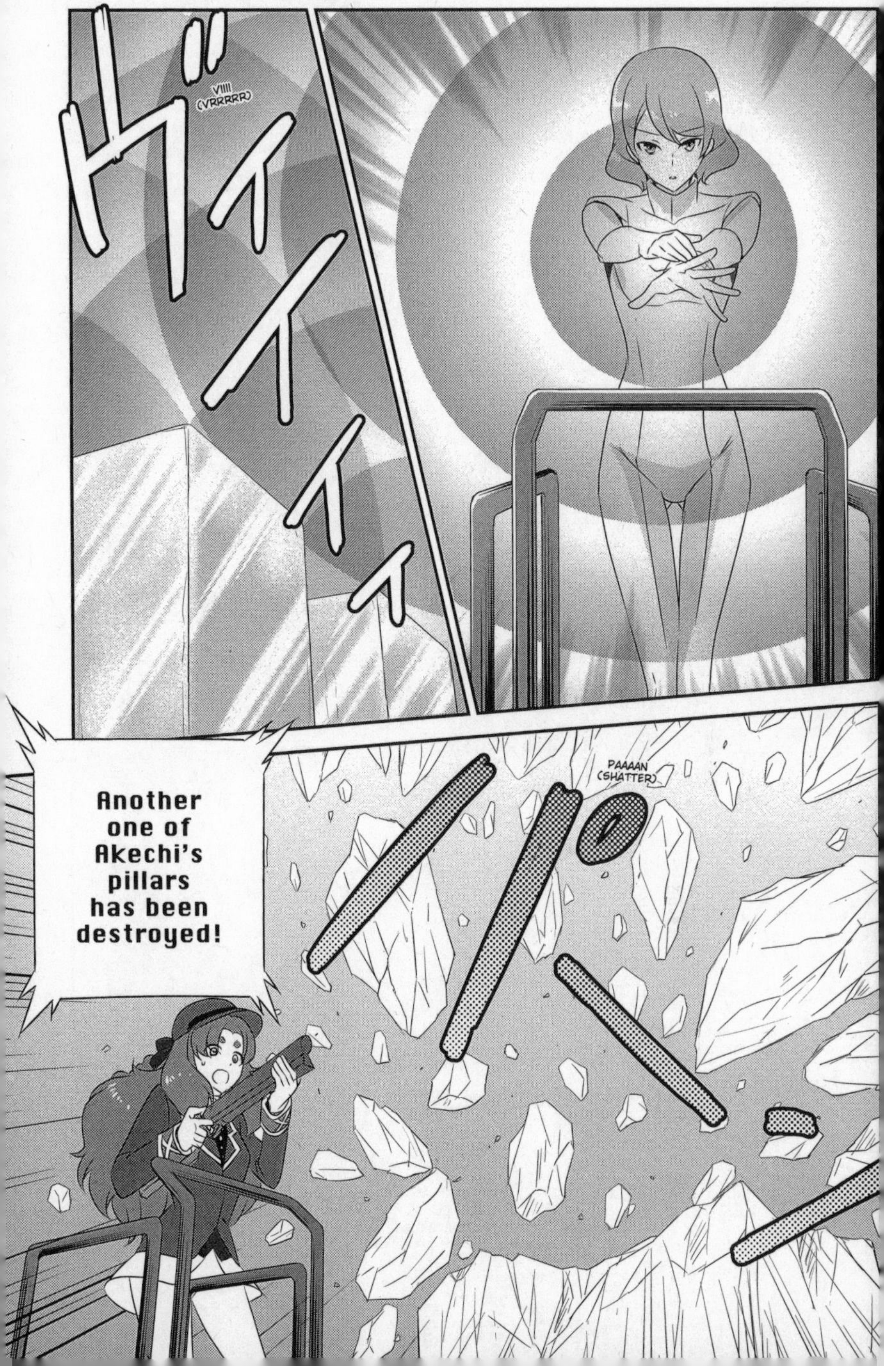
ヴィイイィ
VIIII (VRRRRR)
PAAAAN (SHATTER)
パ
Another one of Akechi's pillars has been destroyed!

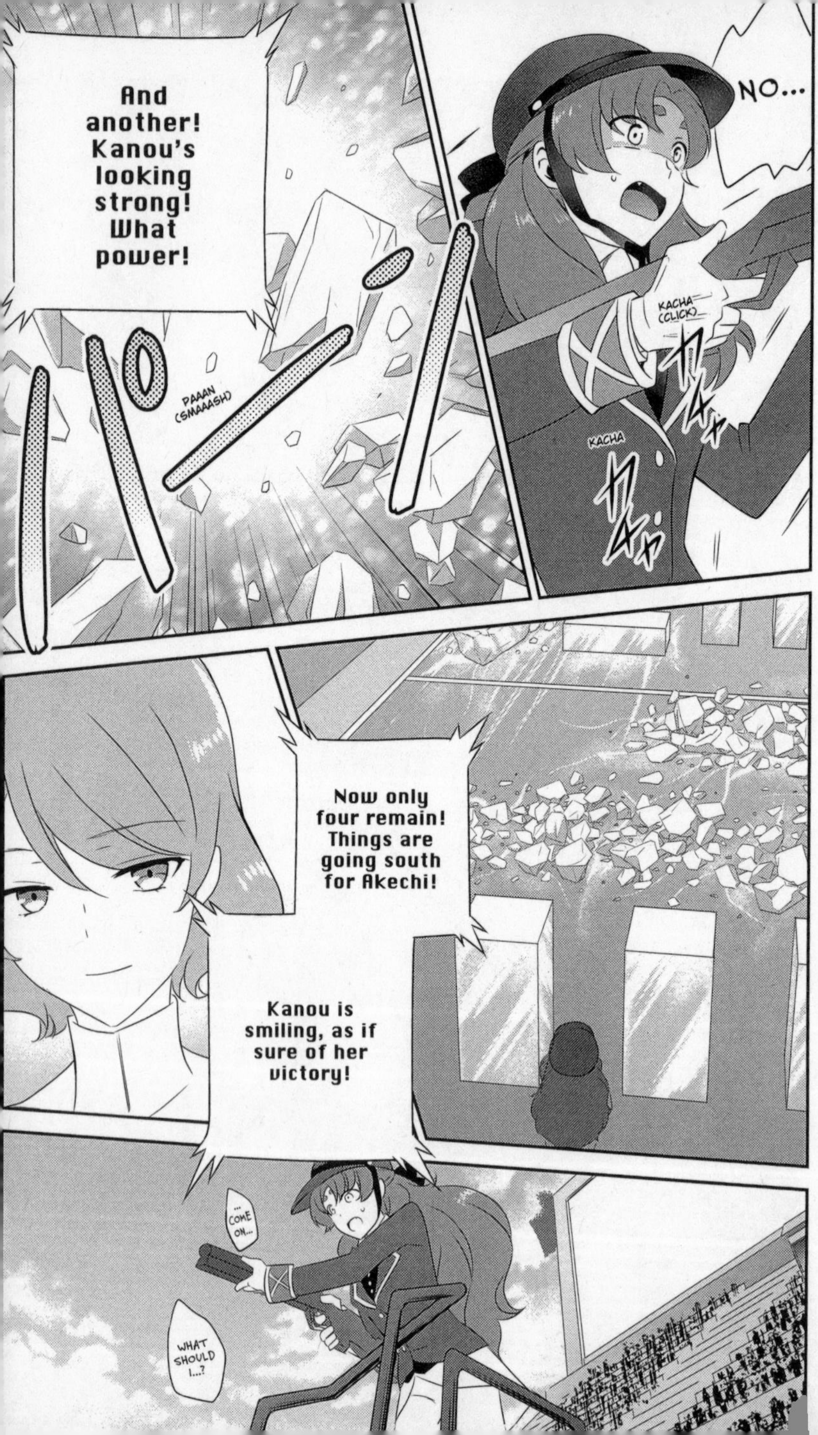
NO...
And another! Kanou's looking strong! What power!
KACHA (CLICK)
KACHA
PAAAN (SMAAASH)
Now only four remain! Things are going south for Akechi!
Kanou is smiling, as if sure of her victory!
...COME ON...
WHAT SHOULD I...?

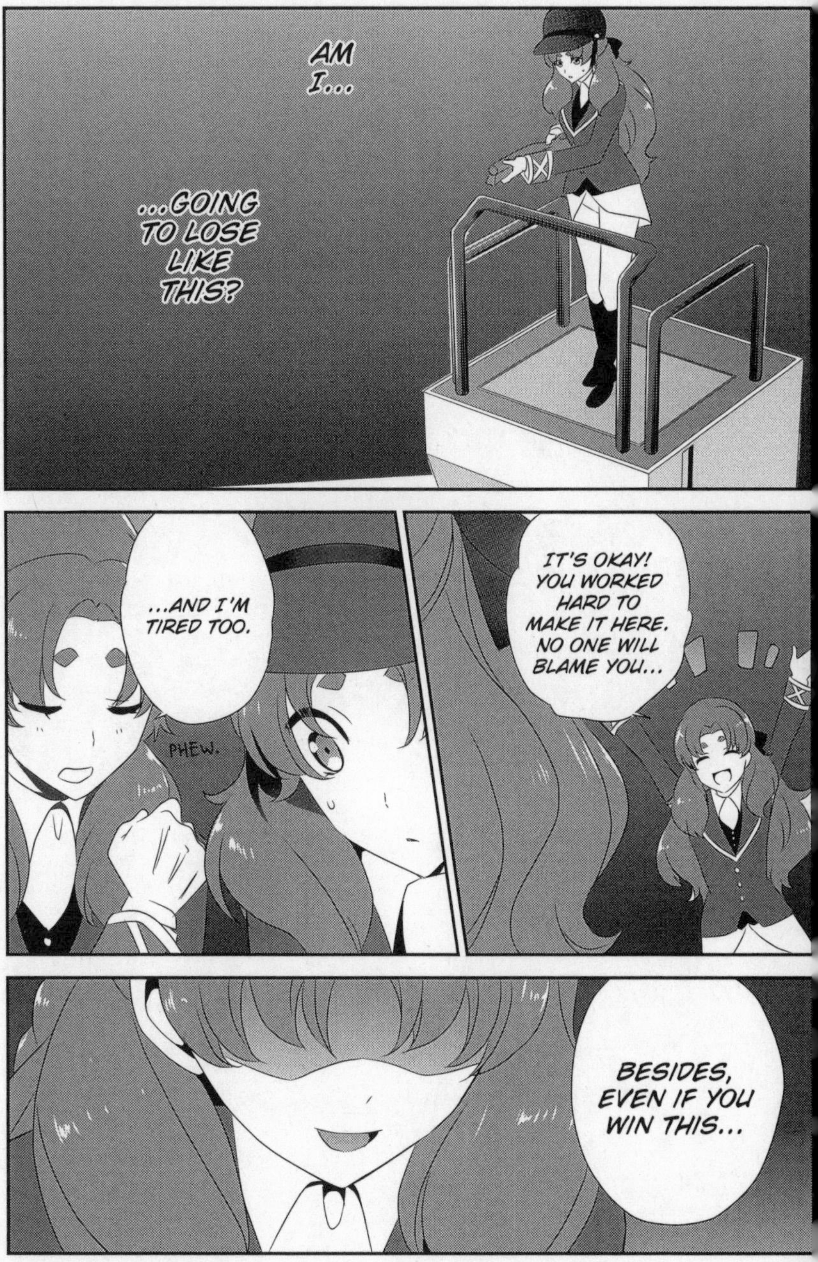
AM I...
...GOING TO LOSE LIKE THIS?
IT'S OKAY! YOU WORKED HARD TO MAKE IT HERE. NO ONE WILL BLAME YOU...
...AND I'M TIRED TOO.
PHEW.
BESIDES, EVEN IF YOU WIN THIS...

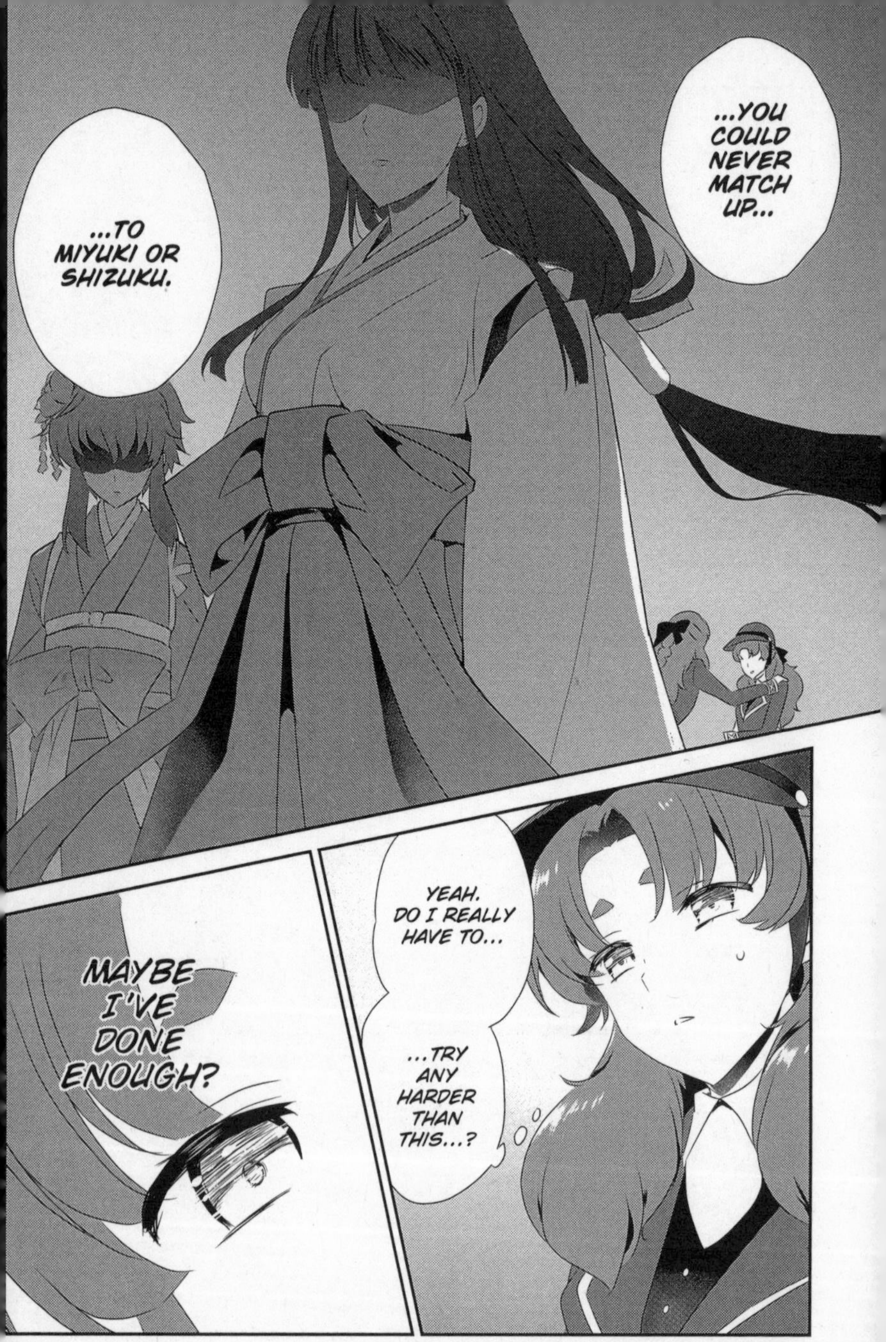
...YOU COULD NEVER MATCH UP...
...TO MIYUKI OR SHIZUKU.
YEAH. DO I REALLY HAVE TO...
...TRY ANY HARDER THAN THIS...?
MAYBE I'VE DONE ENOUGH?

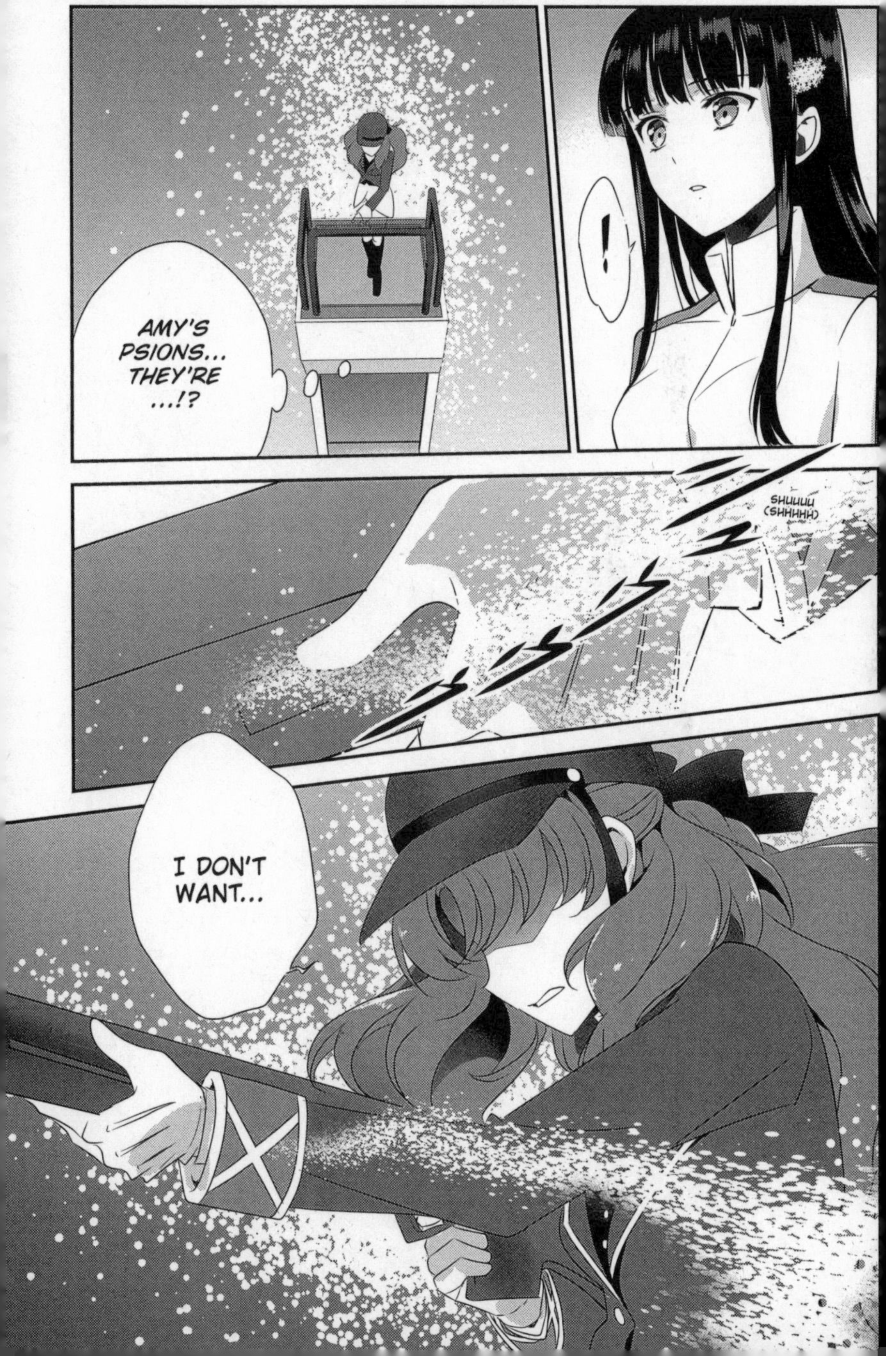
!
AMY'S PSIONS... THEY'RE ...!?
SHUUUU (SHHHHH)
I DON'T WANT...

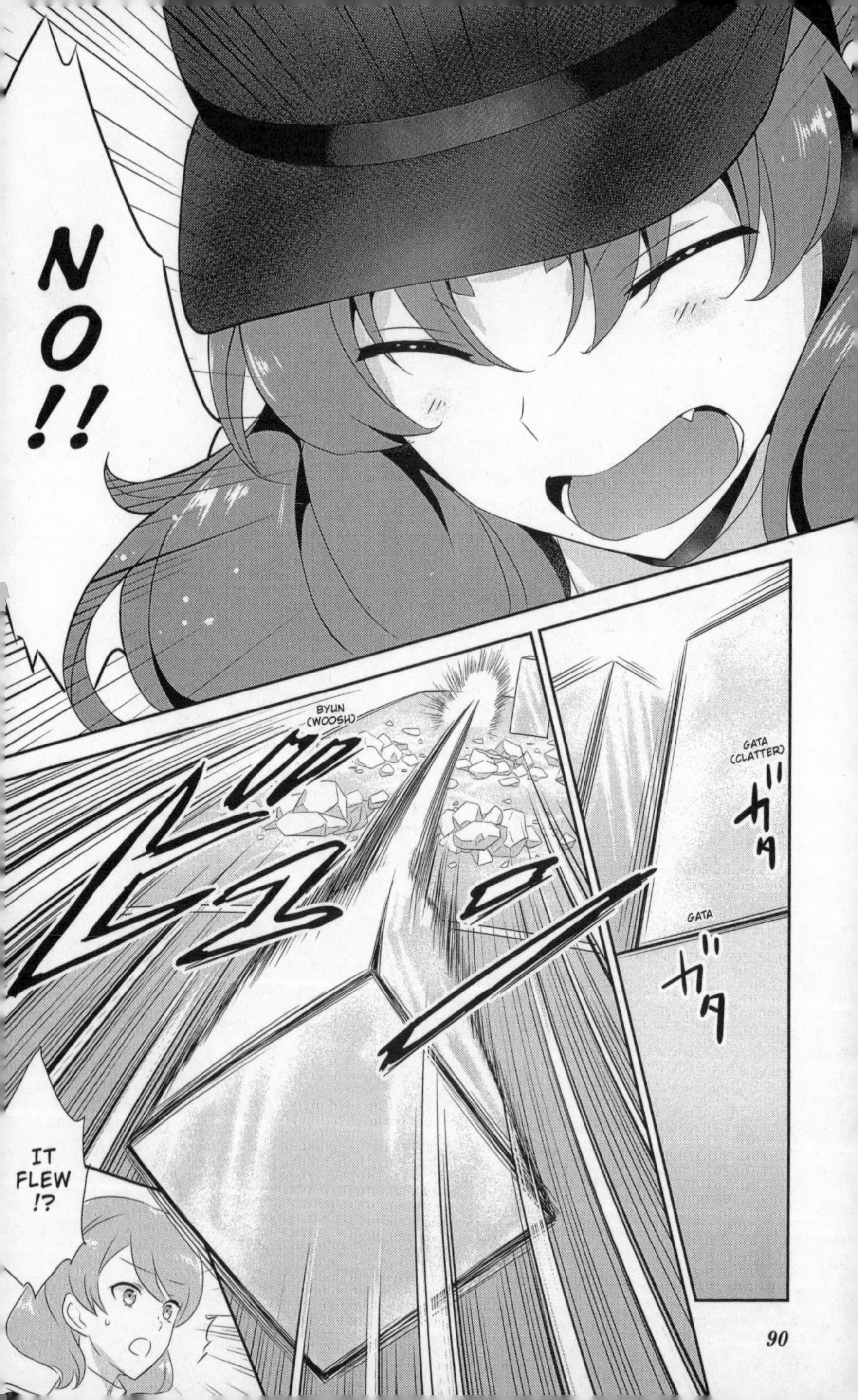
NO!!
GATA (CLATTER)
ガタ
GATA
ガタ
BYUN (WOOSH)
IT FLEW!?

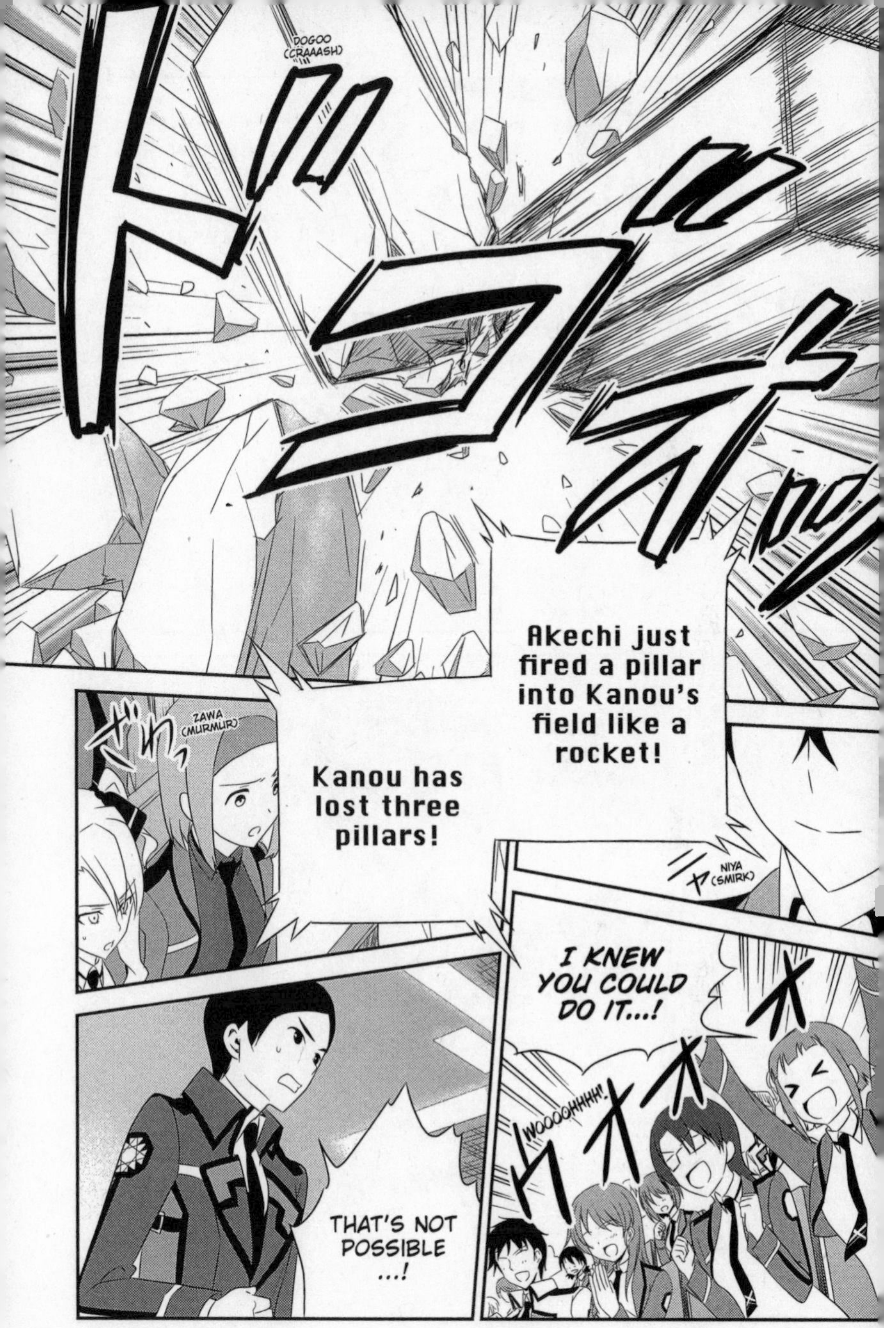
DOGOO (CRAAASH)
Akechi just fired a pillar into Kanou's field like a rocket!
NIYA (SMIRK)
ZAWA (MURMUR)
Kanou has lost three pillars!
I KNEW YOU COULD DO IT...!
WOOOOHHHH!
THAT'S NOT POSSIBLE ...!

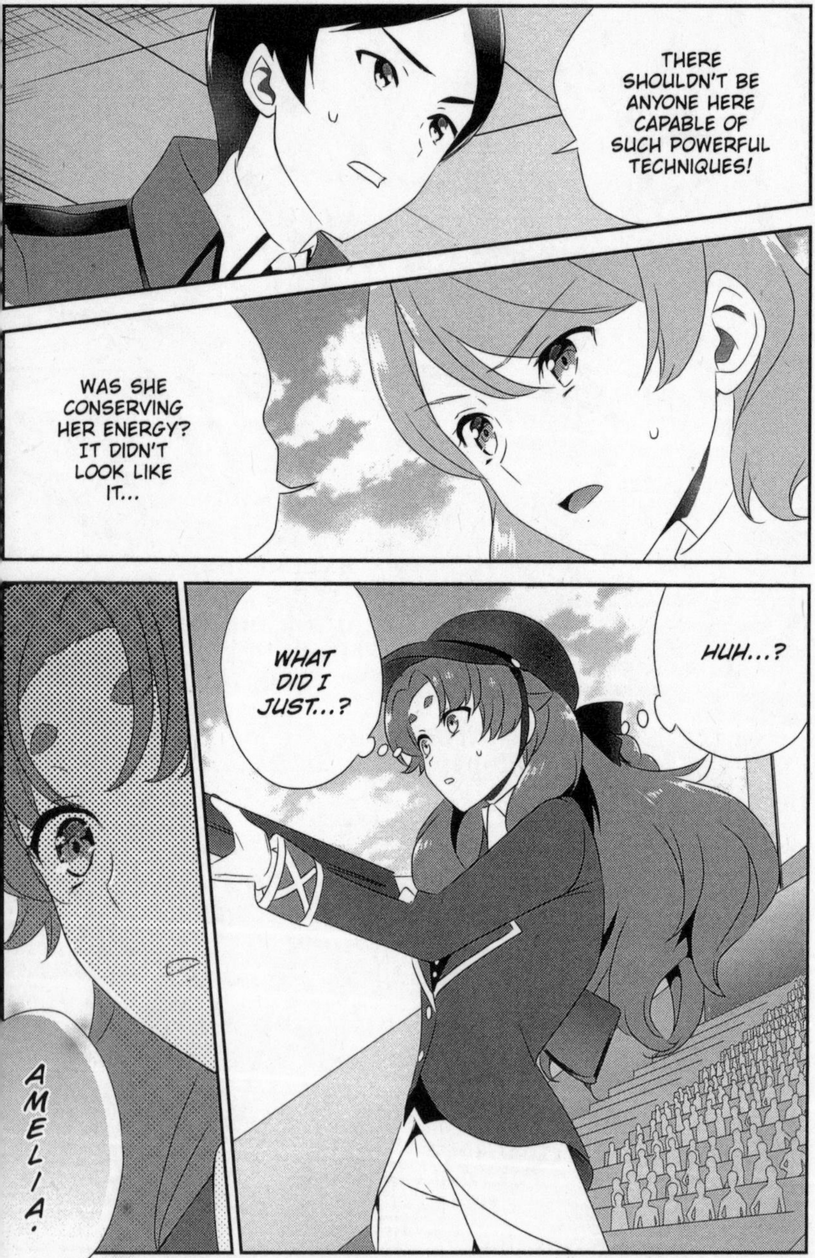
THERE SHOULDN'T BE ANYONE HERE CAPABLE OF SUCH POWERFUL TECHNIQUES!
WAS SHE CONSERVING HER ENERGY? IT DIDN'T LOOK LIKE IT...
HUH...?
WHAT DID I JUST...?
AMELIA.

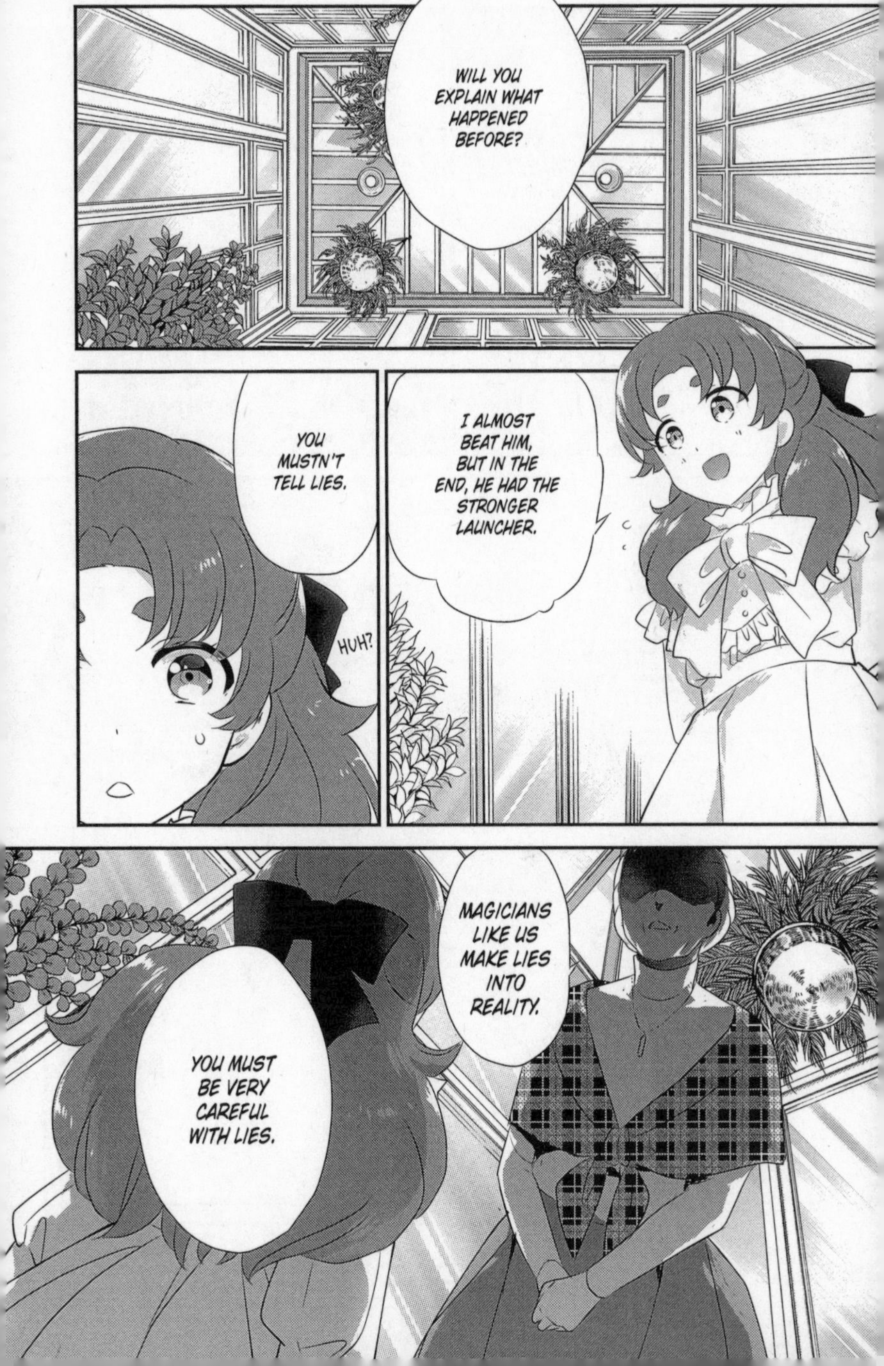
WILL YOU EXPLAIN WHAT HAPPENED BEFORE?
I ALMOST BEAT HIM, BUT IN THE END, HE HAD THE STRONGER LAUNCHER.
YOU MUSTN'T TELL LIES.
HUH?
MAGICIANS LIKE US MAKE LIES INTO REALITY.
YOU MUST BE VERY CAREFUL WITH LIES.

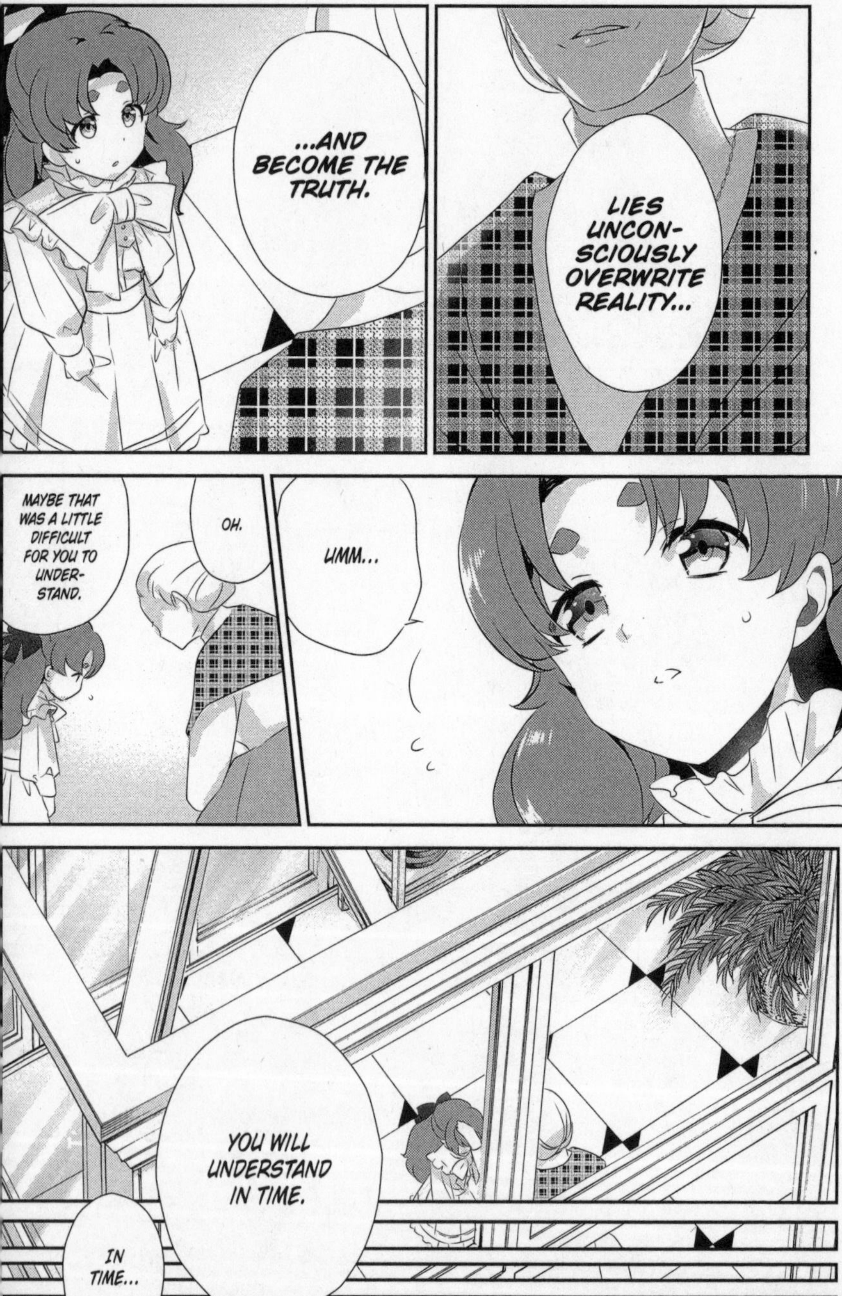
LIES UNCON-SCIOUSLY OVERWRITE REALITY...
...AND BECOME THE TRUTH.
UMM...
OH.
MAYBE THAT WAS A LITTLE DIFFICULT FOR YOU TO UNDER-STAND.
YOU WILL UNDERSTAND IN TIME.
IN TIME...

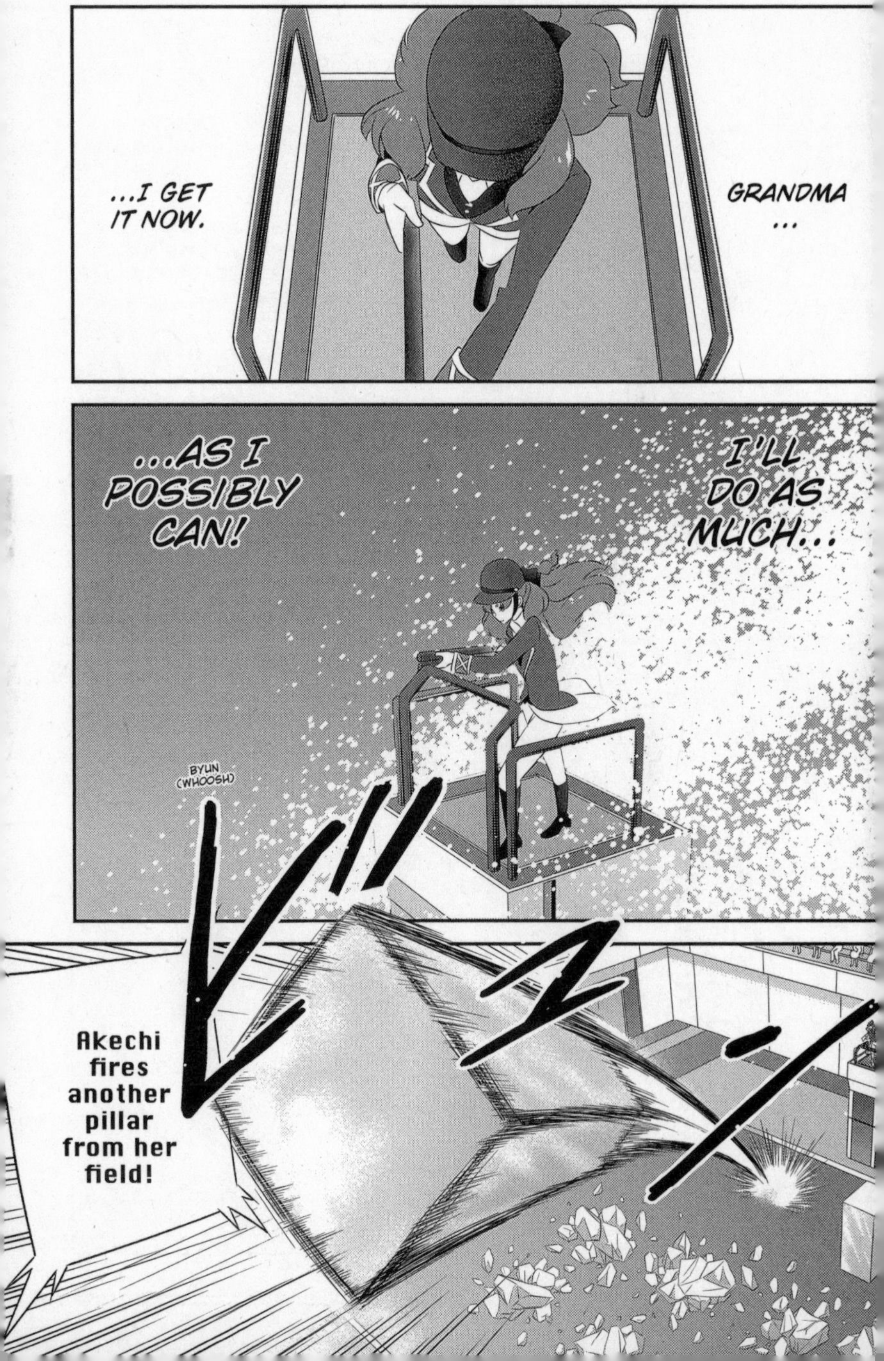
GRANDMA...
...I GET IT NOW.
I'LL DO AS MUCH...
...AS I POSSIBLY CAN!
BYUN (WHOOSH)
Akechi fires another pillar from her field!

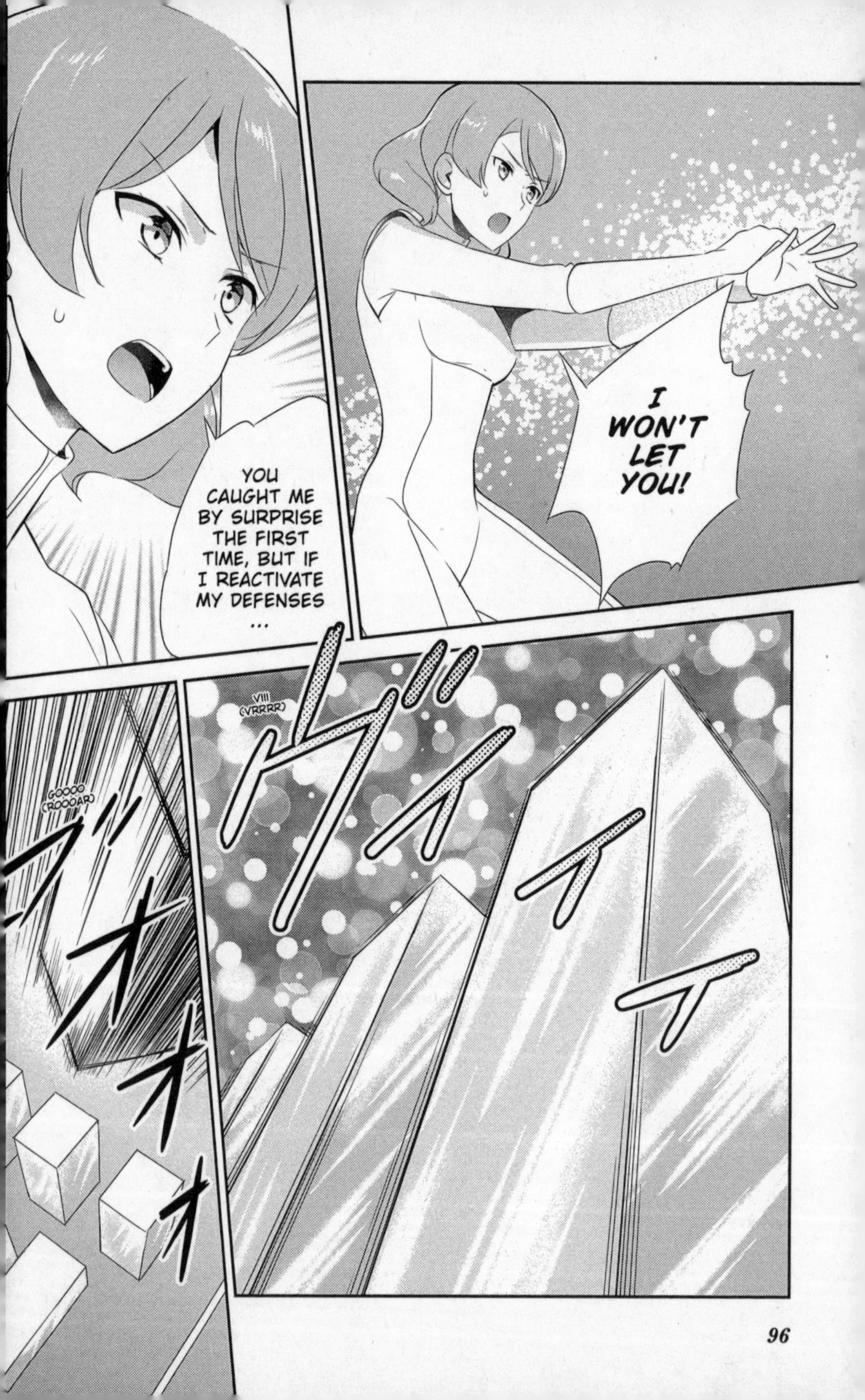
I WON'T LET YOU!
YOU CAUGHT ME BY SURPRISE THE FIRST TIME, BUT IF I REACTIVATE MY DEFENSES ...
VIII (VRRRR)
GOOOO (ROOOAR)

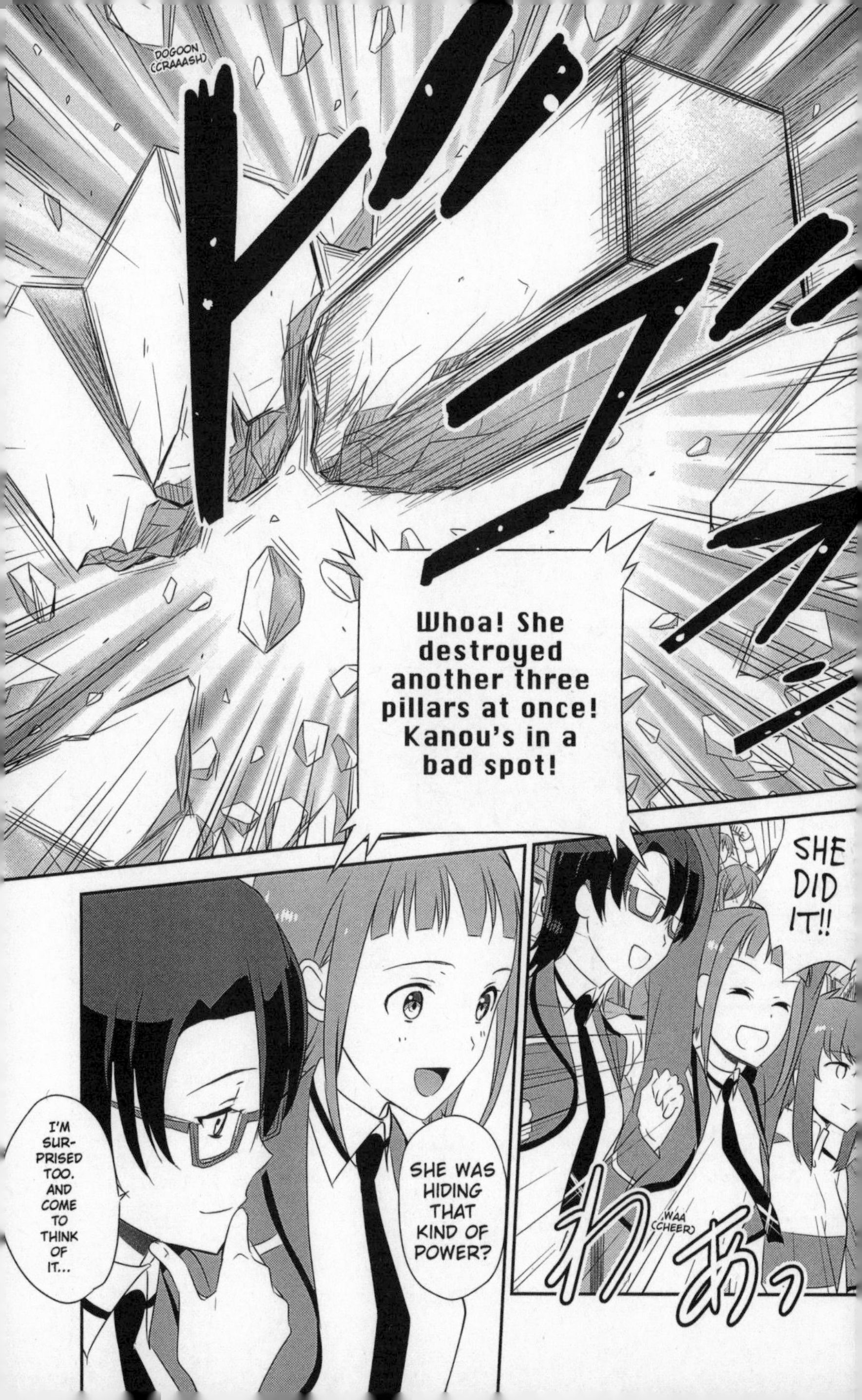
DOGOON (CRAAASH)
Whoa! She destroyed another three pillars at once! Kanou's in a bad spot!
SHE DID IT!!
WAA (CHEER)
SHE WAS HIDING THAT KIND OF POWER?
I'M SUR-PRISED TOO. AND COME TO THINK OF IT...

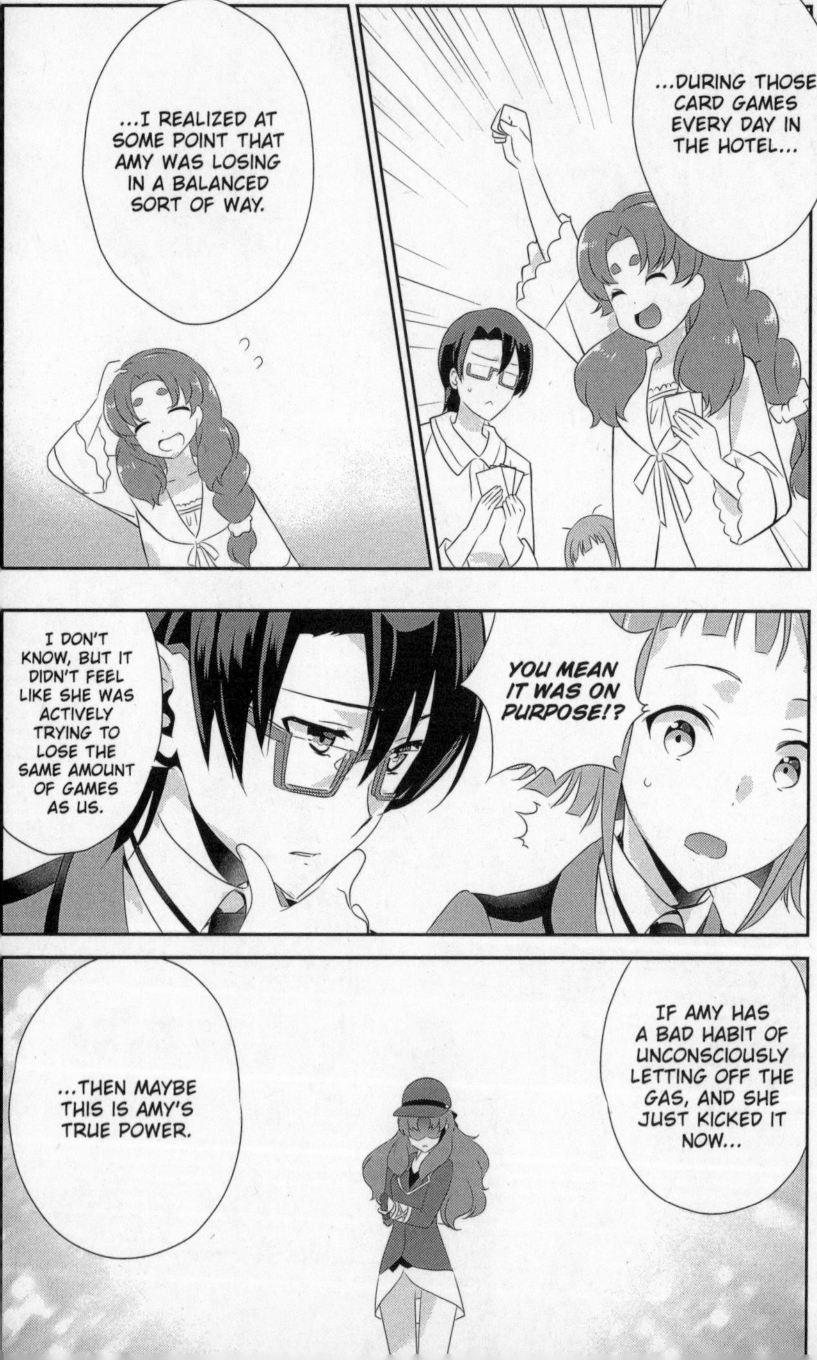
...DURING THOSE CARD GAMES EVERY DAY IN THE HOTEL...
...I REALIZED AT SOME POINT THAT AMY WAS LOSING IN A BALANCED SORT OF WAY.
YOU MEAN IT WAS ON PURPOSE!?
I DON'T KNOW, BUT IT DIDN'T FEEL LIKE SHE WAS ACTIVELY TRYING TO LOSE THE SAME AMOUNT OF GAMES AS US.
IF AMY HAS A BAD HABIT OF UNCONSCIOUSLY LETTING OFF THE GAS, AND SHE JUST KICKED IT NOW...
...THEN MAYBE THIS IS AMY'S TRUE POWER.

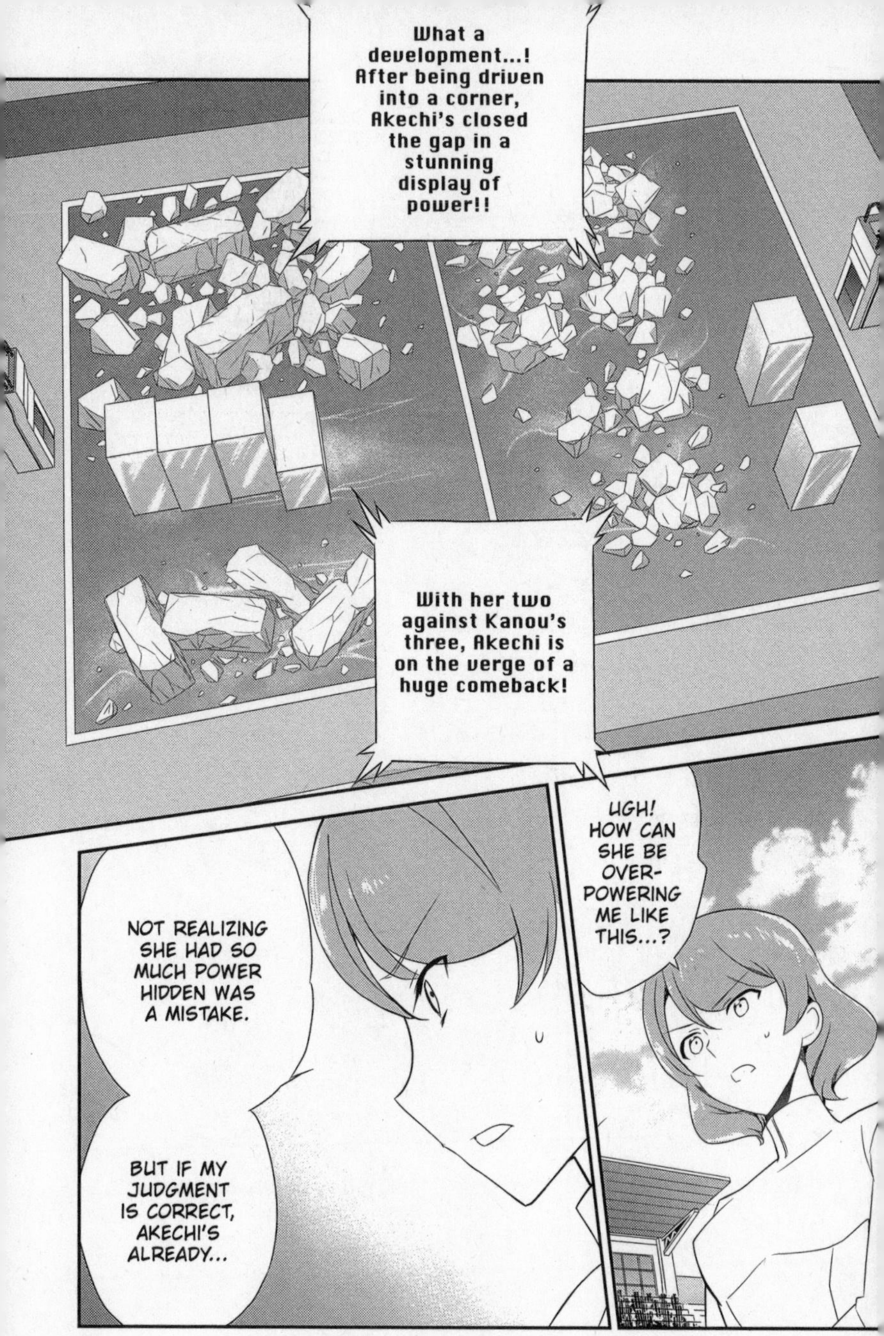
What a development...! After being driven into a corner, Akechi's closed the gap in a stunning display of power!!
With her two against Kanou's three, Akechi is on the verge of a huge comeback!
UGH! HOW CAN SHE BE OVER-POWERING ME LIKE THIS...?
NOT REALIZING SHE HAD SO MUCH POWER HIDDEN WAS A MISTAKE.
BUT IF MY JUDGMENT IS CORRECT, AKECHI'S ALREADY...

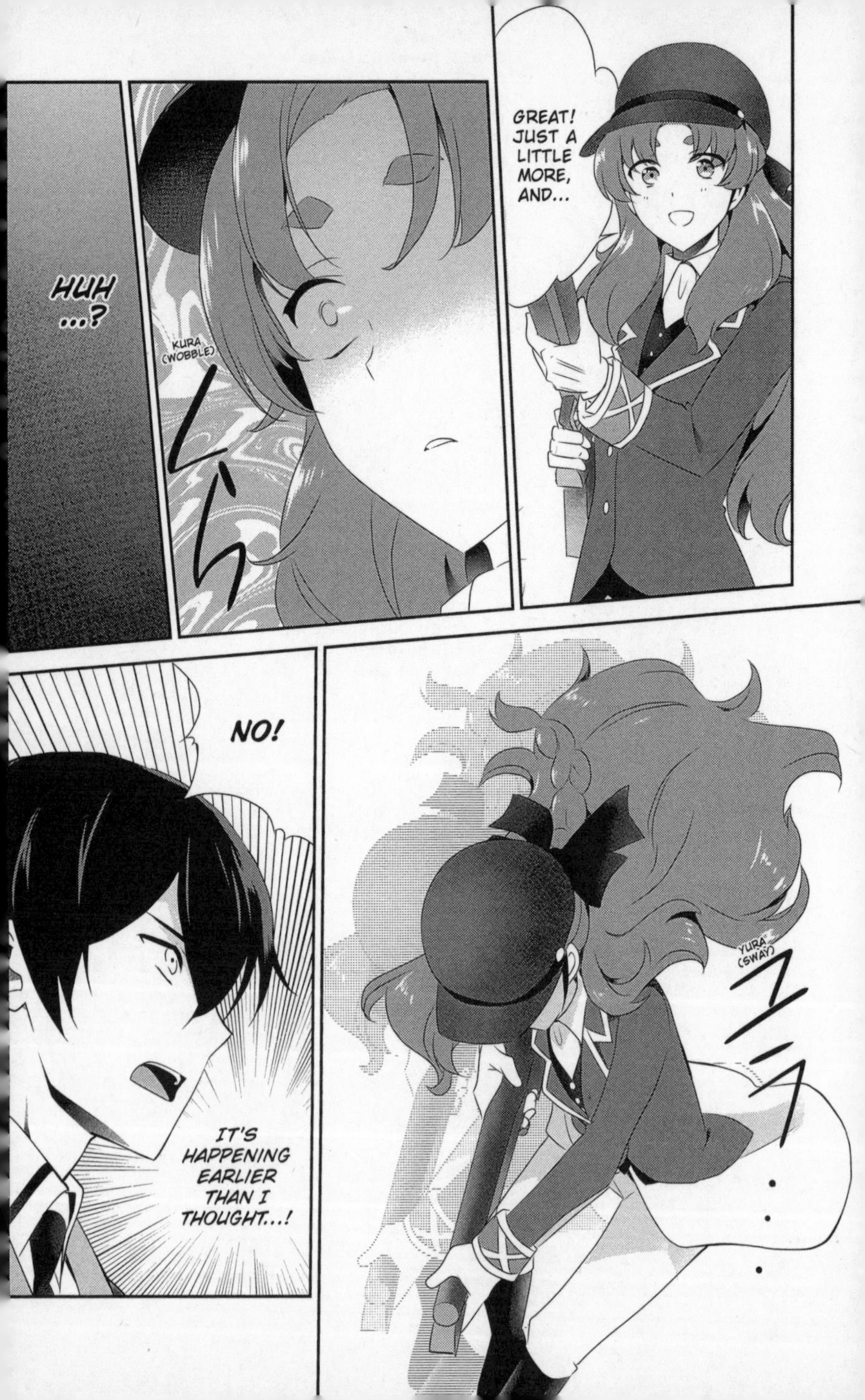
GREAT! JUST A LITTLE MORE, AND...
KURA (WOBBLE)
HUH ...?
YURA (SWAY)
NO!
IT'S HAPPENING EARLIER THAN I THOUGHT...!

THE
HONOR
STUDENT
AT
Magic High
School

THIS MATCH IS DECIDED ...!!

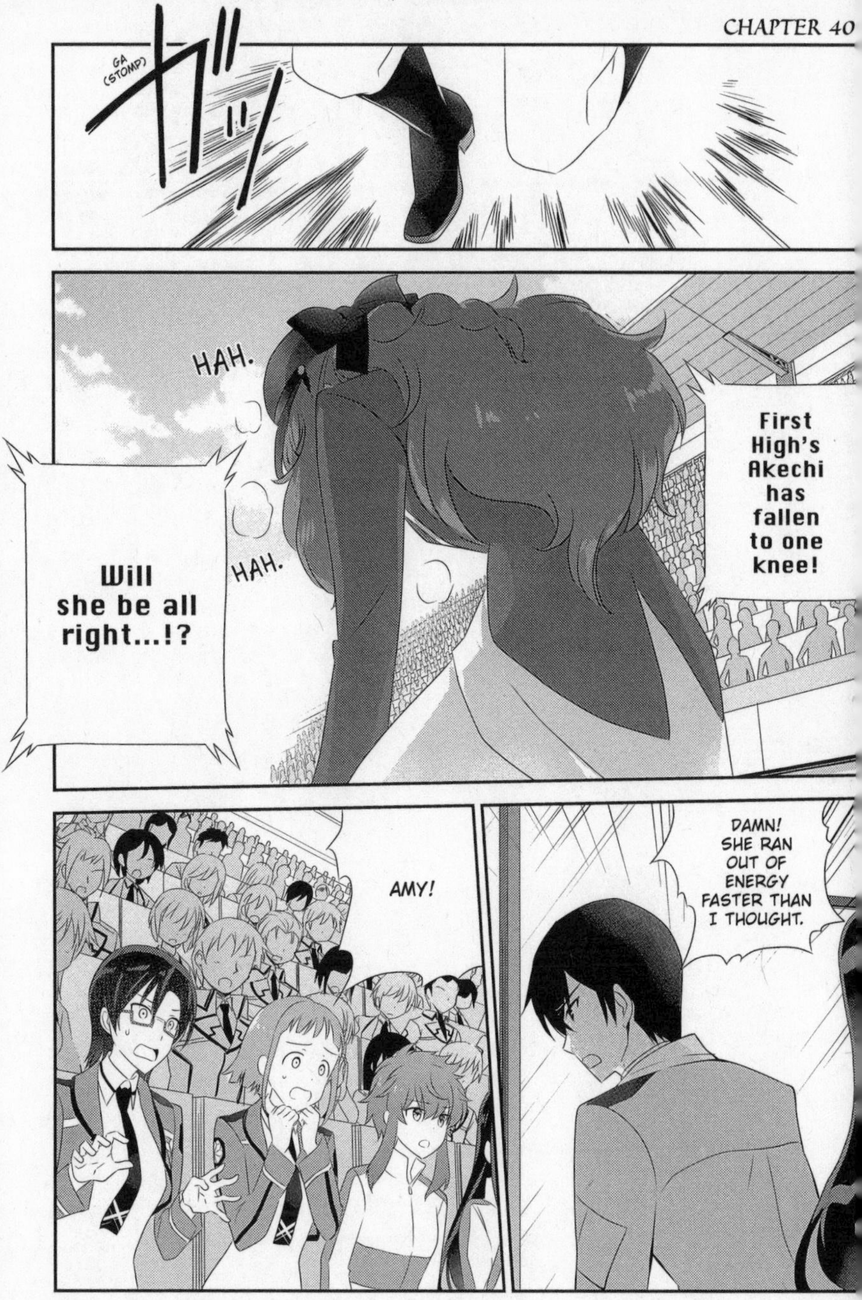
GA (STOMP)
First High's Akechi has fallen to one knee!
HAH.
HAH.
Will she be all right...!?
DAMN! SHE RAN OUT OF ENERGY FASTER THAN I THOUGHT.
AMY!

CHAPTER 40

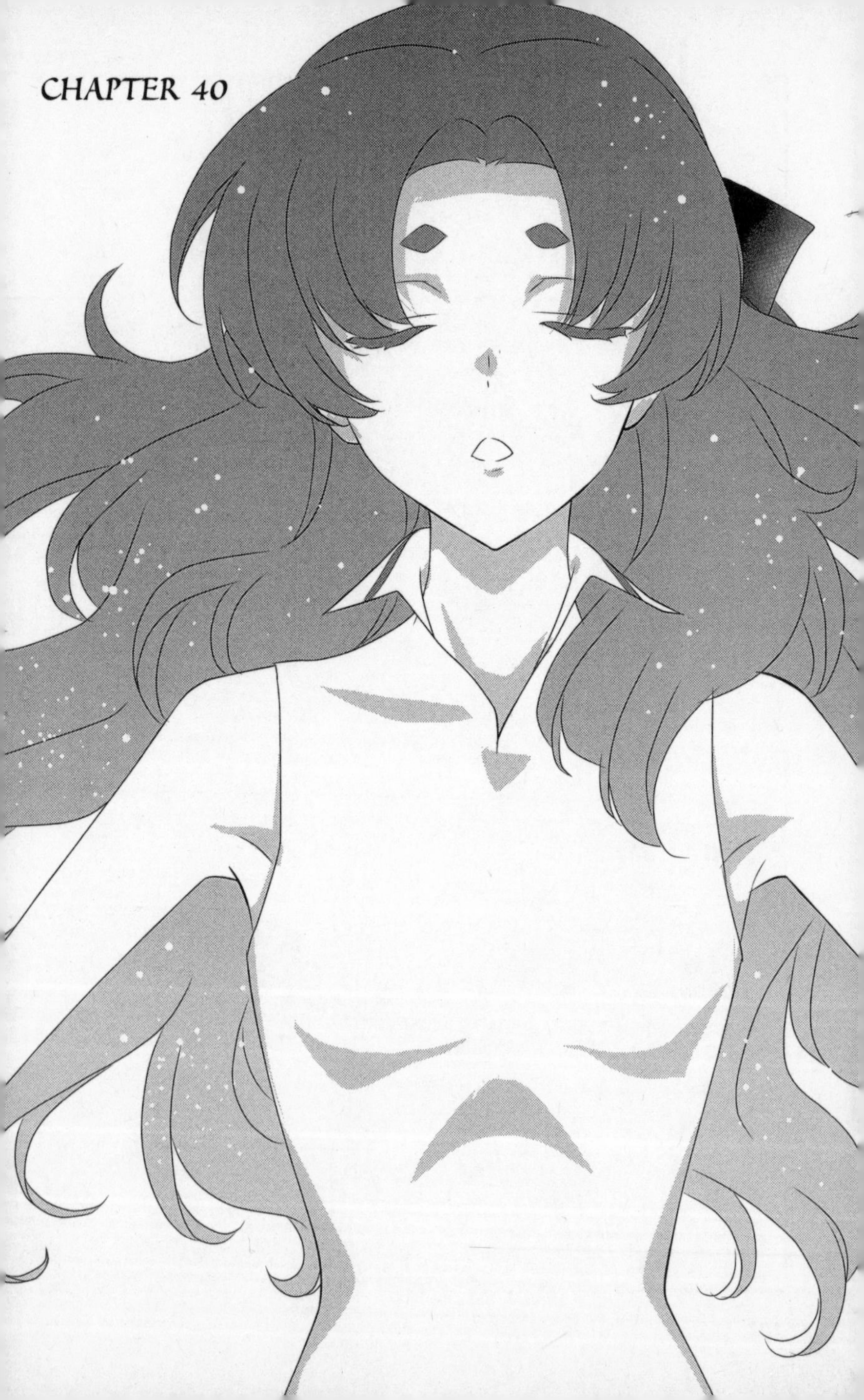

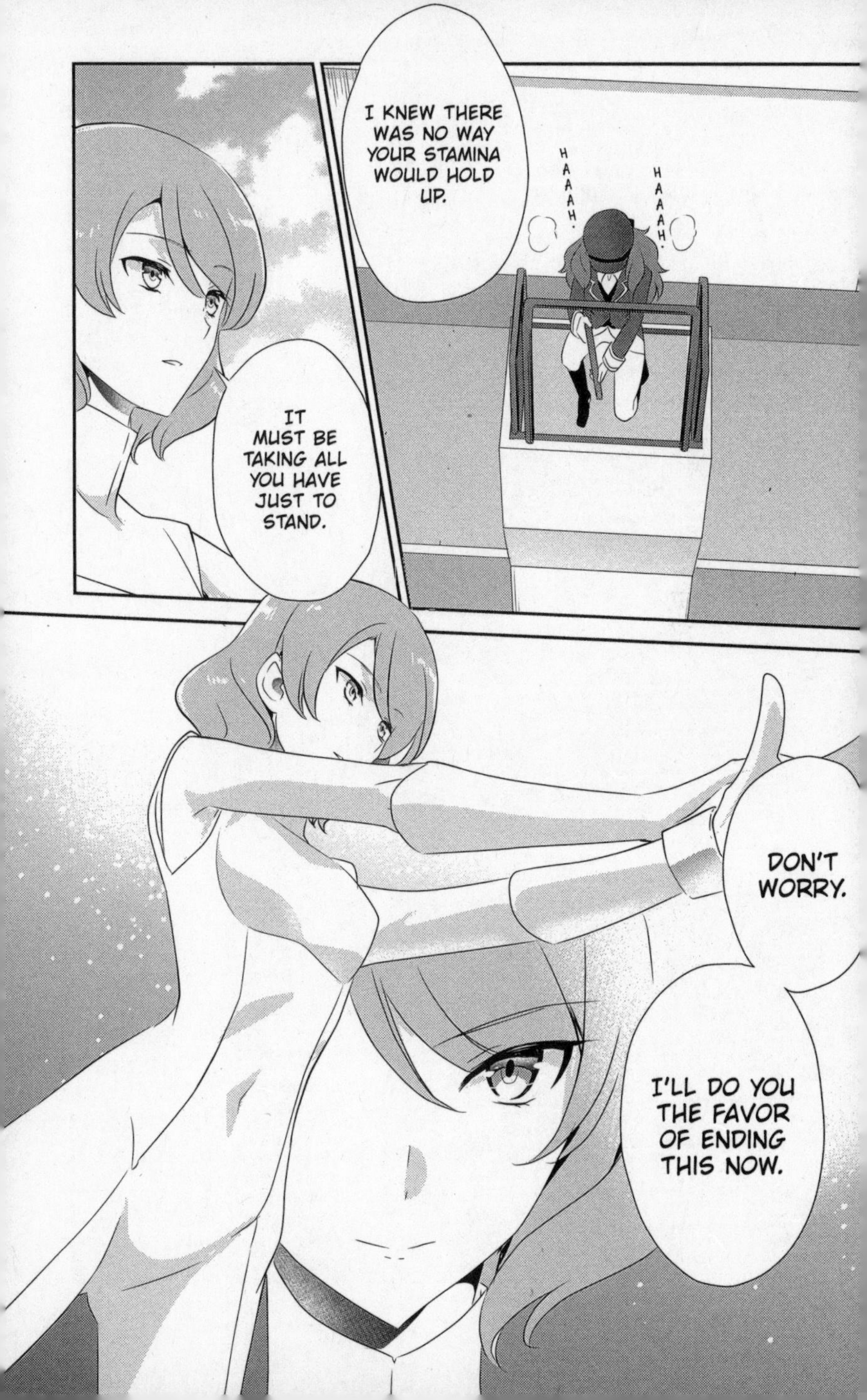
I KNEW THERE WAS NO WAY YOUR STAMINA WOULD HOLD UP.
HAAAH.
HAAAH.
IT MUST BE TAKING ALL YOU HAVE JUST TO STAND.
DON'T WORRY.
I'LL DO YOU THE FAVOR OF ENDING THIS NOW.

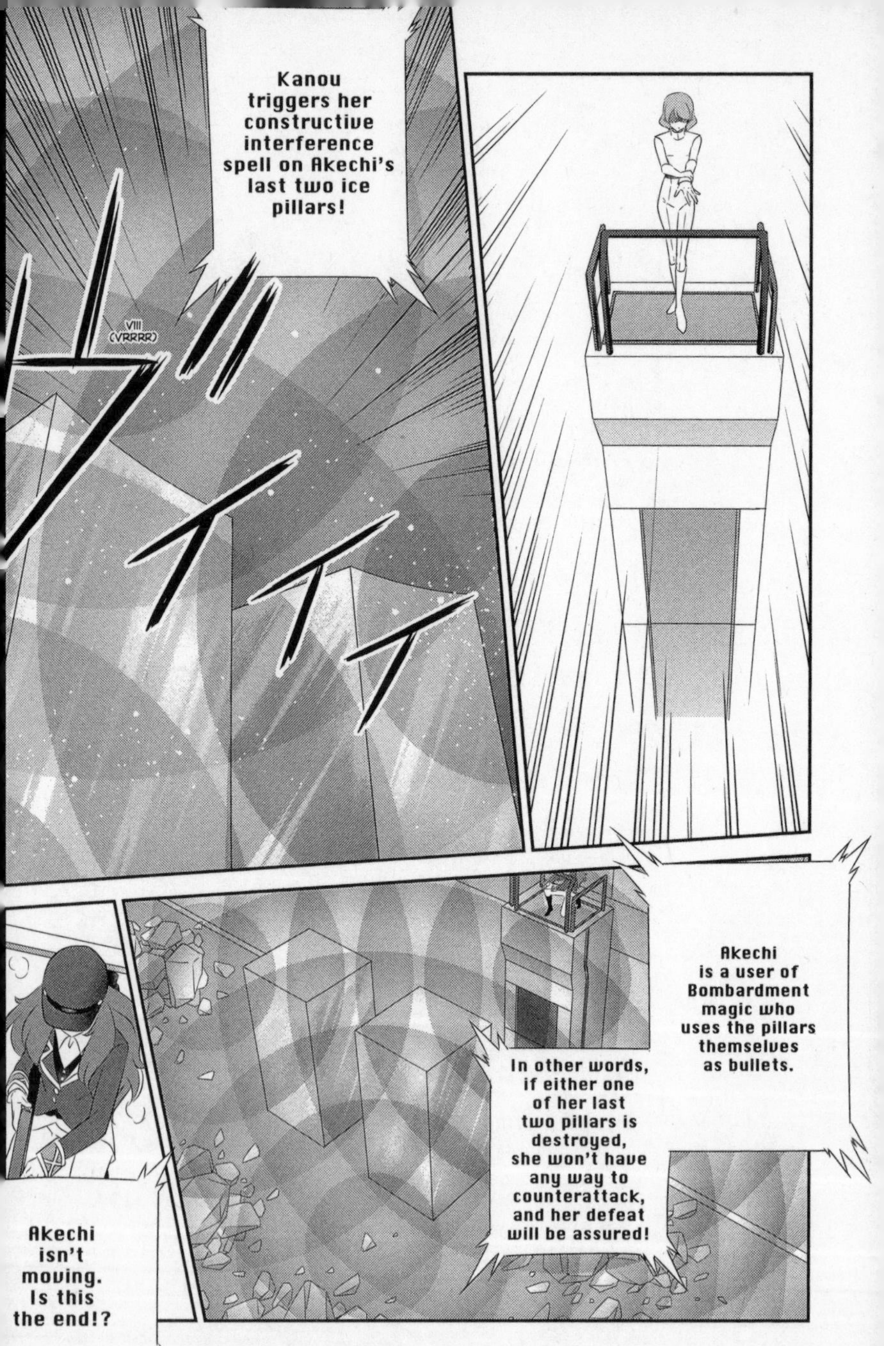
Kanou triggers her constructive interference spell on Akechi's last two ice pillars!
VIII (VRRRR)
Akechi is a user of Bombardment magic who uses the pillars themselves as bullets.
In other words, if either one of her last two pillars is destroyed, she won't have any way to counterattack, and her defeat will be assured!
Akechi isn't moving. Is this the end!?

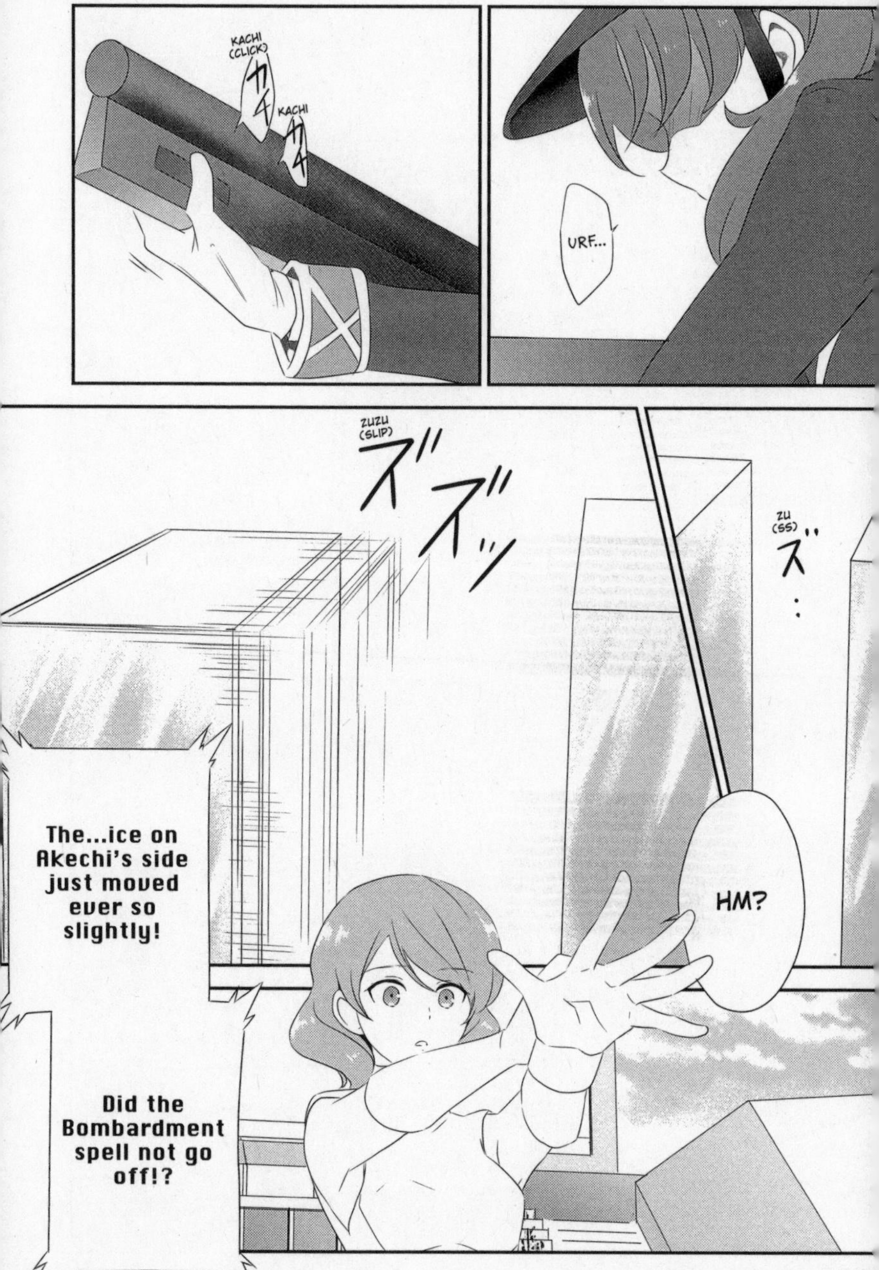
URF...
KACHI (CLICK)
カチ
KACHI
カチ
ZU (SS)
ズ
HM?
ZUZU (SLIP)
ズズッ
The...ice on Akechi's side just moved ever so slightly!
Did the Bombardment spell not go off!?

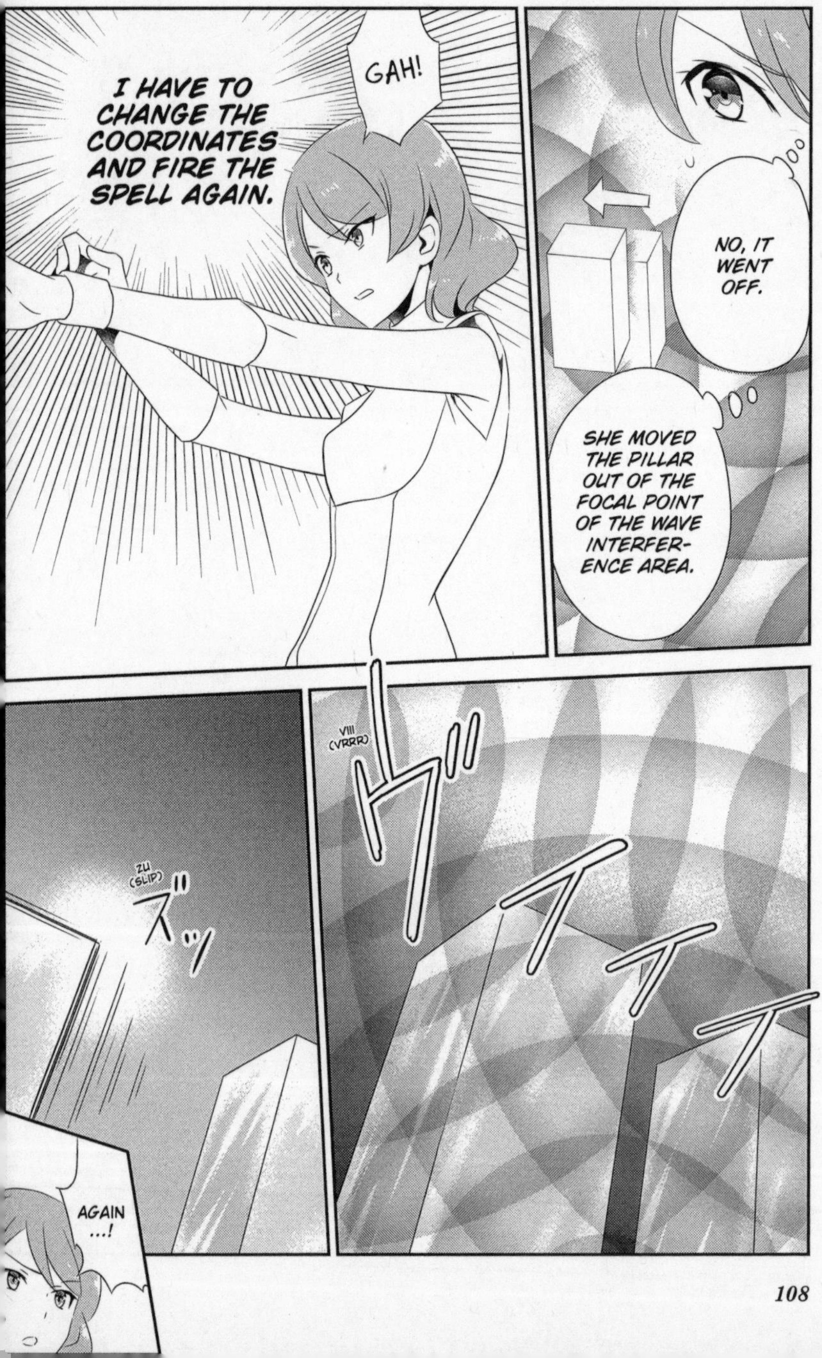
NO, IT WENT OFF.
SHE MOVED THE PILLAR OUT OF THE FOCAL POINT OF THE WAVE INTERFERENCE AREA.
GAH!
I HAVE TO CHANGE THE COORDINATES AND FIRE THE SPELL AGAIN.
VIII (VRRR)
ZU (SLIP)
AGAIN ...!

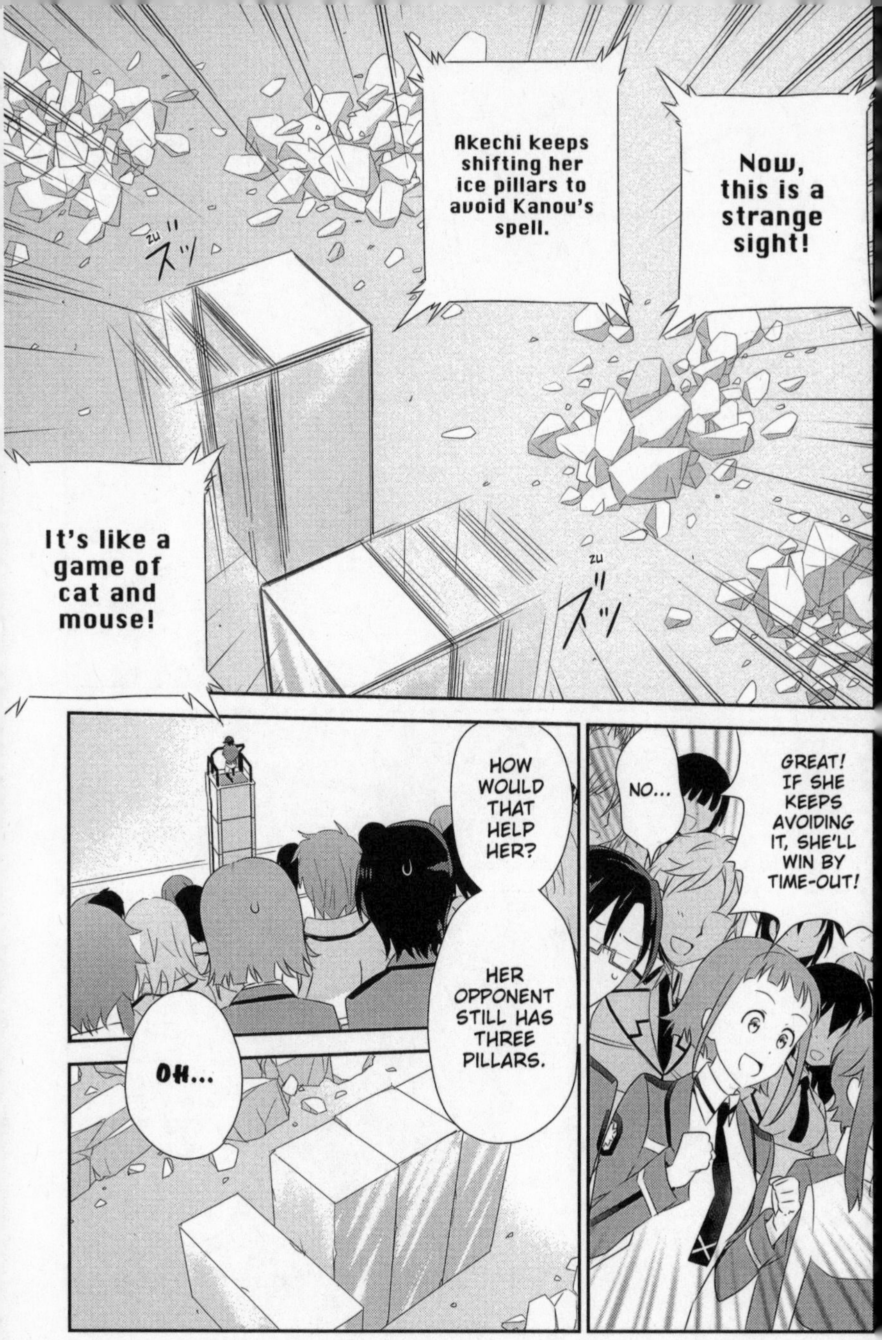
Now, this is a strange sight!
Akechi keeps shifting her ice pillars to avoid Kanou's spell.
zu ズッ
zu ズッ
It's like a game of cat and mouse!
GREAT! IF SHE KEEPS AVOIDING IT, SHE'LL WIN BY TIME-OUT!
NO...
HOW WOULD THAT HELP HER?
HER OPPONENT STILL HAS THREE PILLARS.
OH...

ARE YOU GOING TO PLAY THIS GAME OF TAG FOREVER?

I MEAN, I'LL GO ALONG WITH IT, BUT...

SIGH...

...I DIDN'T THINK YOU WOULD CHOOSE A FUTILE WAR OF ATTRITION.

WHAT A LETDOWN.

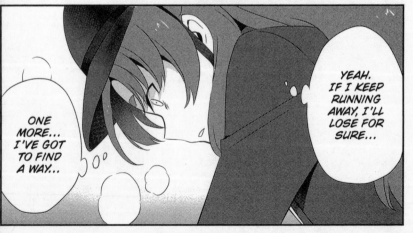

YEAH. IF I KEEP RUNNING AWAY, I'LL LOSE FOR SURE...

ONE MORE... I'VE GOT TO FIND A WAY...

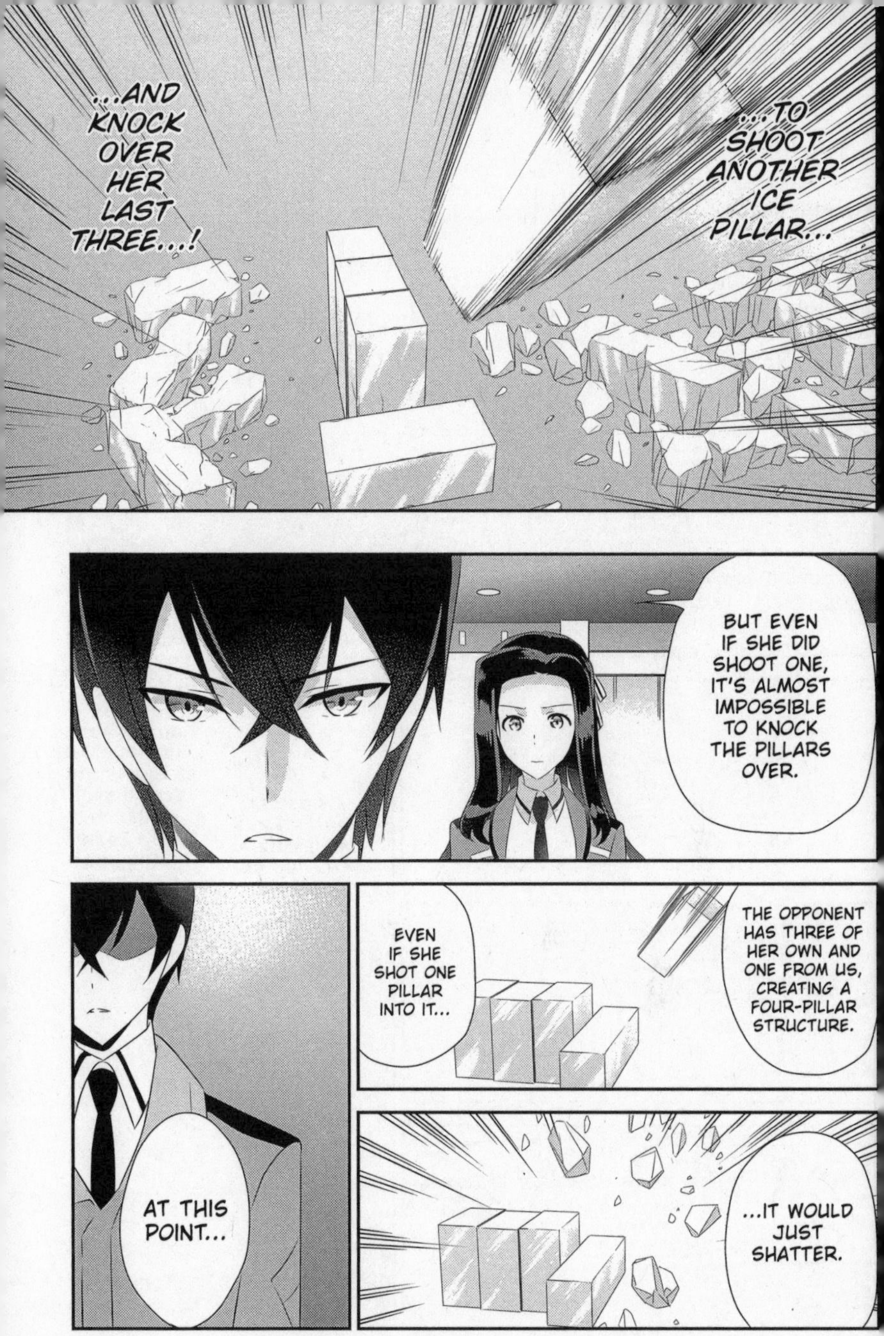
...TO SHOOT ANOTHER ICE PILLAR...
...AND KNOCK OVER HER LAST THREE...!
BUT EVEN IF SHE DID SHOOT ONE, IT'S ALMOST IMPOSSIBLE TO KNOCK THE PILLARS OVER.
THE OPPONENT HAS THREE OF HER OWN AND ONE FROM US, CREATING A FOUR-PILLAR STRUCTURE.
EVEN IF SHE SHOT ONE PILLAR INTO IT...
...IT WOULD JUST SHATTER.
AT THIS POINT...

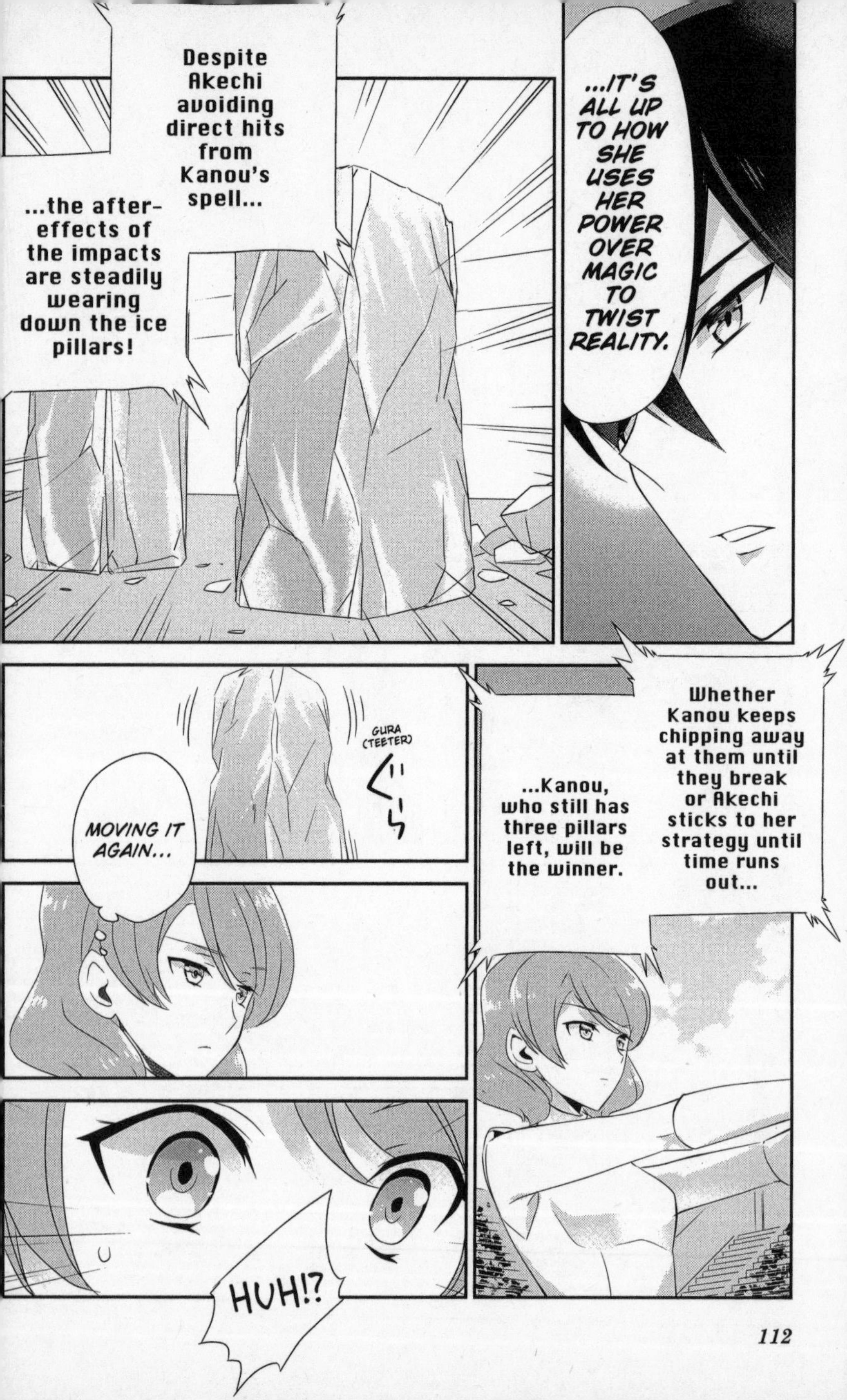
...IT'S ALL UP TO HOW SHE USES HER POWER OVER MAGIC TO TWIST REALITY.
Despite Akechi avoiding direct hits from Kanou's spell...
...the after-effects of the impacts are steadily wearing down the ice pillars!
Whether Kanou keeps chipping away at them until they break or Akechi sticks to her strategy until time runs out...
...Kanou, who still has three pillars left, will be the winner.
GURA (TEETER)
ぐら
MOVING IT AGAIN...
HUH!?

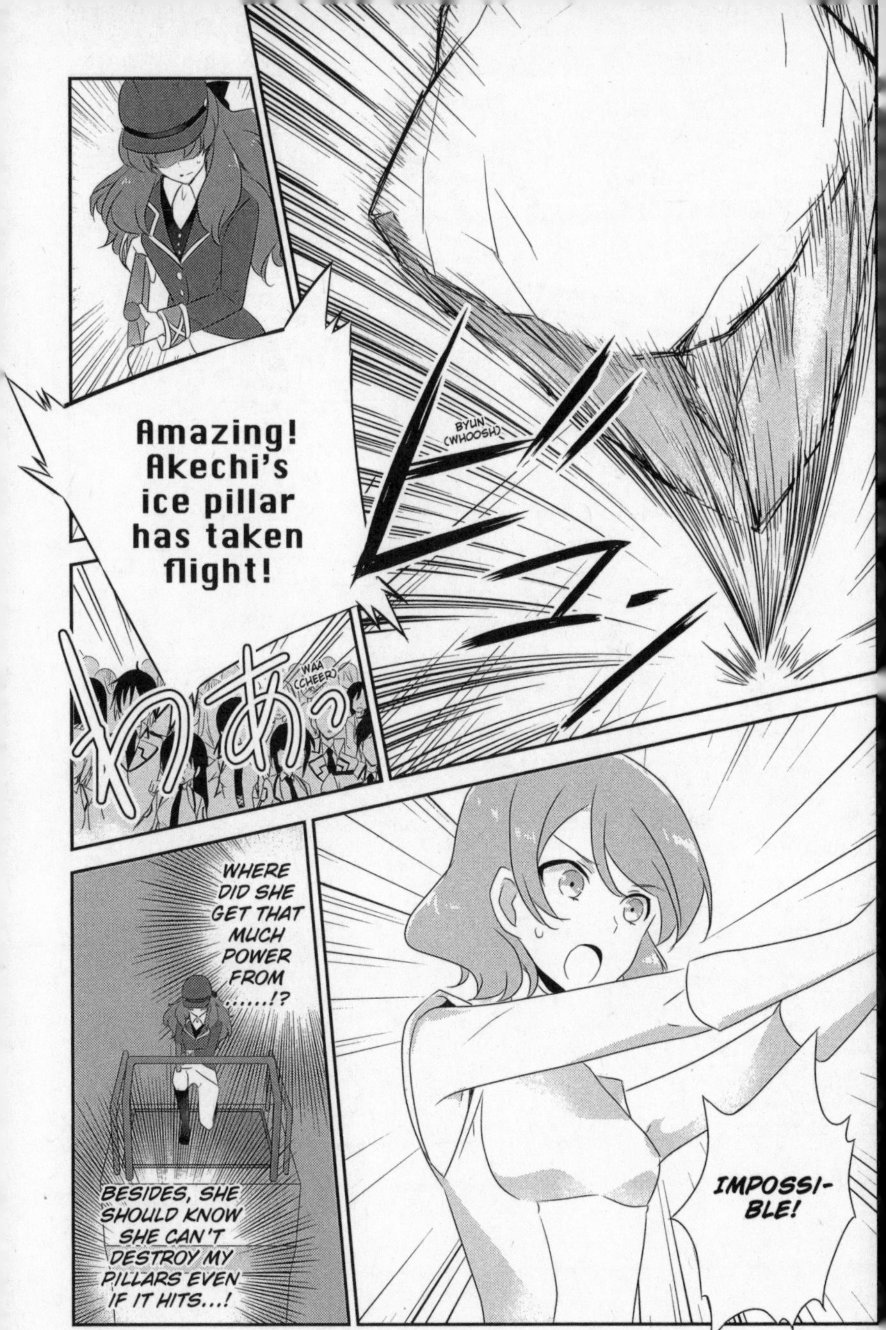

BYUN (WHOOSH)
Amazing! Akechi's ice pillar has taken flight!
WAA (CHEER)
IMPOSSI-BLE!
WHERE DID SHE GET THAT MUCH POWER FROM ......!?
BESIDES, SHE SHOULD KNOW SHE CAN'T DESTROY MY PILLARS EVEN IF IT HITS...!

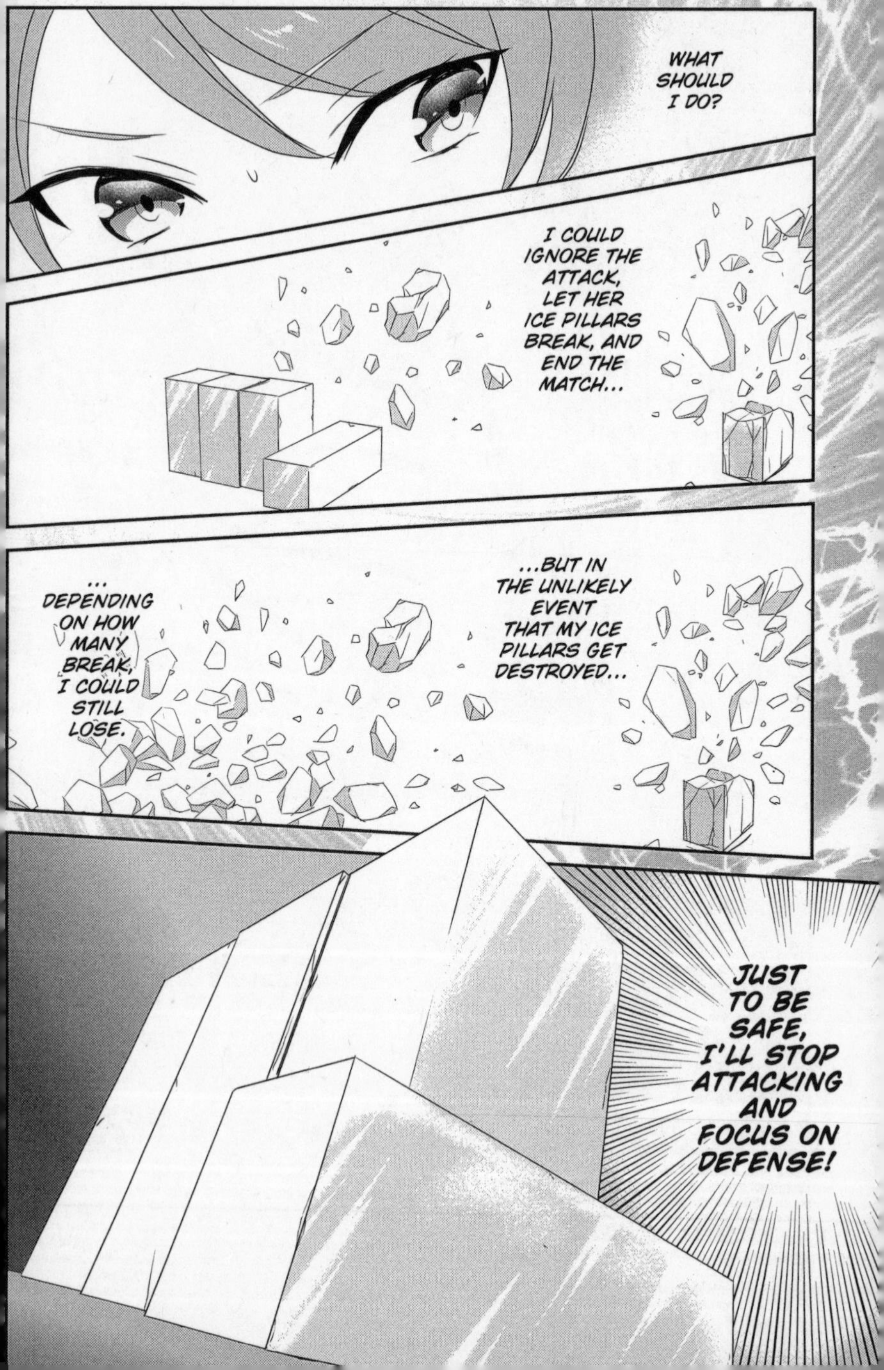
WHAT SHOULD I DO?
I COULD IGNORE THE ATTACK, LET HER ICE PILLARS BREAK, AND END THE MATCH...
...BUT IN THE UNLIKELY EVENT THAT MY ICE PILLARS GET DESTROYED...
...DEPENDING ON HOW MANY BREAK, I COULD STILL LOSE.
JUST TO BE SAFE, I'LL STOP ATTACKING AND FOCUS ON DEFENSE!

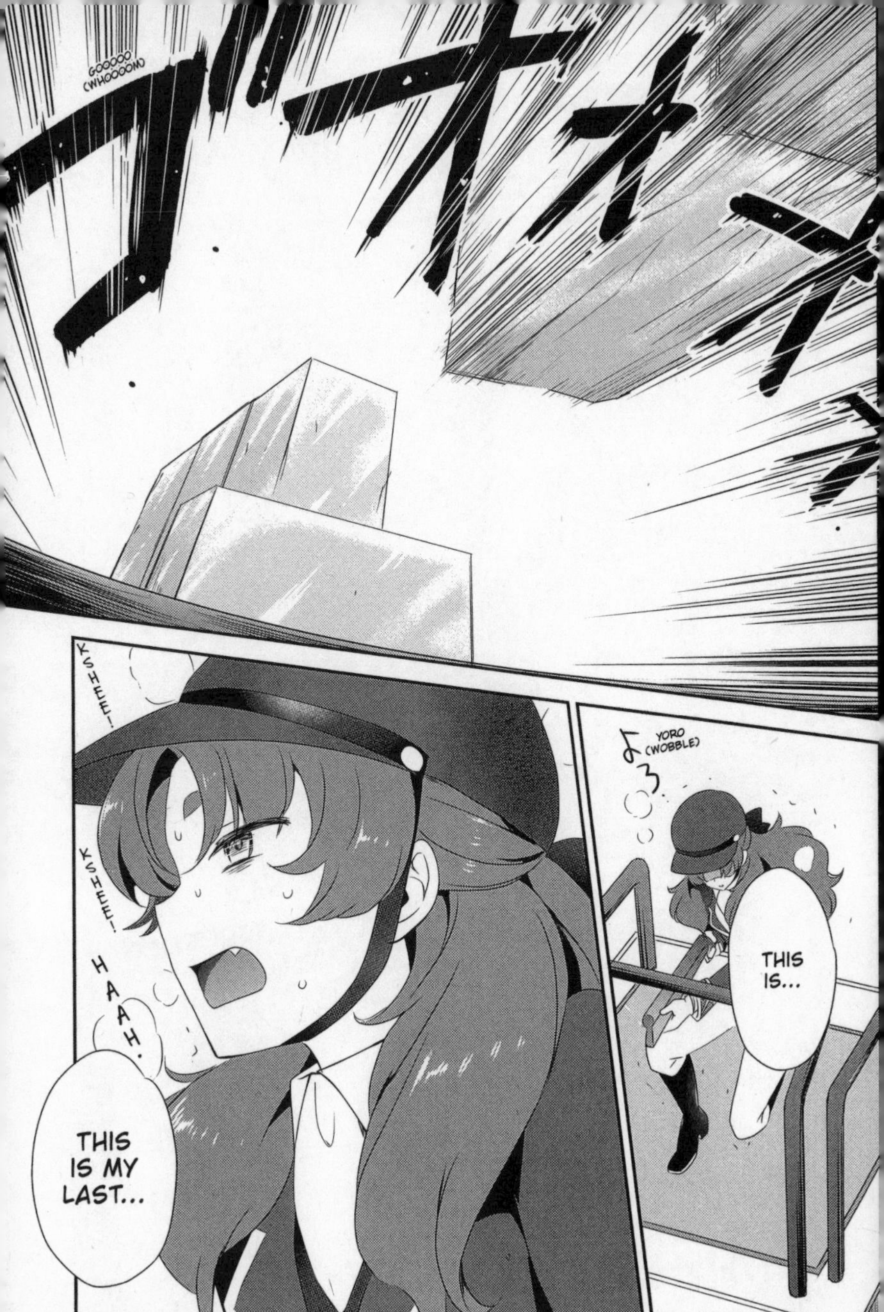
GOOOOO (WHOOOOM)
YORO (WOBBLE)
THIS IS...
KSHEE!
KSHEE!
HAAAH!
THIS IS MY LAST...

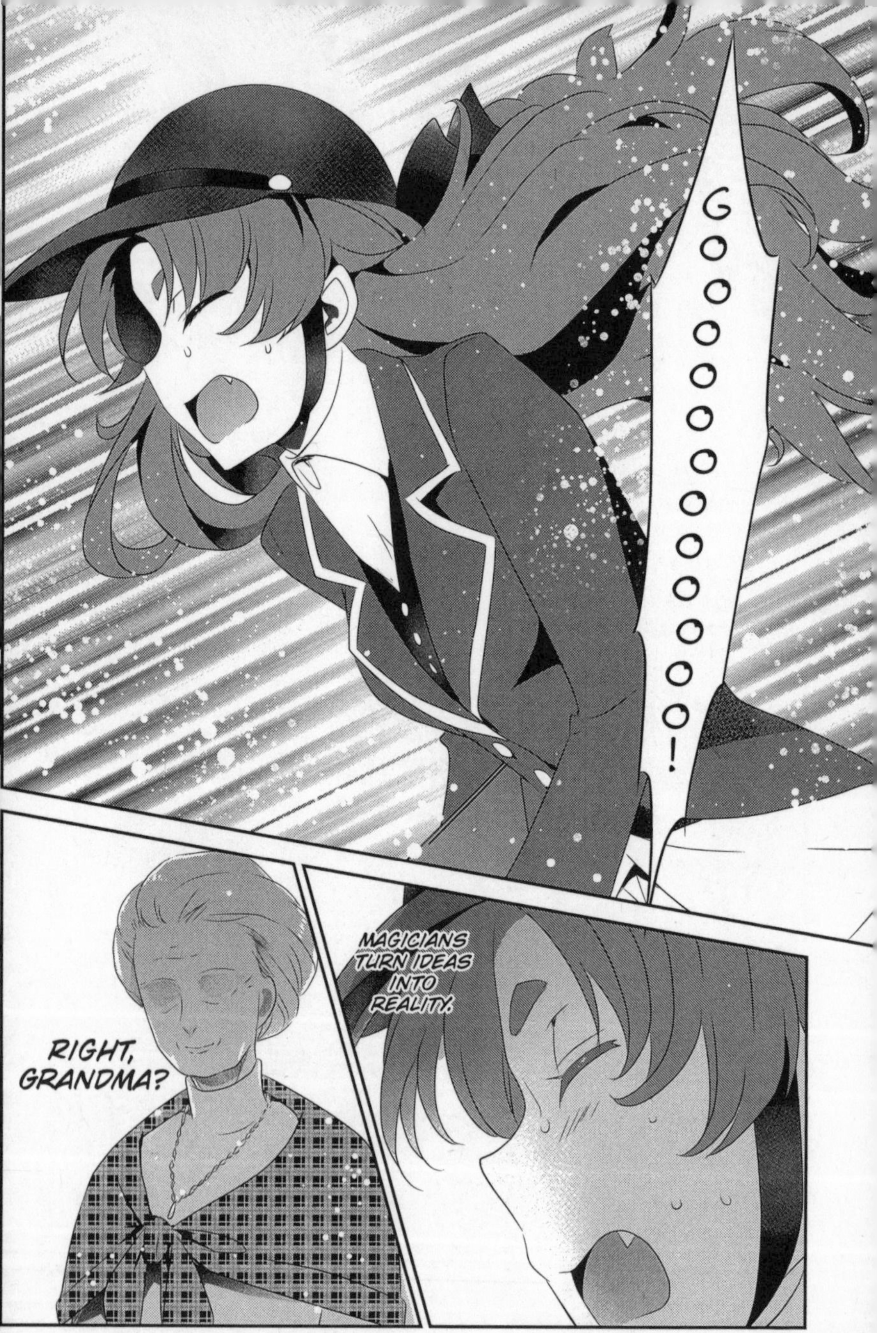
GOOOOOOOOOOOO!
MAGICIANS TURN IDEAS INTO REALITY.
RIGHT, GRANDMA?

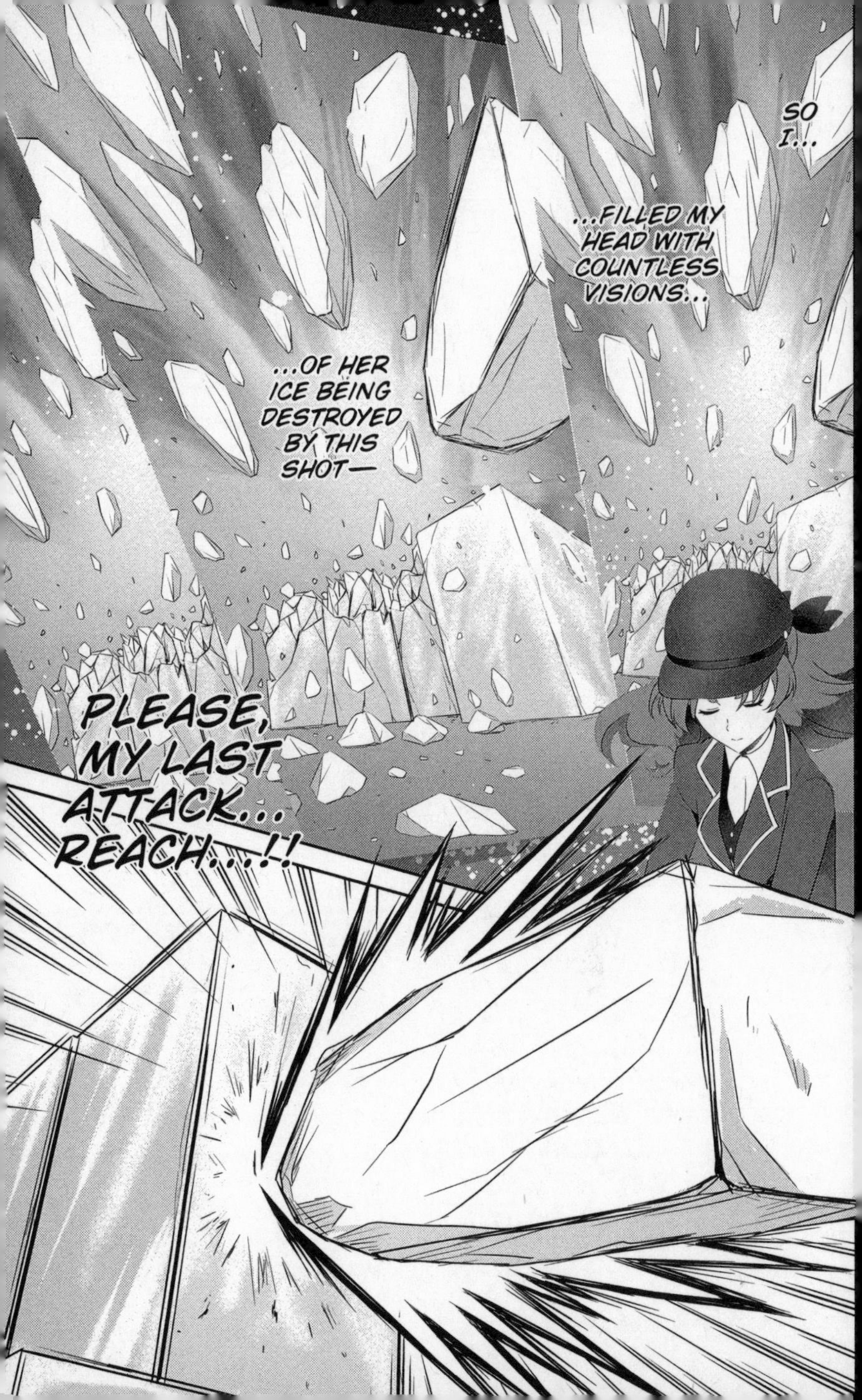
SO I...
...FILLED MY HEAD WITH COUNTLESS VISIONS...
...OF HER ICE BEING DESTROYED BY THIS SHOT—
PLEASE, MY LAST ATTACK... REACH...!!

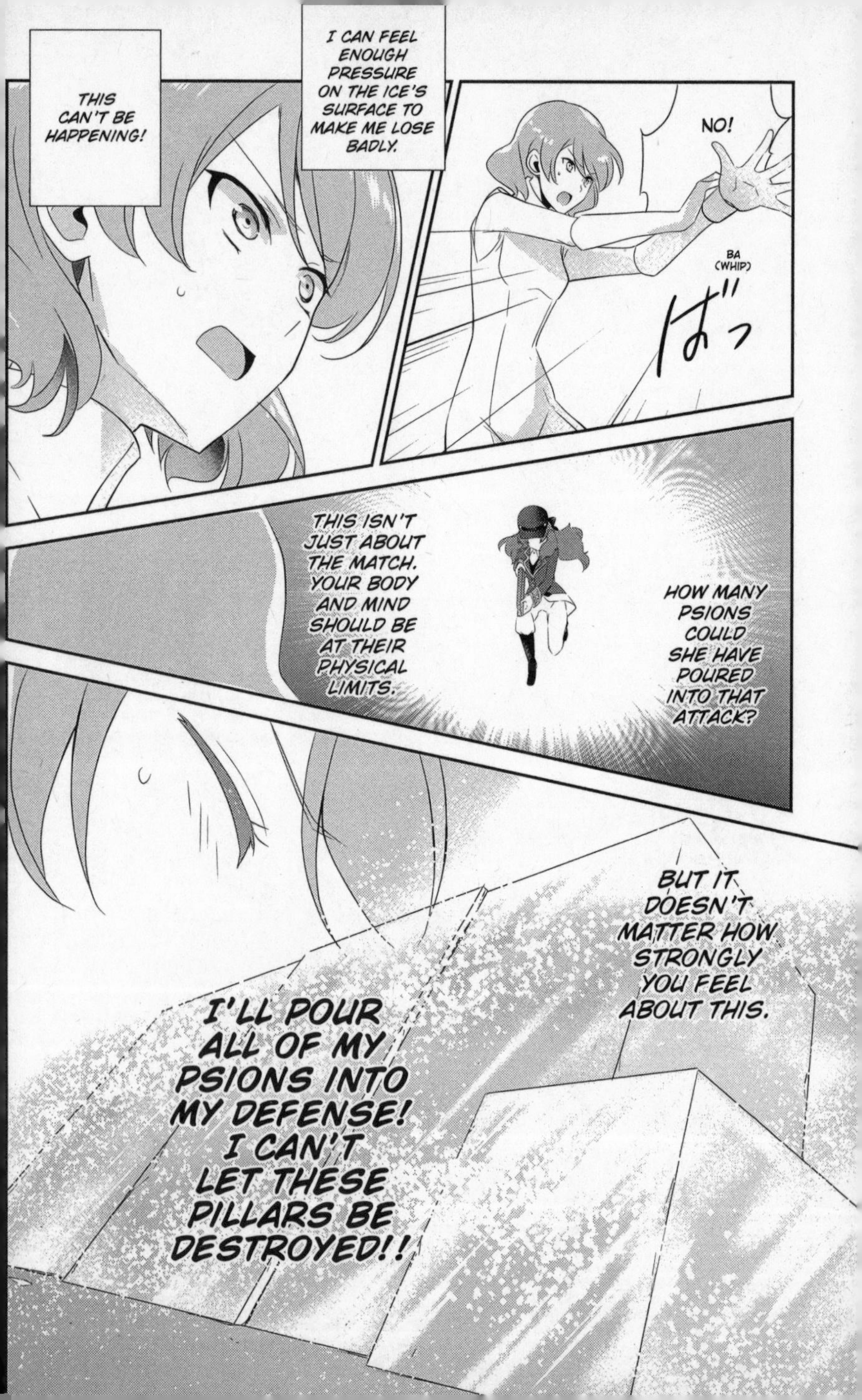
NO!
ばっ
BA (WHIP)
I CAN FEEL ENOUGH PRESSURE ON THE ICE'S SURFACE TO MAKE ME LOSE BADLY.
THIS CAN'T BE HAPPENING!
HOW MANY PSIONS COULD SHE HAVE POURED INTO THAT ATTACK?
THIS ISN'T JUST ABOUT THE MATCH. YOUR BODY AND MIND SHOULD BE AT THEIR PHYSICAL LIMITS.
BUT IT DOESN'T MATTER HOW STRONGLY YOU FEEL ABOUT THIS.
I'LL POUR ALL OF MY PSIONS INTO MY DEFENSE! I CAN'T LET THESE PILLARS BE DESTROYED!!

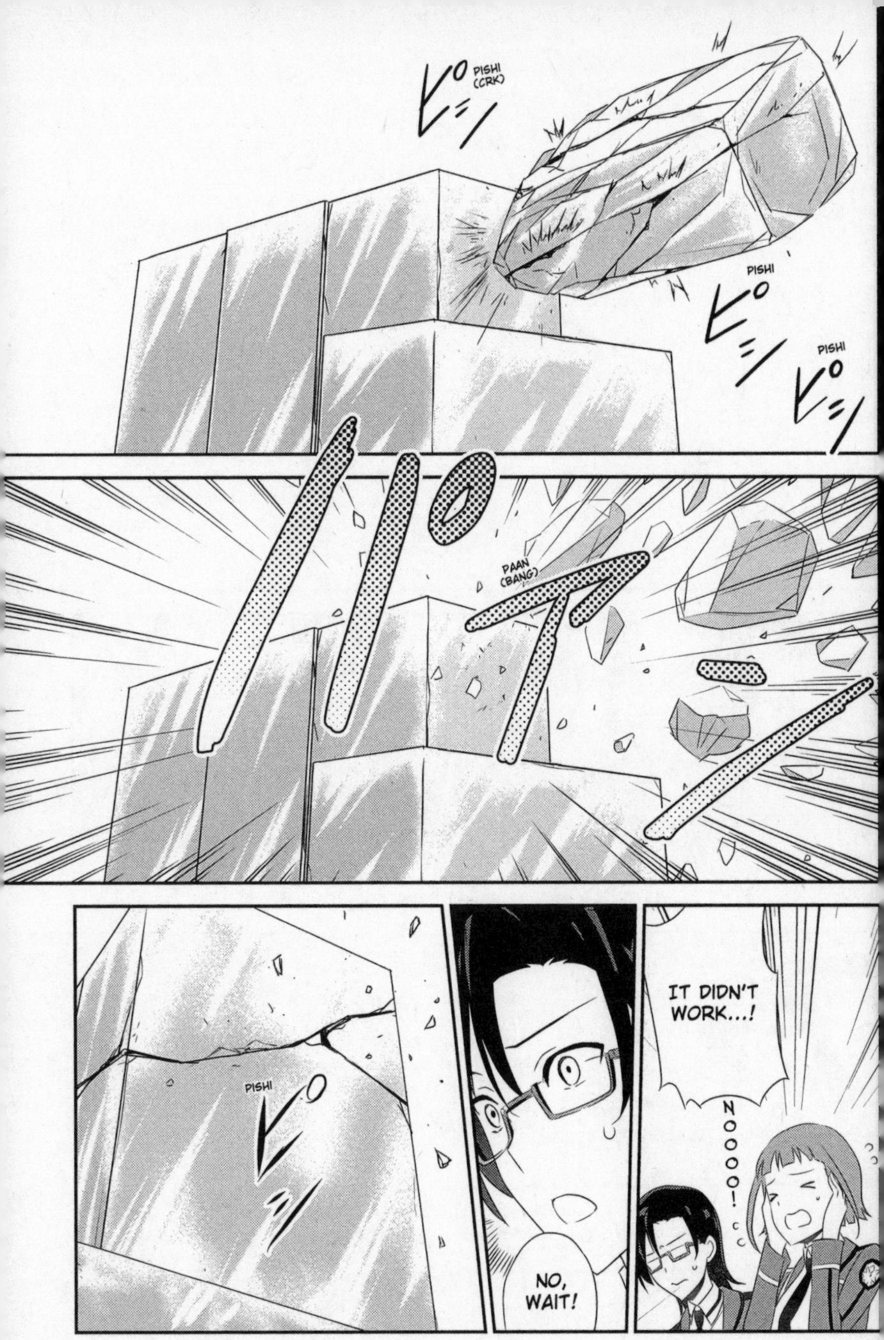
PISHI (CRK)
PISHI
PISHI
PAAN (BANG)
IT DIDN'T WORK...!
NOOOOO!
NO, WAIT!
PISHI

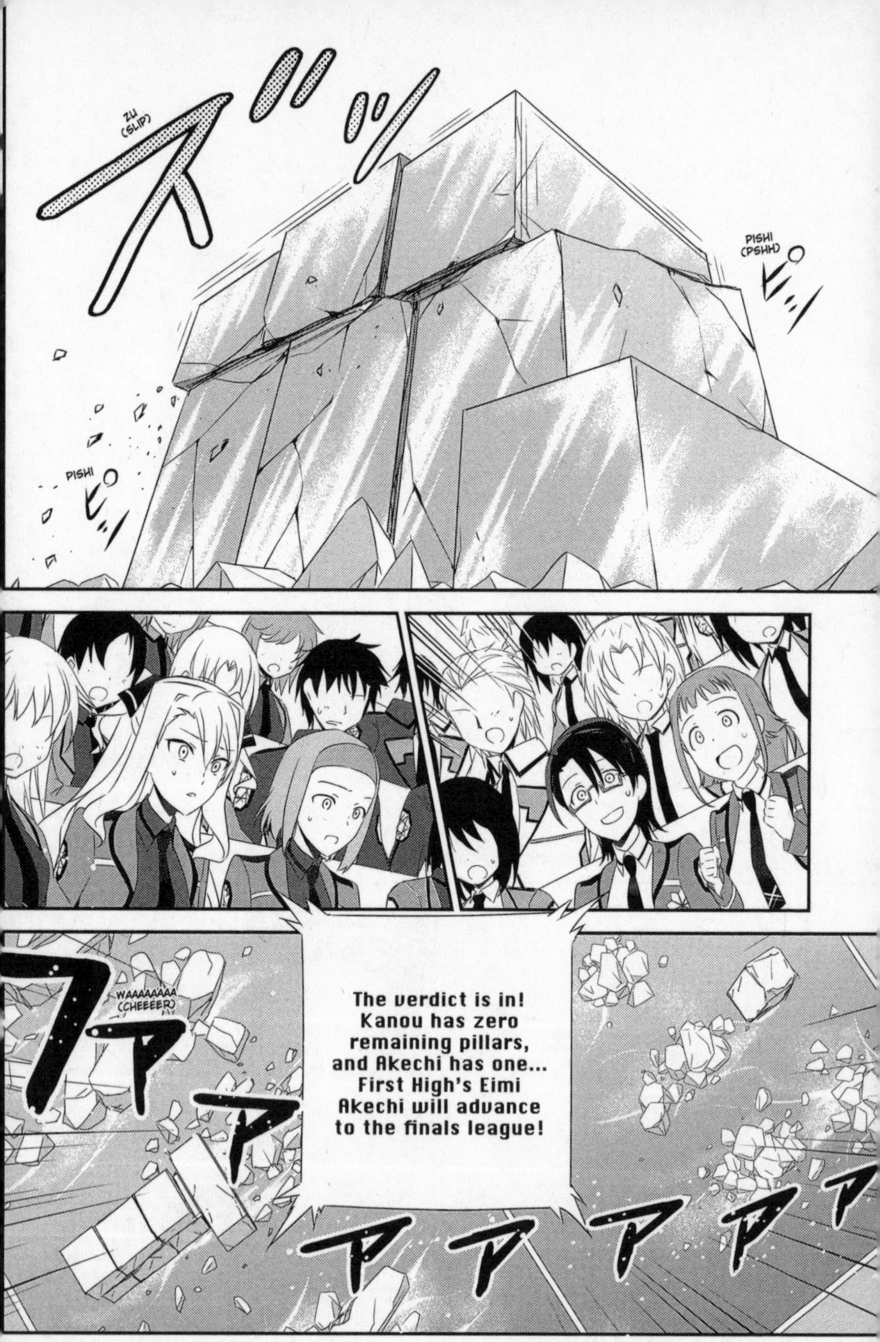

ZU (SLIP)
PISHI (PSHH)
PISHI
WAAAAAAA (CHEEEER)
The verdict is in! Kanou has zero remaining pillars, and Akechi has one... First High's Eimi Akechi will advance to the finals league!

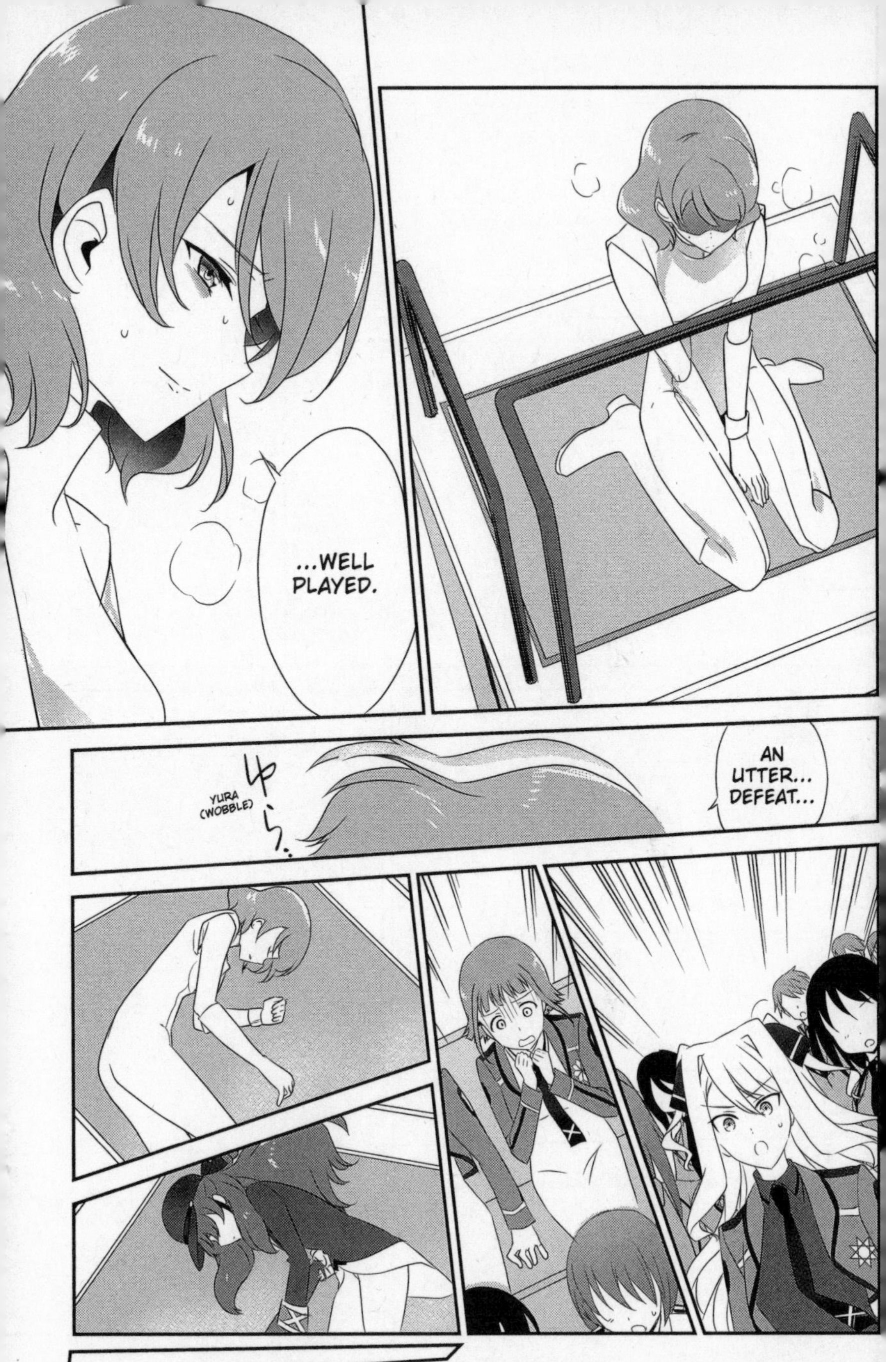
...WELL PLAYED.
AN UTTER... DEFEAT...
ゆら…
YURA (WOBBLE)

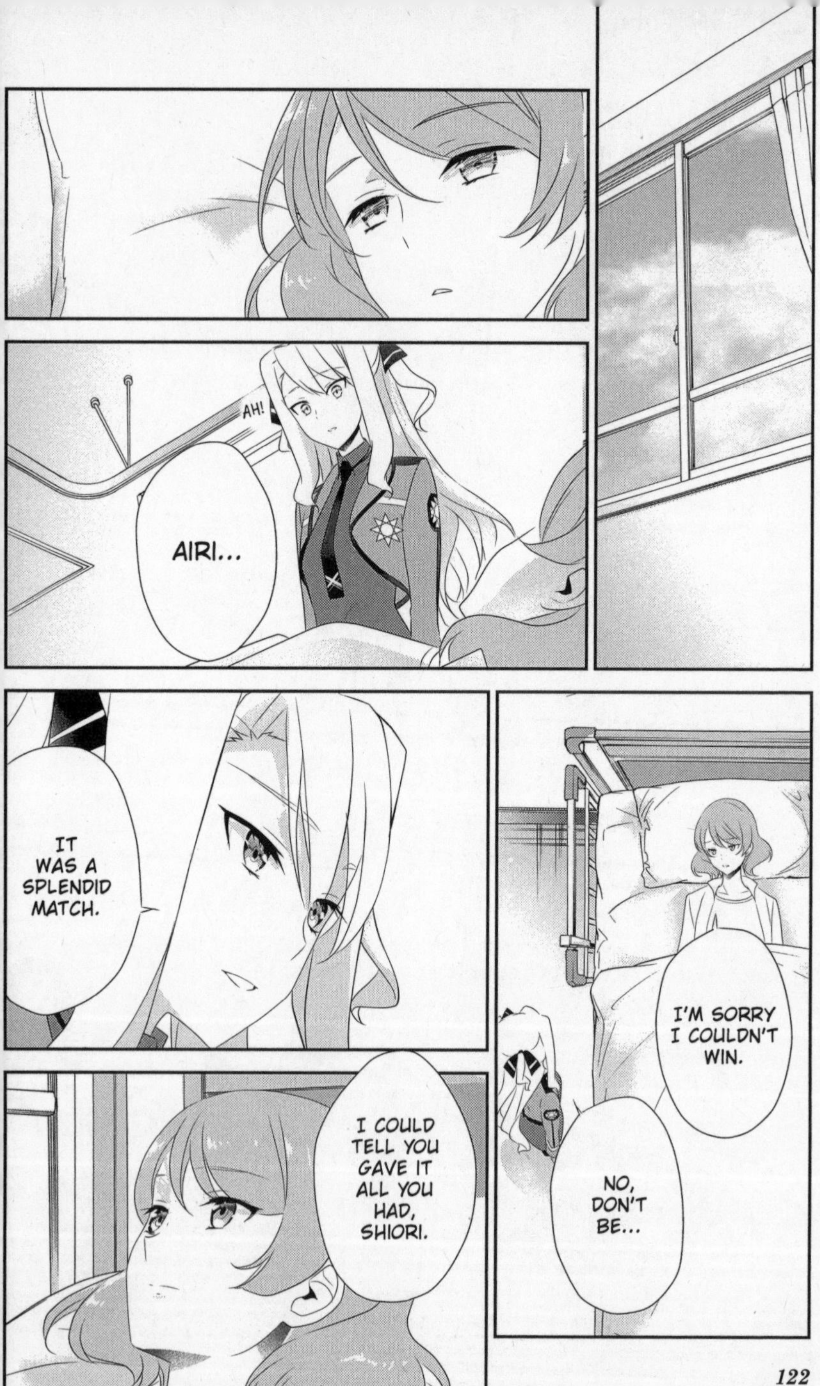
AH!
AIRI...
I'M SORRY I COULDN'T WIN.
NO, DON'T BE...
IT WAS A SPLENDID MATCH.
I COULD TELL YOU GAVE IT ALL YOU HAD, SHIORI.

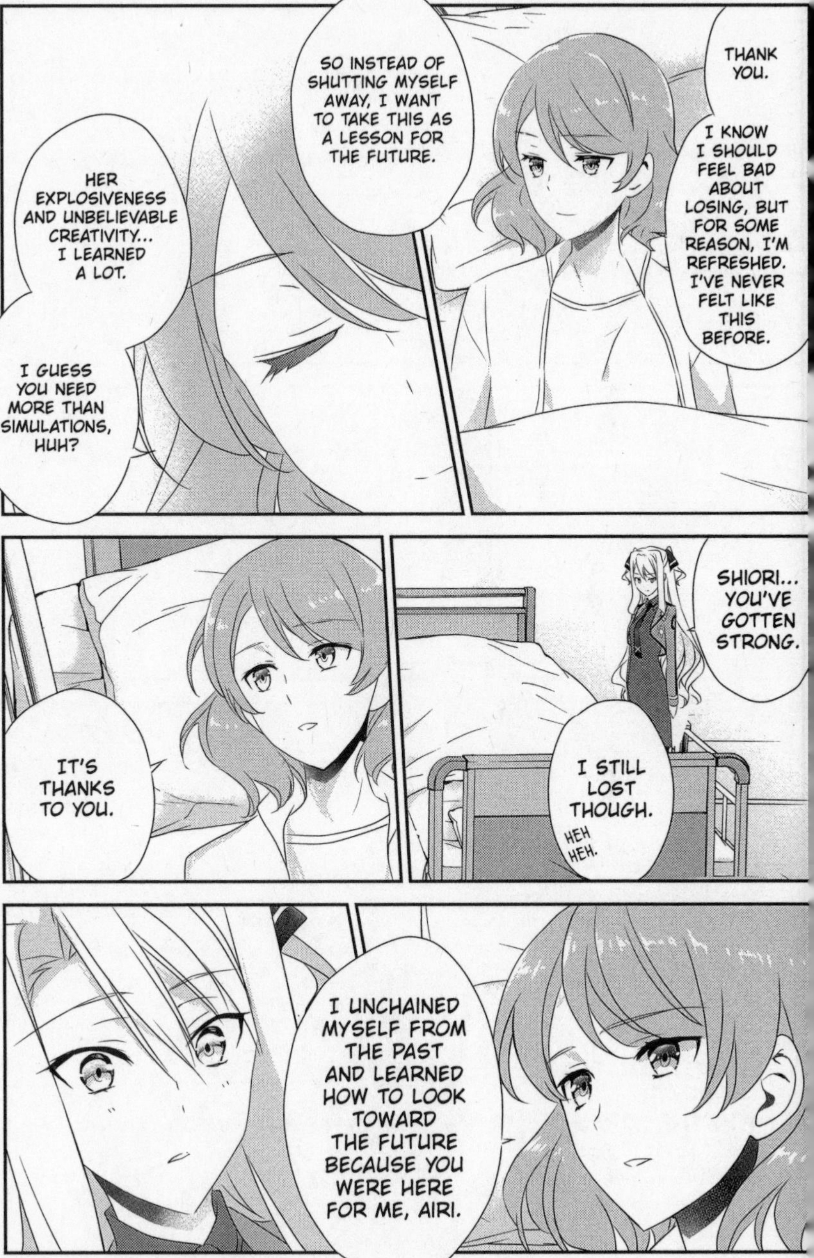
THANK YOU.
I KNOW I SHOULD FEEL BAD ABOUT LOSING, BUT FOR SOME REASON, I'M REFRESHED. I'VE NEVER FELT LIKE THIS BEFORE.
SO INSTEAD OF SHUTTING MYSELF AWAY, I WANT TO TAKE THIS AS A LESSON FOR THE FUTURE.
HER EXPLOSIVENESS AND UNBELIEVABLE CREATIVITY... I LEARNED A LOT.
I GUESS YOU NEED MORE THAN SIMULATIONS, HUH?
SHIORI... YOU'VE GOTTEN STRONG.
I STILL LOST THOUGH.
HEH HEH.
IT'S THANKS TO YOU.
I UNCHAINED MYSELF FROM THE PAST AND LEARNED HOW TO LOOK TOWARD THE FUTURE BECAUSE YOU WERE HERE FOR ME, AIRI.

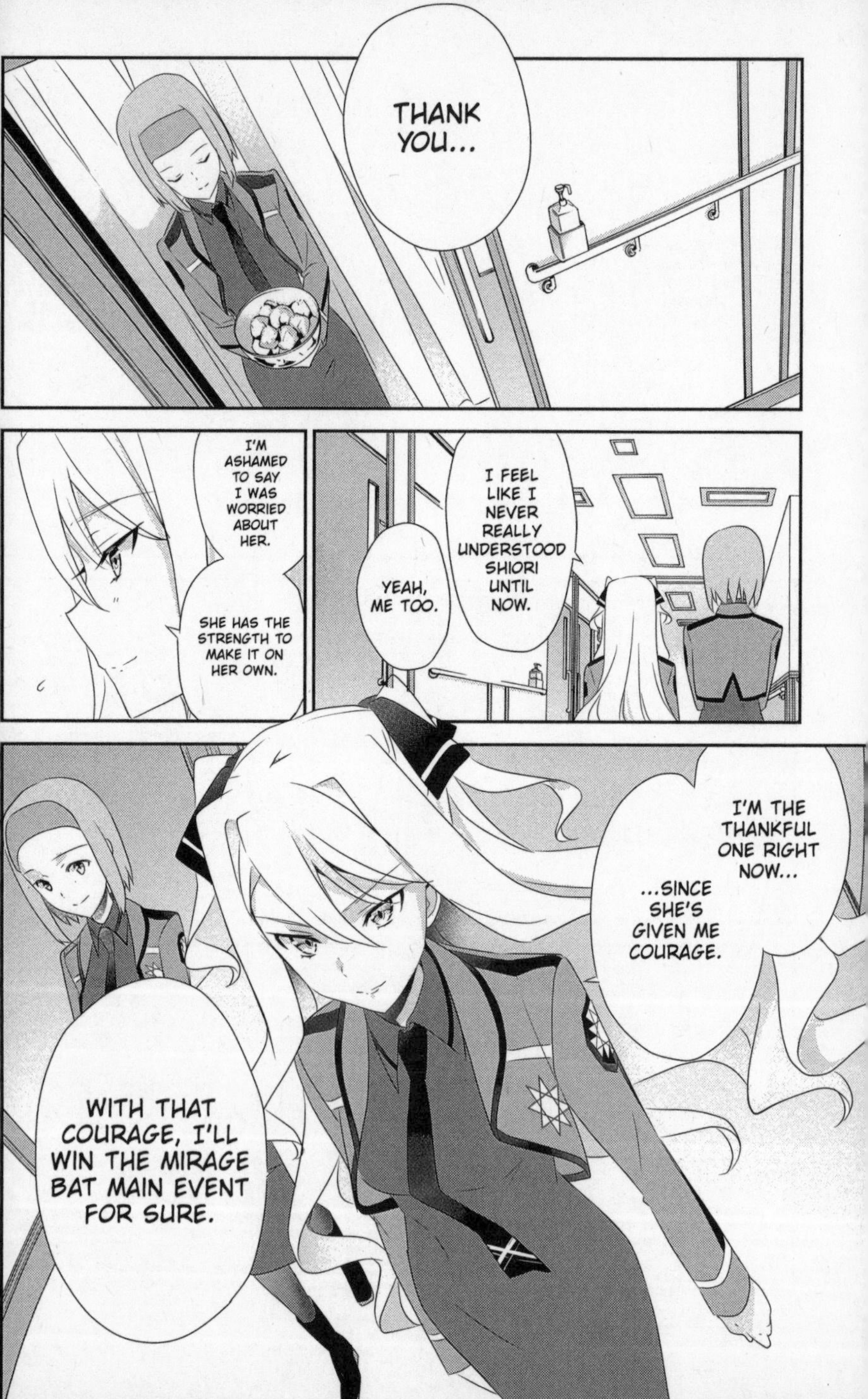
THANK YOU...
I FEEL LIKE I NEVER REALLY UNDERSTOOD SHIORI UNTIL NOW.
YEAH, ME TOO.
I'M ASHAMED TO SAY I WAS WORRIED ABOUT HER.
SHE HAS THE STRENGTH TO MAKE IT ON HER OWN.
I'M THE THANKFUL ONE RIGHT NOW...
...SINCE SHE'S GIVEN ME COURAGE.
WITH THAT COURAGE, I'LL WIN THE MIRAGE BAT MAIN EVENT FOR SURE.

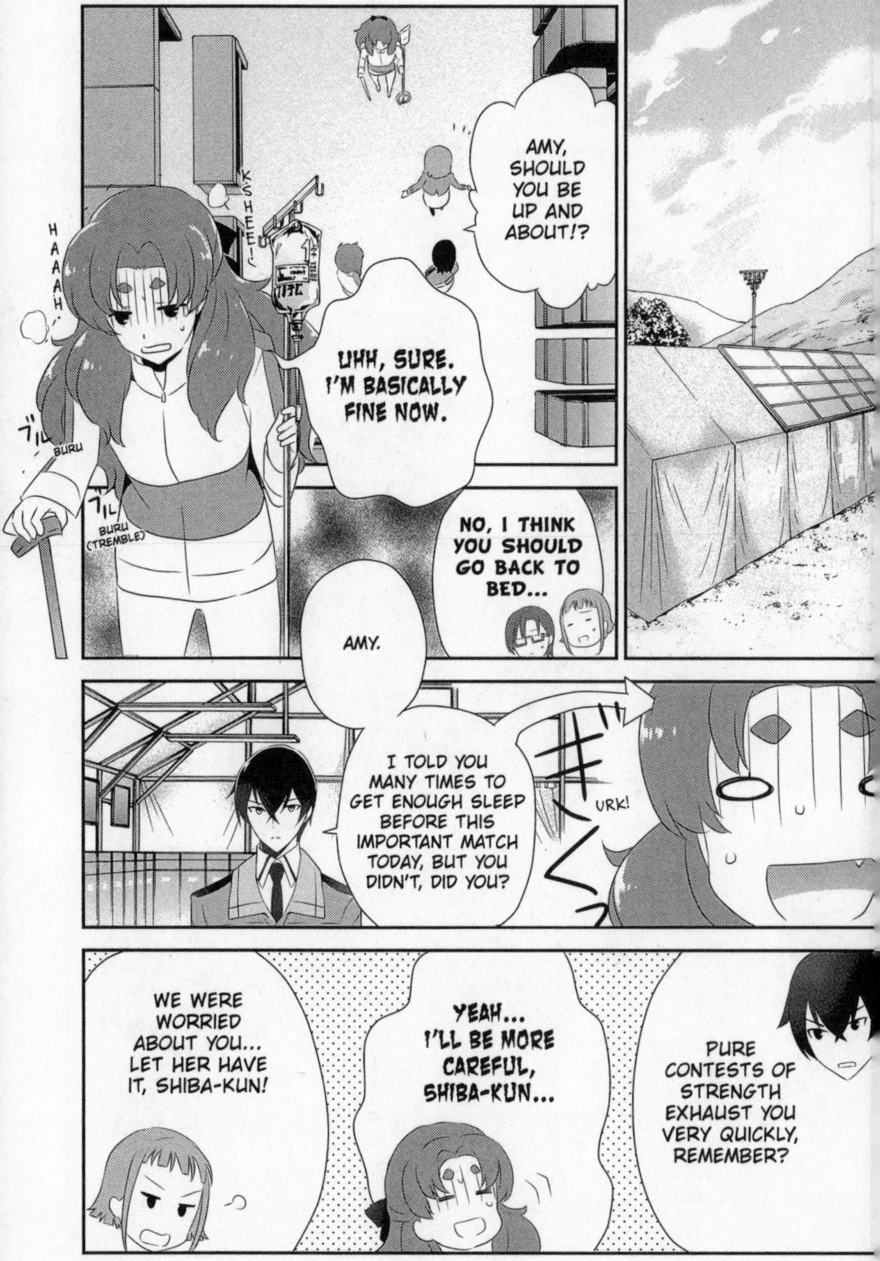
AMY, SHOULD YOU BE UP AND ABOUT!?
KSHEE!
HAAAAH
UHH, SURE. I'M BASICALLY FINE NOW.
ブル BURU
ブル BURU (TREMBLE)
NO, I THINK YOU SHOULD GO BACK TO BED...
AMY.
URK!
I TOLD YOU MANY TIMES TO GET ENOUGH SLEEP BEFORE THIS IMPORTANT MATCH TODAY, BUT YOU DIDN'T, DID YOU?
PURE CONTESTS OF STRENGTH EXHAUST YOU VERY QUICKLY, REMEMBER?
YEAH... I'LL BE MORE CAREFUL, SHIBA-KUN...
WE WERE WORRIED ABOUT YOU... LET HER HAVE IT, SHIBA-KUN!

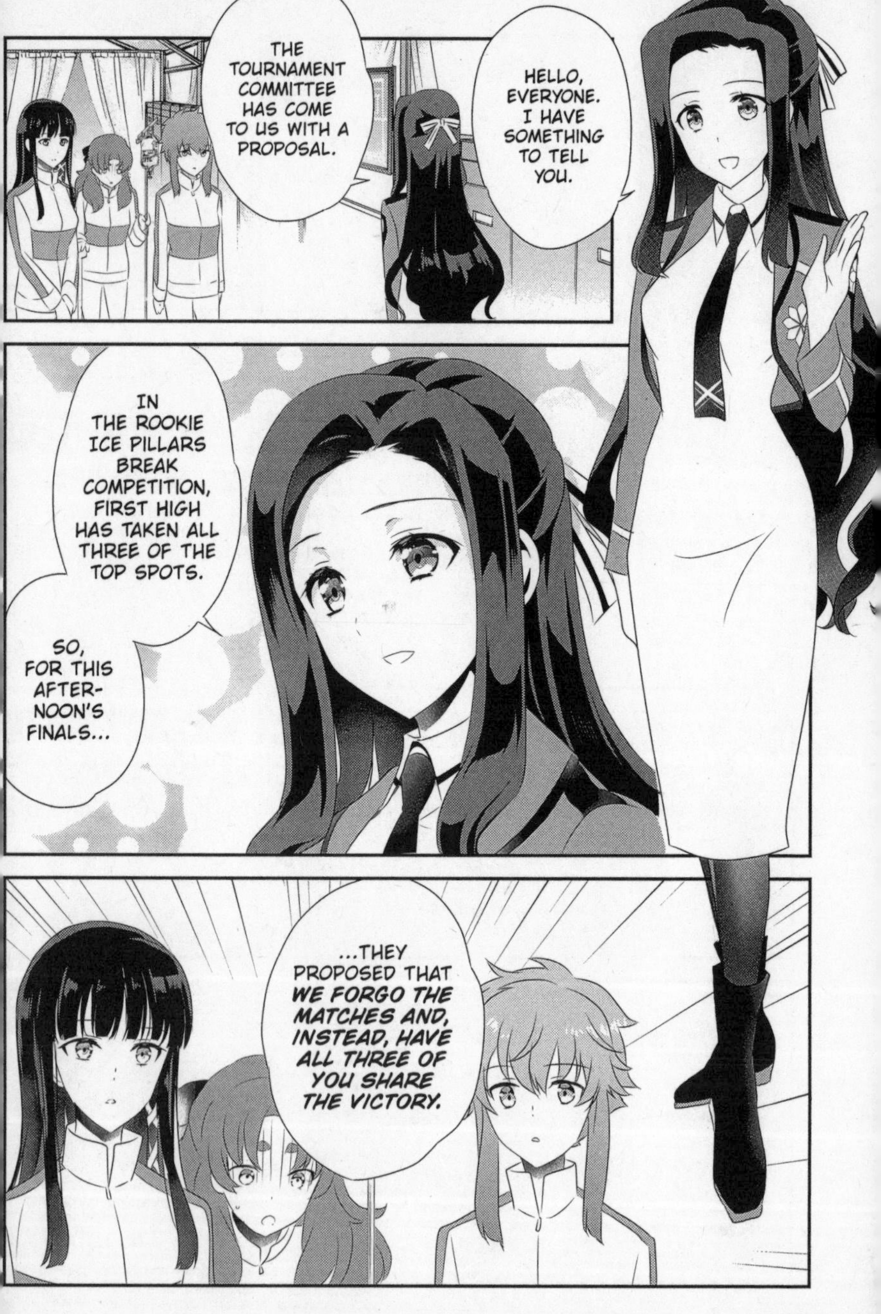
HELLO, EVERYONE. I HAVE SOMETHING TO TELL YOU.
THE TOURNAMENT COMMITTEE HAS COME TO US WITH A PROPOSAL.
IN THE ROOKIE ICE PILLARS BREAK COMPETITION, FIRST HIGH HAS TAKEN ALL THREE OF THE TOP SPOTS.
SO, FOR THIS AFTER-NOON'S FINALS...
...THEY PROPOSED THAT *WE FORGO THE MATCHES AND, INSTEAD, HAVE ALL THREE OF YOU SHARE THE VICTORY.*

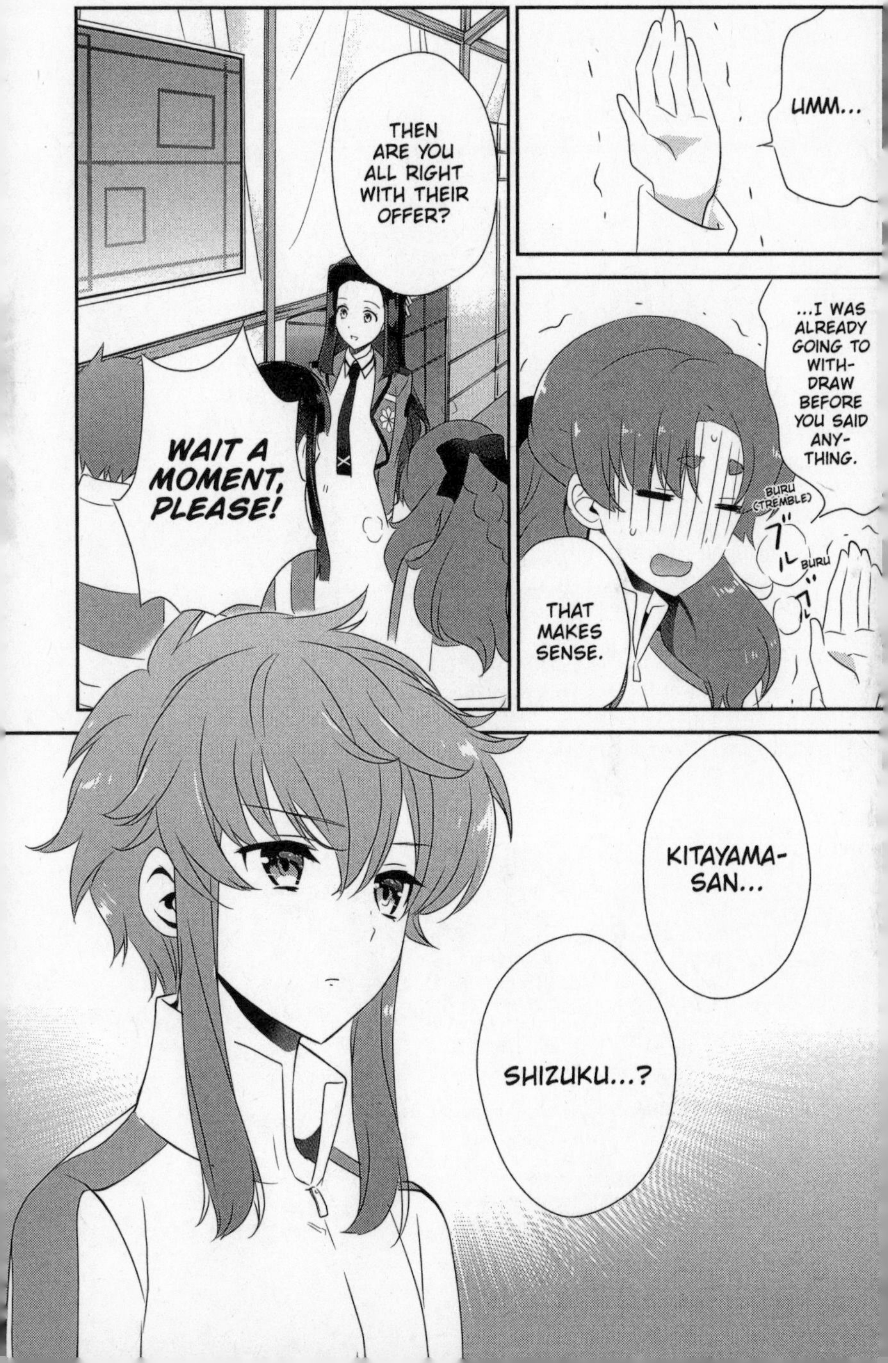
UMM...
...I WAS ALREADY GOING TO WITH-DRAW BEFORE YOU SAID ANY-THING.
BURU (TREMBLE)
BURU
THAT MAKES SENSE.
THEN ARE YOU ALL RIGHT WITH THEIR OFFER?
WAIT A MOMENT, PLEASE!
KITAYAMA-SAN...
SHIZUKU...?

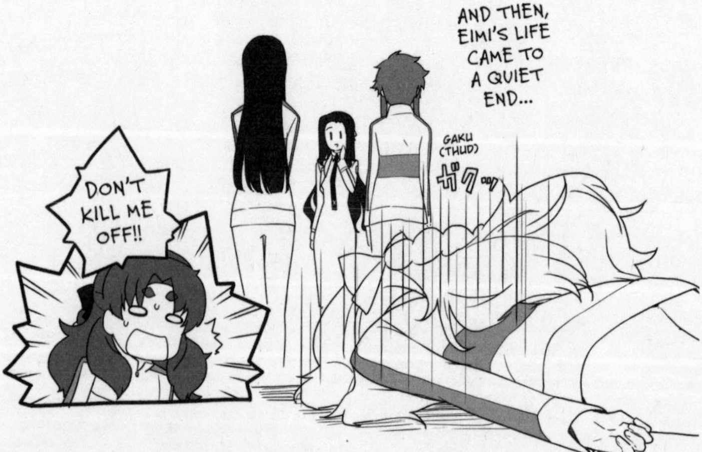
AND THEN, EIMI'S LIFE CAME TO A QUIET END...
GAKU (THUD)
ガク
DON'T KILL ME OFF!!

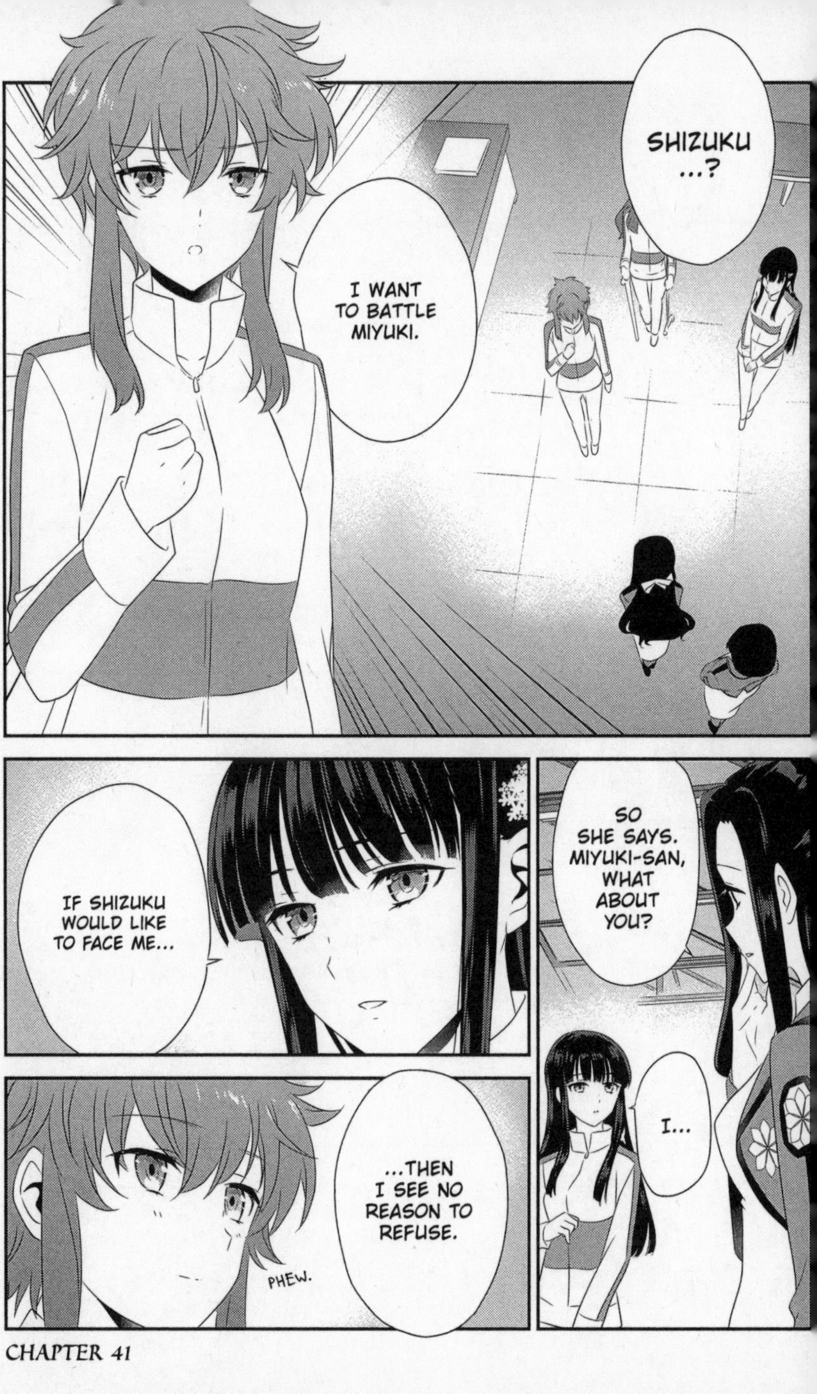
SHIZUKU ...?
I WANT TO BATTLE MIYUKI.
SO SHE SAYS. MIYUKI-SAN, WHAT ABOUT YOU?
I...
IF SHIZUKU WOULD LIKE TO FACE ME...
...THEN I SEE NO REASON TO REFUSE.
PHEW.

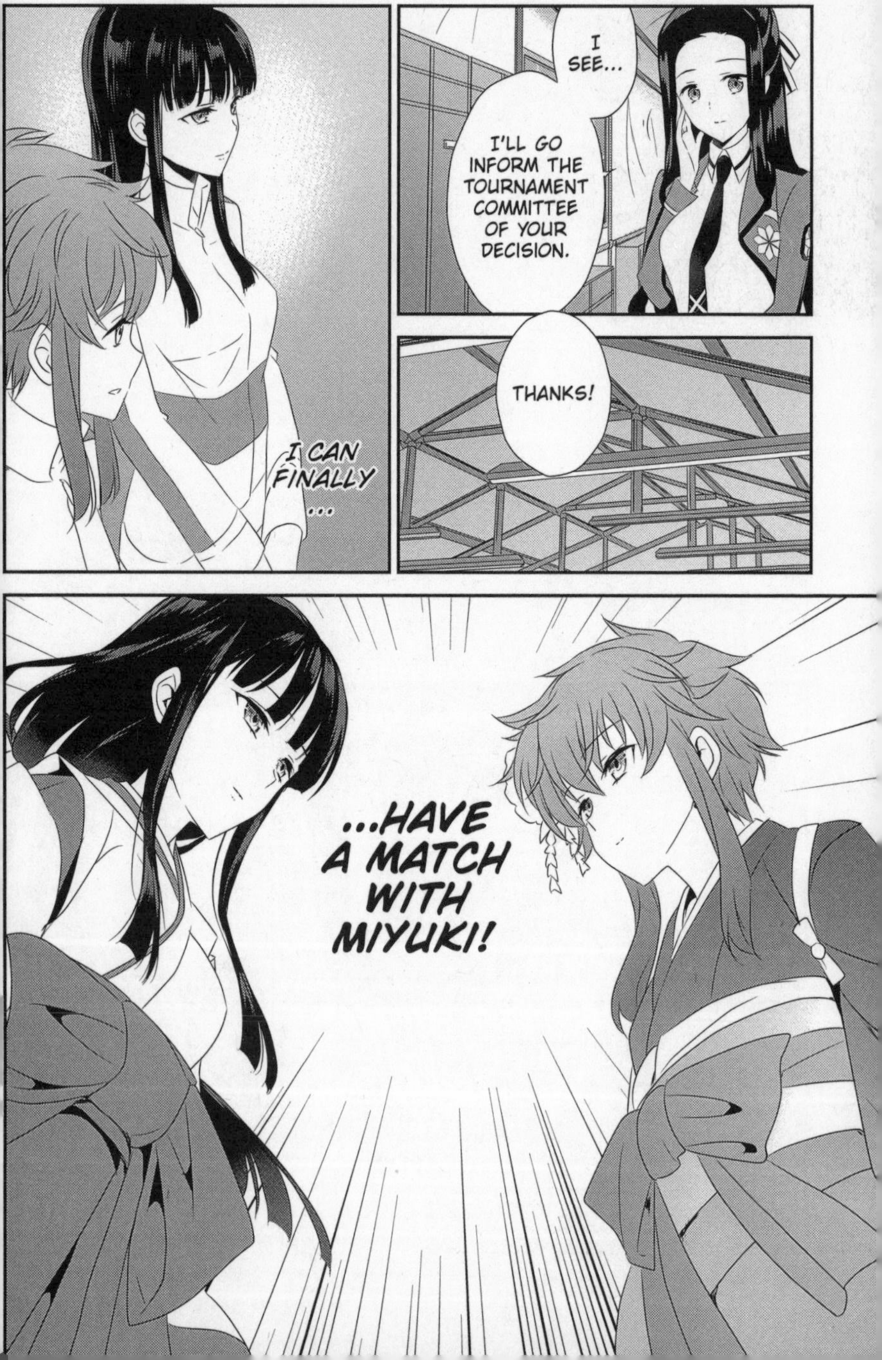
I SEE...
I'LL GO INFORM THE TOURNAMENT COMMITTEE OF YOUR DECISION.
THANKS!
I CAN FINALLY ...
...HAVE A MATCH WITH MIYUKI!

CHAPTER 41

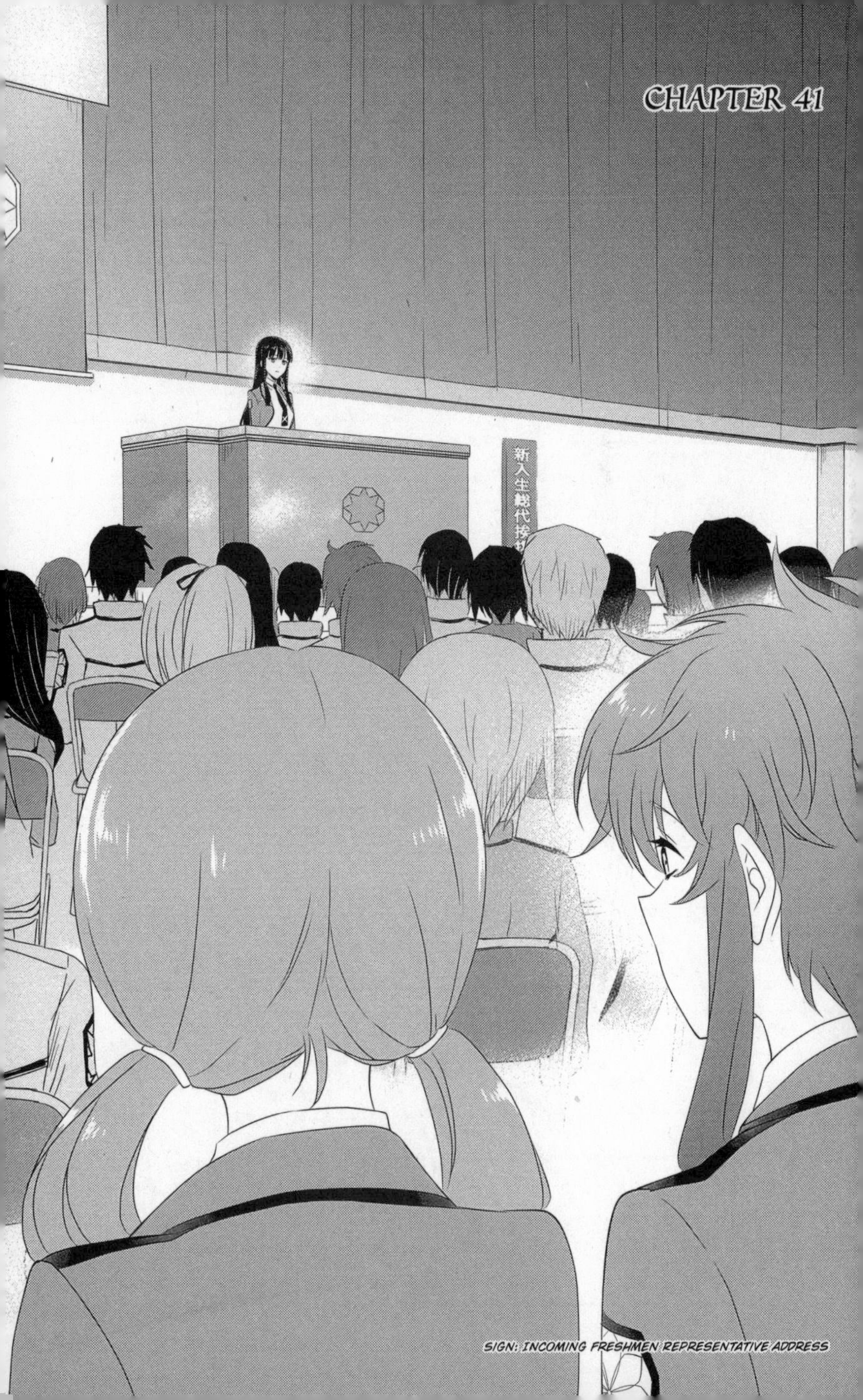
新入生総代挨
SIGN: INCOMING FRESHMEN REPRESENTATIVE ADDRESS

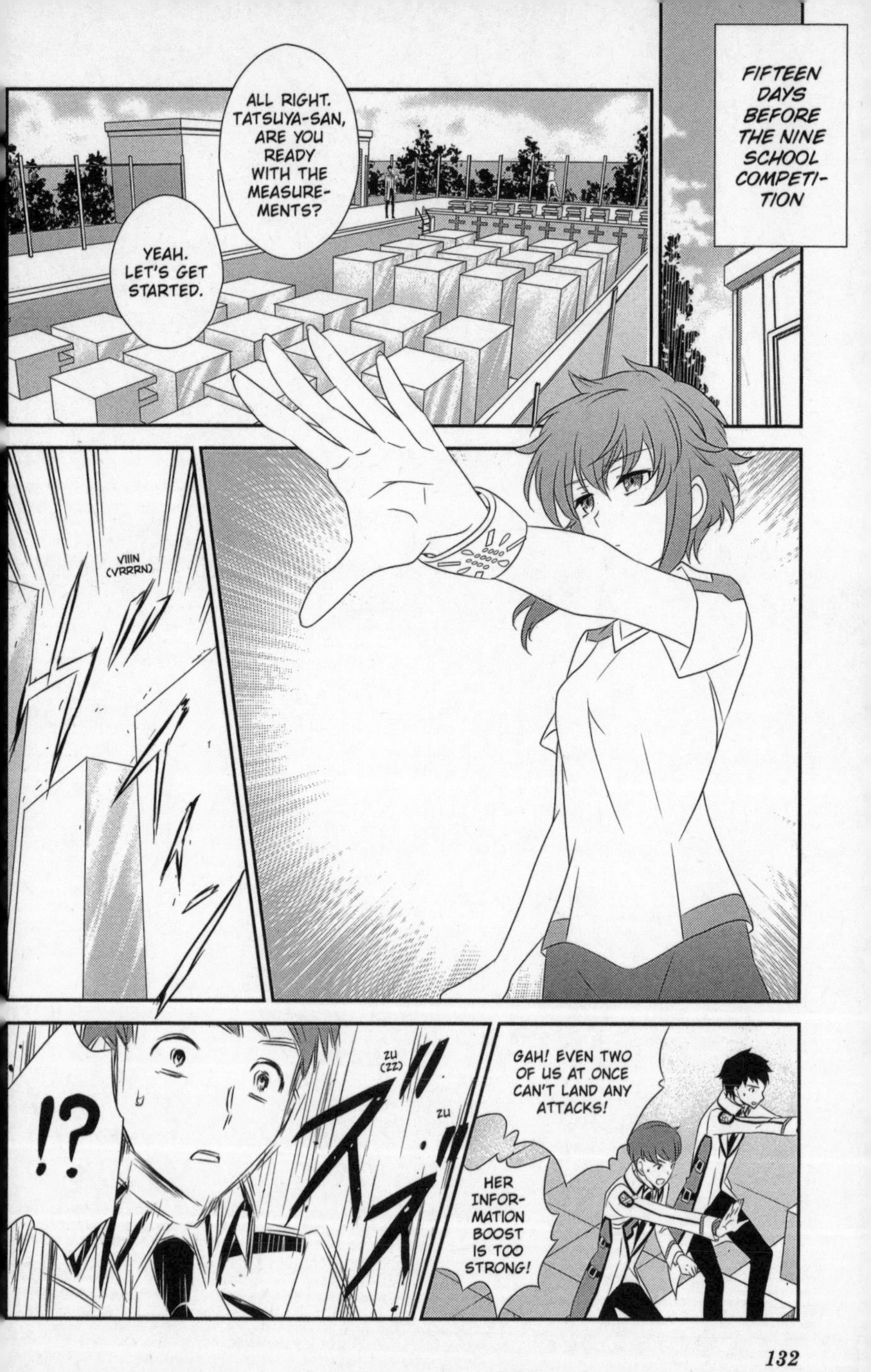
FIFTEEN DAYS BEFORE THE NINE SCHOOL COMPETITION
ALL RIGHT. TATSUYA-SAN, ARE YOU READY WITH THE MEASUREMENTS?
YEAH. LET'S GET STARTED.
VIIN (VRRRN)
GAH! EVEN TWO OF US AT ONCE CAN'T LAND ANY ATTACKS!
HER INFORMATION BOOST IS TOO STRONG!
ZU (ZZ)
ZU
!?

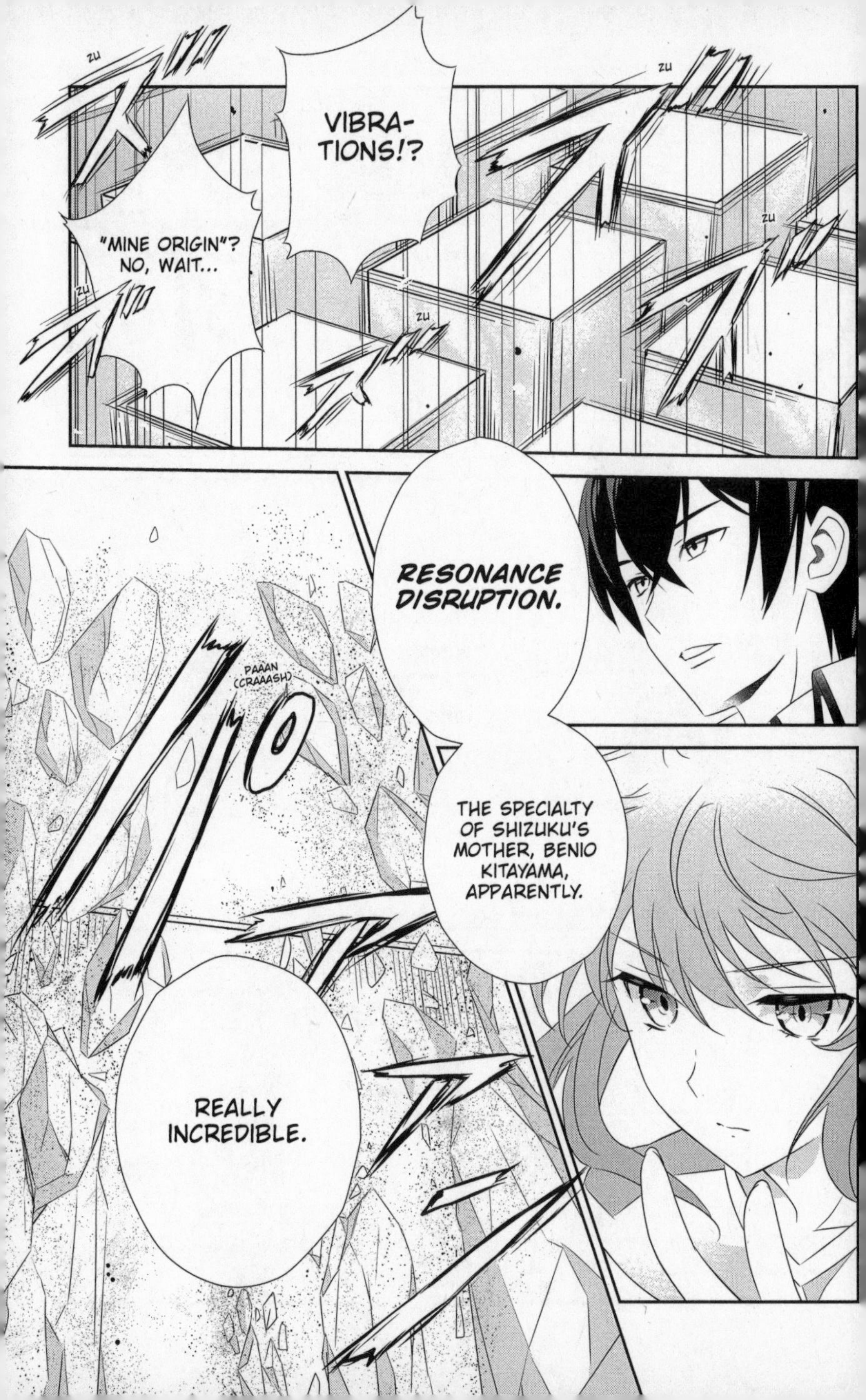
zu
zu
VIBRATIONS!?
zu
zu
"MINE ORIGIN"? NO, WAIT...
zu
zu
RESONANCE DISRUPTION.
THE SPECIALTY OF SHIZUKU'S MOTHER, BENIO KITAYAMA, APPARENTLY.
PAAAN (CRAAASH)
REALLY INCREDIBLE.

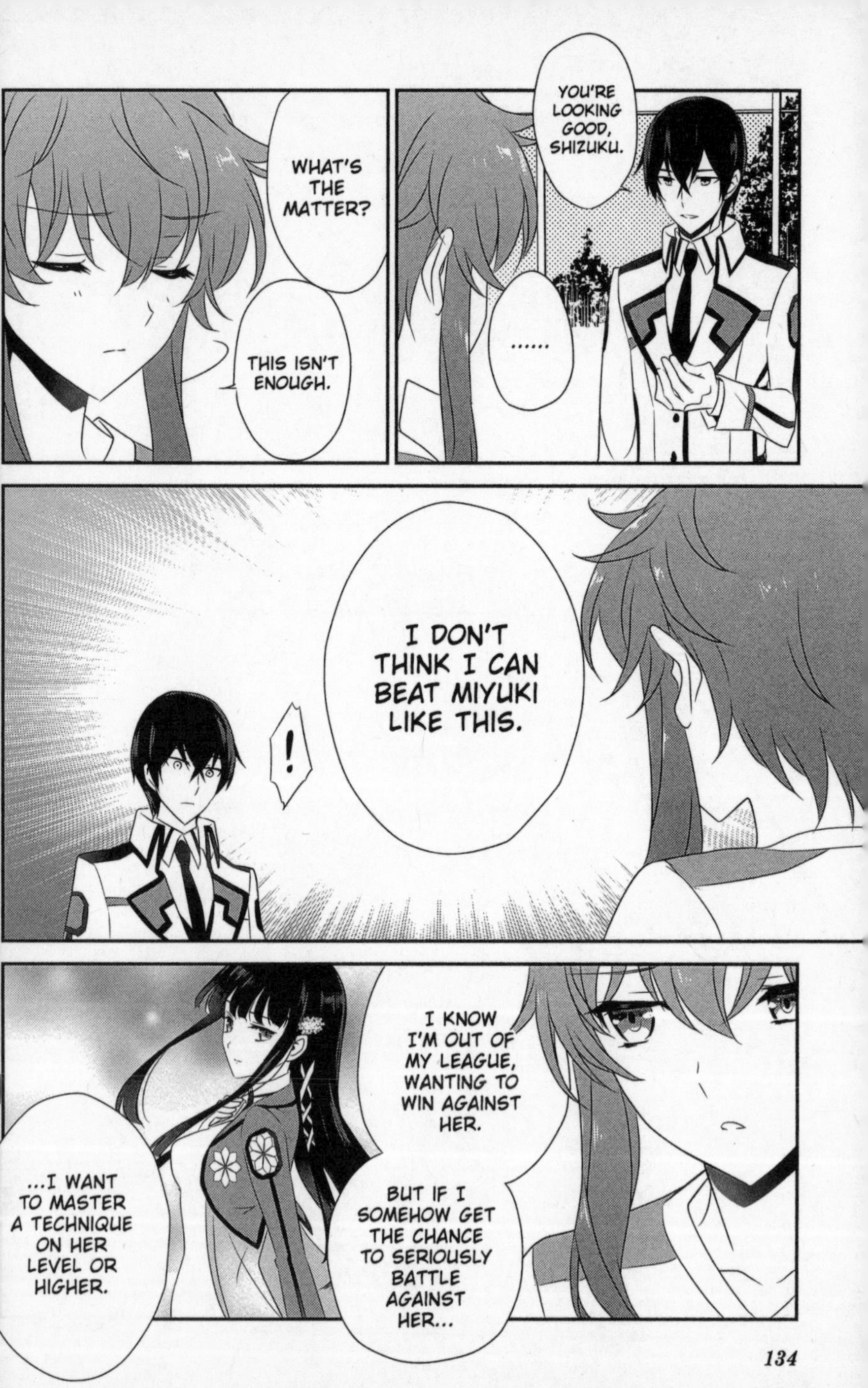
YOU'RE LOOKING GOOD, SHIZUKU.
......
WHAT'S THE MATTER?
THIS ISN'T ENOUGH.
I DON'T THINK I CAN BEAT MIYUKI LIKE THIS.
!
I KNOW I'M OUT OF MY LEAGUE, WANTING TO WIN AGAINST HER.
BUT IF I SOMEHOW GET THE CHANCE TO SERIOUSLY BATTLE AGAINST HER...
...I WANT TO MASTER A TECHNIQUE ON HER LEVEL OR HIGHER.

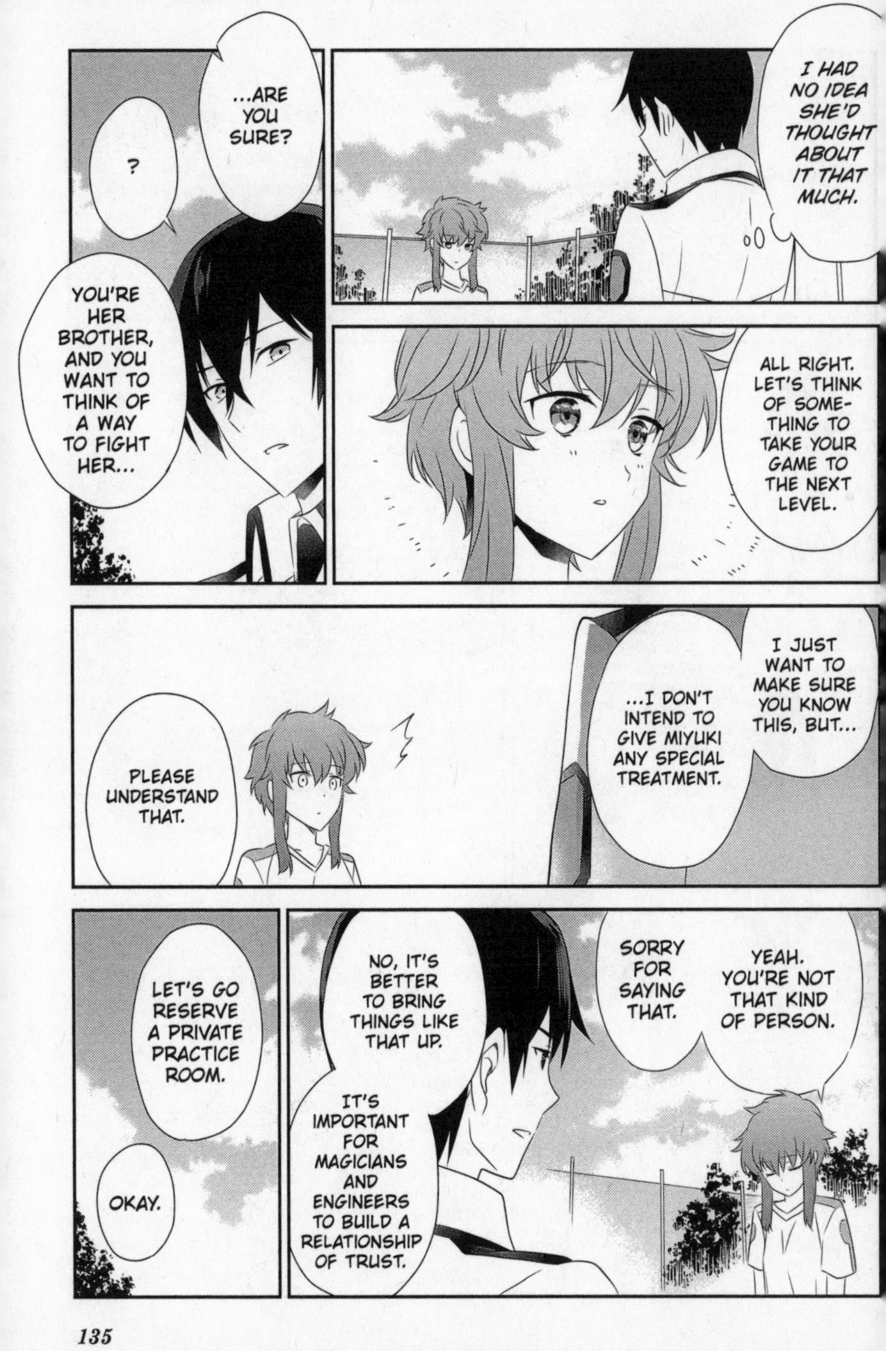
I HAD NO IDEA SHE'D THOUGHT ABOUT IT THAT MUCH.
ALL RIGHT. LET'S THINK OF SOME-THING TO TAKE YOUR GAME TO THE NEXT LEVEL.
...ARE YOU SURE?
?
YOU'RE HER BROTHER, AND YOU WANT TO THINK OF A WAY TO FIGHT HER...
I JUST WANT TO MAKE SURE YOU KNOW THIS, BUT...
...I DON'T INTEND TO GIVE MIYUKI ANY SPECIAL TREATMENT.
PLEASE UNDERSTAND THAT.
YEAH. YOU'RE NOT THAT KIND OF PERSON.
SORRY FOR SAYING THAT.
NO, IT'S BETTER TO BRING THINGS LIKE THAT UP.
IT'S IMPORTANT FOR MAGICIANS AND ENGINEERS TO BUILD A RELATIONSHIP OF TRUST.
LET'S GO RESERVE A PRIVATE PRACTICE ROOM.
OKAY.

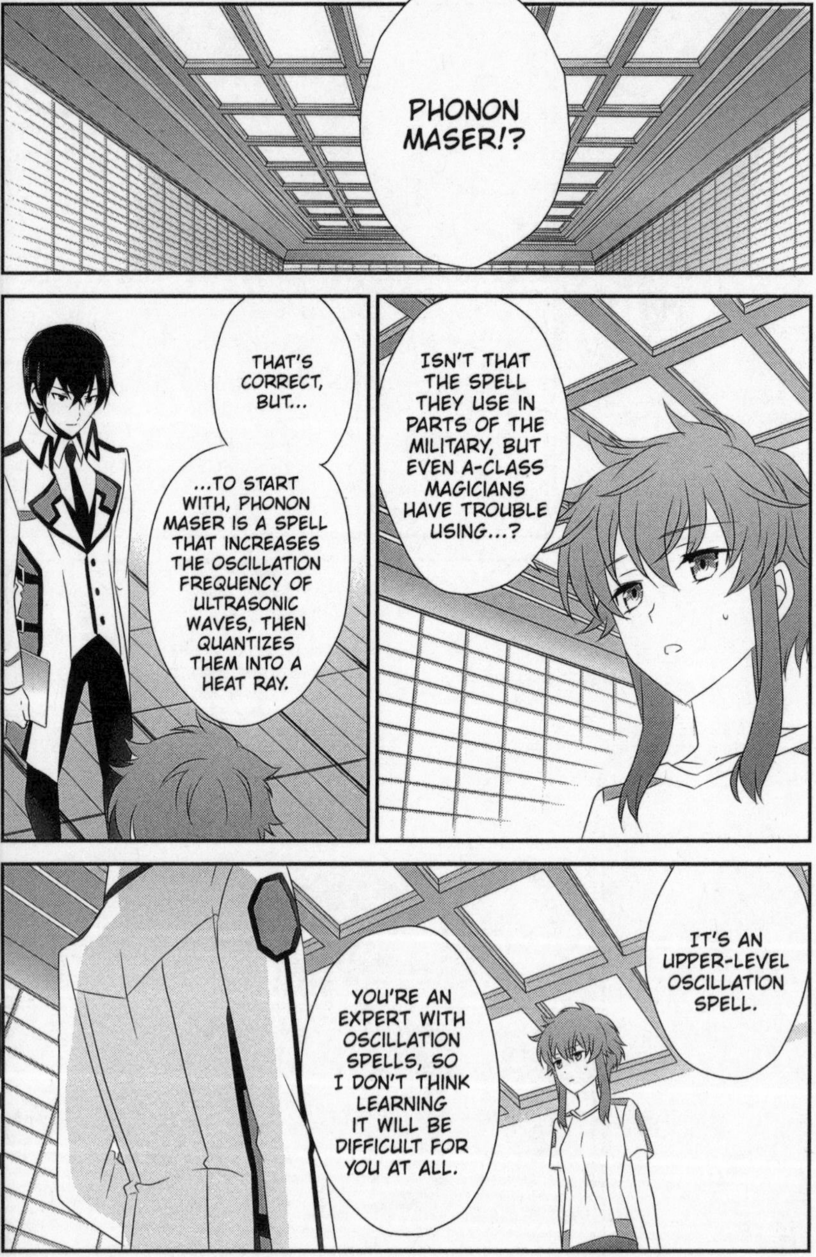
PHONON MASER!?
ISN'T THAT THE SPELL THEY USE IN PARTS OF THE MILITARY, BUT EVEN A-CLASS MAGICIANS HAVE TROUBLE USING...?
THAT'S CORRECT, BUT...
...TO START WITH, PHONON MASER IS A SPELL THAT INCREASES THE OSCILLATION FREQUENCY OF ULTRASONIC WAVES, THEN QUANTIZES THEM INTO A HEAT RAY.
IT'S AN UPPER-LEVEL OSCILLATION SPELL.
YOU'RE AN EXPERT WITH OSCILLATION SPELLS, SO I DON'T THINK LEARNING IT WILL BE DIFFICULT FOR YOU AT ALL.

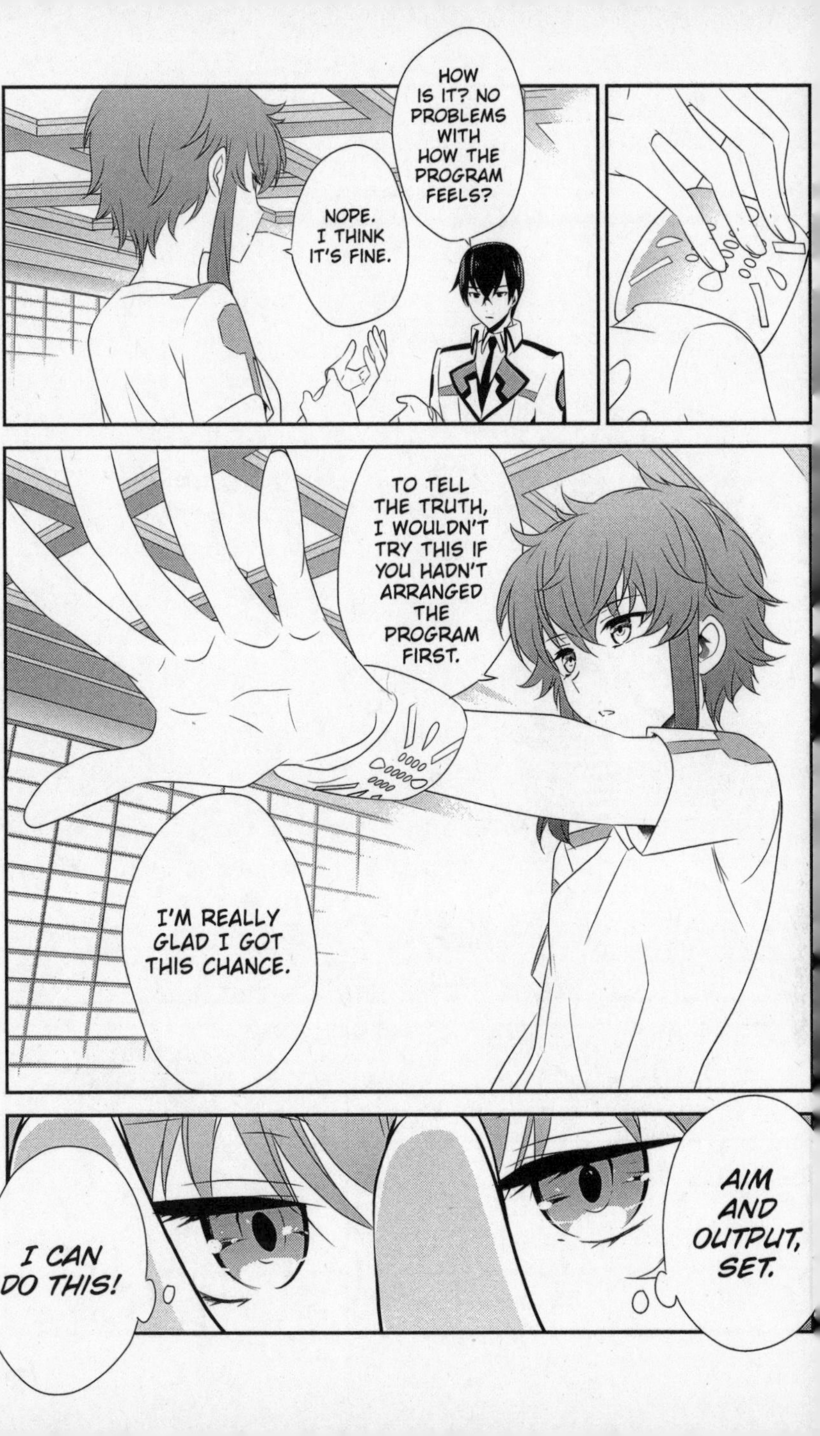
HOW IS IT? NO PROBLEMS WITH HOW THE PROGRAM FEELS?
NOPE. I THINK IT'S FINE.
TO TELL THE TRUTH, I WOULDN'T TRY THIS IF YOU HADN'T ARRANGED THE PROGRAM FIRST.
I'M REALLY GLAD I GOT THIS CHANCE.
AIM AND OUTPUT, SET.
I CAN DO THIS!

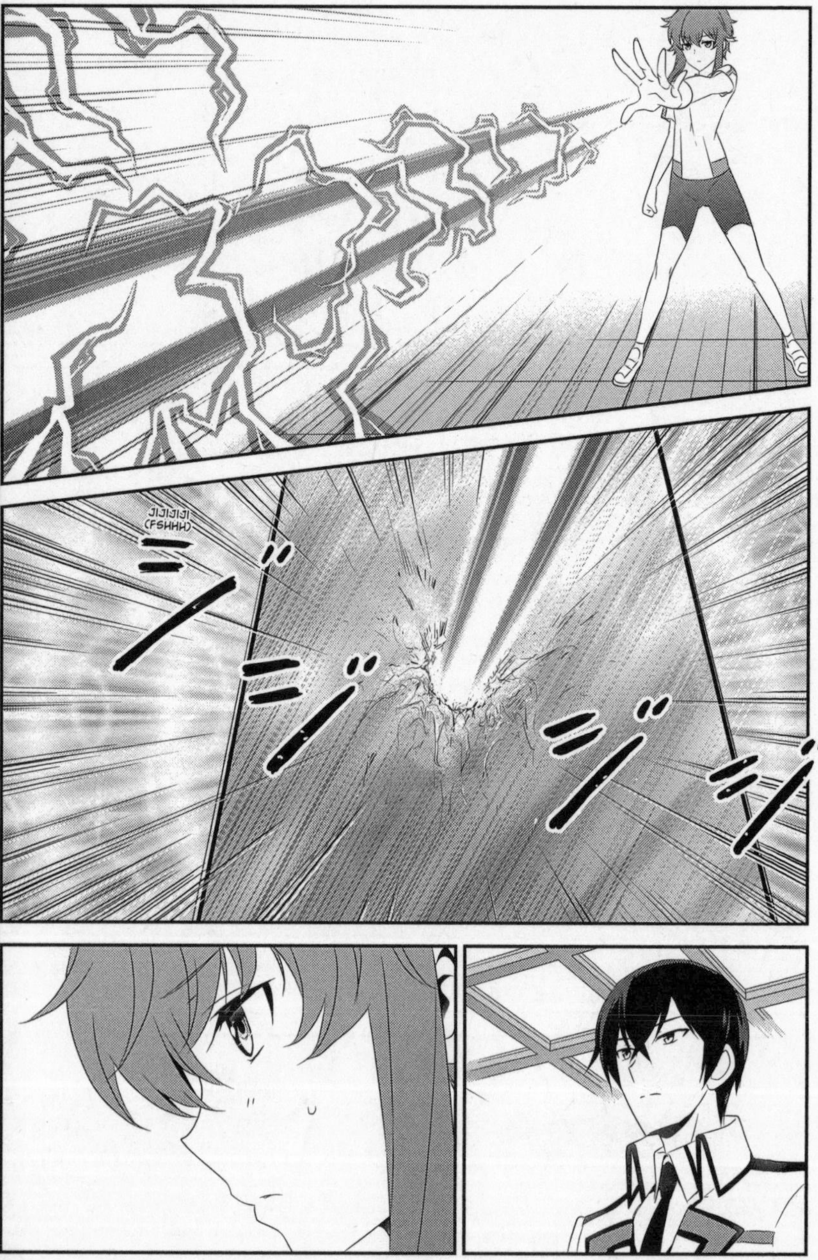
JIJIJIJI
(FSHHH)
ジジジジ

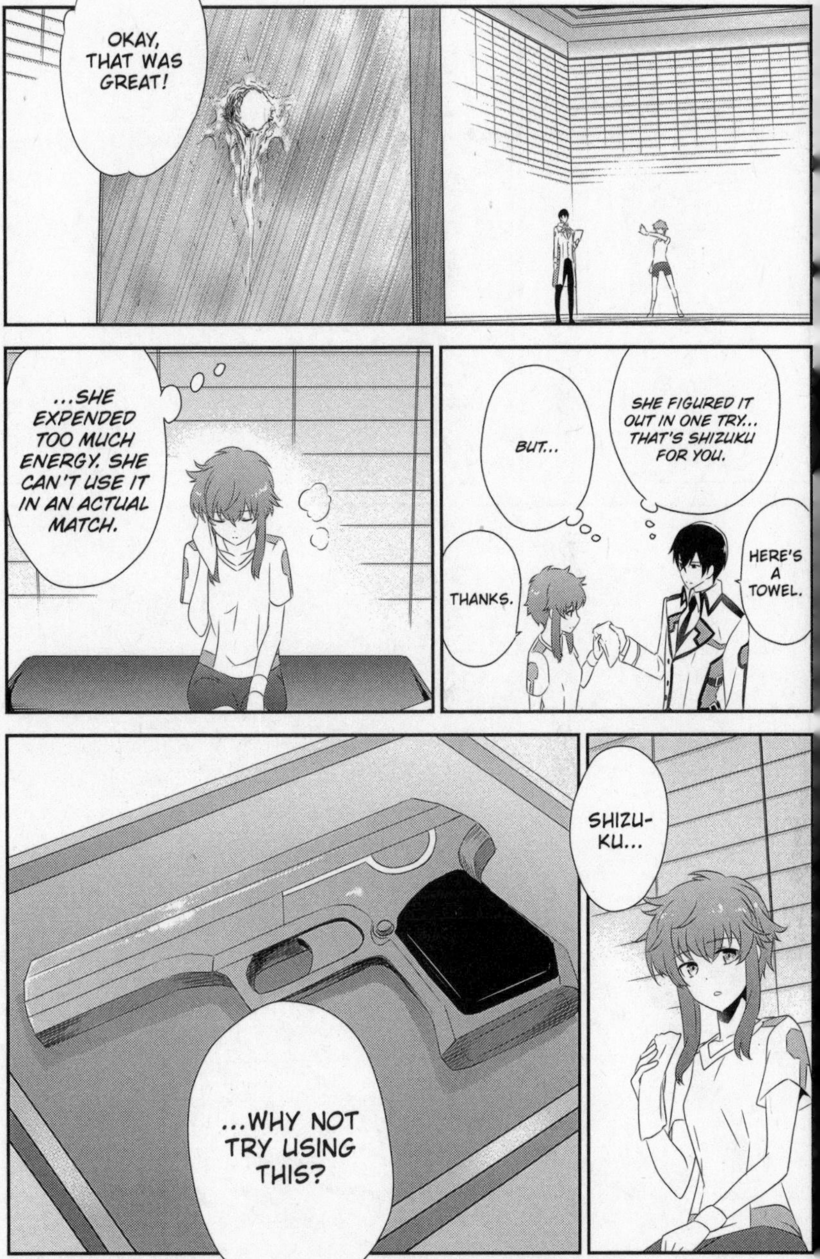
OKAY, THAT WAS GREAT!
SHE FIGURED IT OUT IN ONE TRY... THAT'S SHIZUKU FOR YOU.
BUT...
HERE'S A TOWEL.
THANKS.
...SHE EXPENDED TOO MUCH ENERGY. SHE CAN'T USE IT IN AN ACTUAL MATCH.
SHIZU-KU...
...WHY NOT TRY USING THIS?

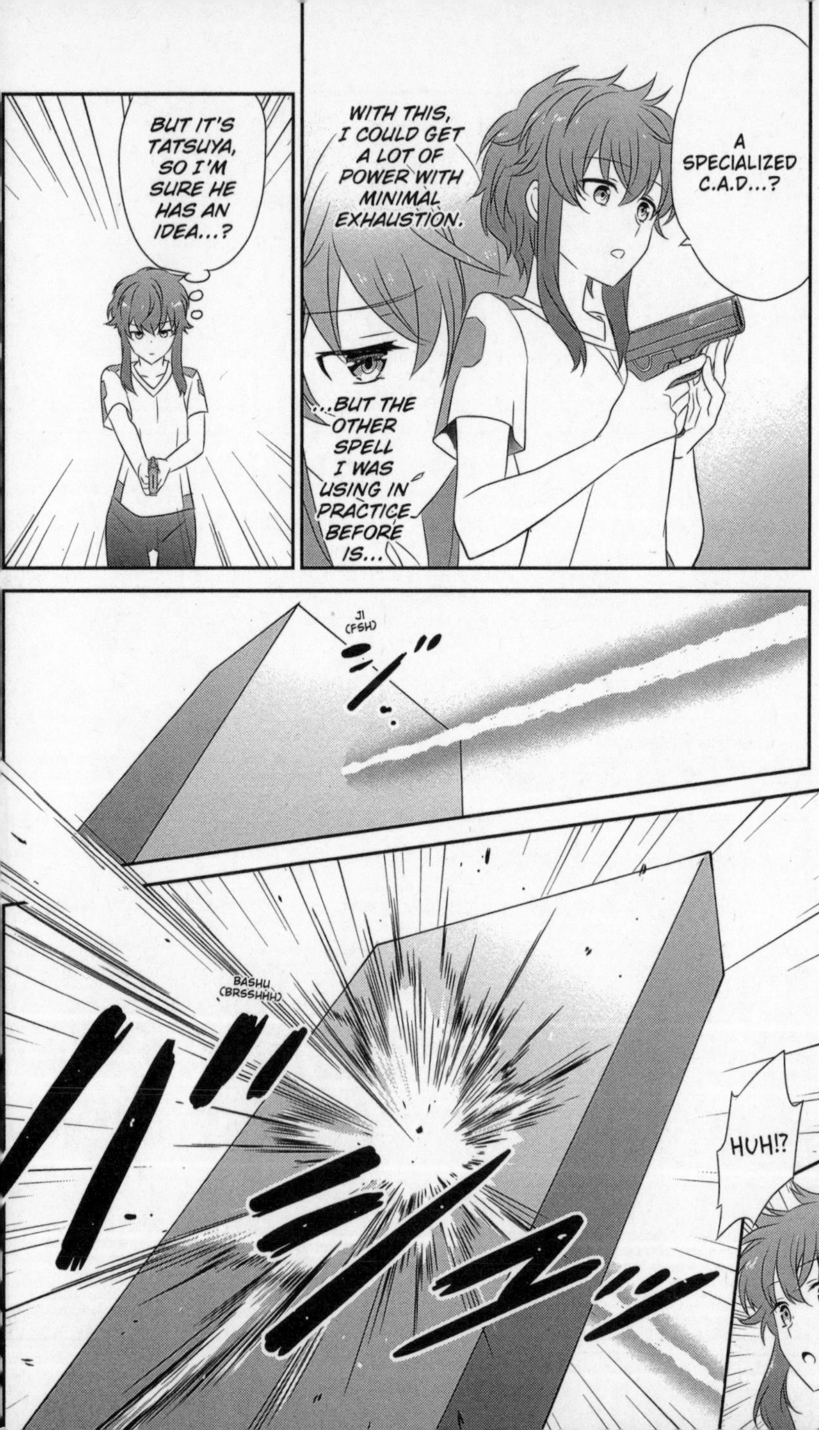

A SPECIALIZED C.A.D...?
WITH THIS, I COULD GET A LOT OF POWER WITH MINIMAL EXHAUSTION.
...BUT THE OTHER SPELL I WAS USING IN PRACTICE BEFORE IS...
BUT IT'S TATSUYA, SO I'M SURE HE HAS AN IDEA...?
JI (FSH)
HUH!?
BASHU (BRSSHHH)

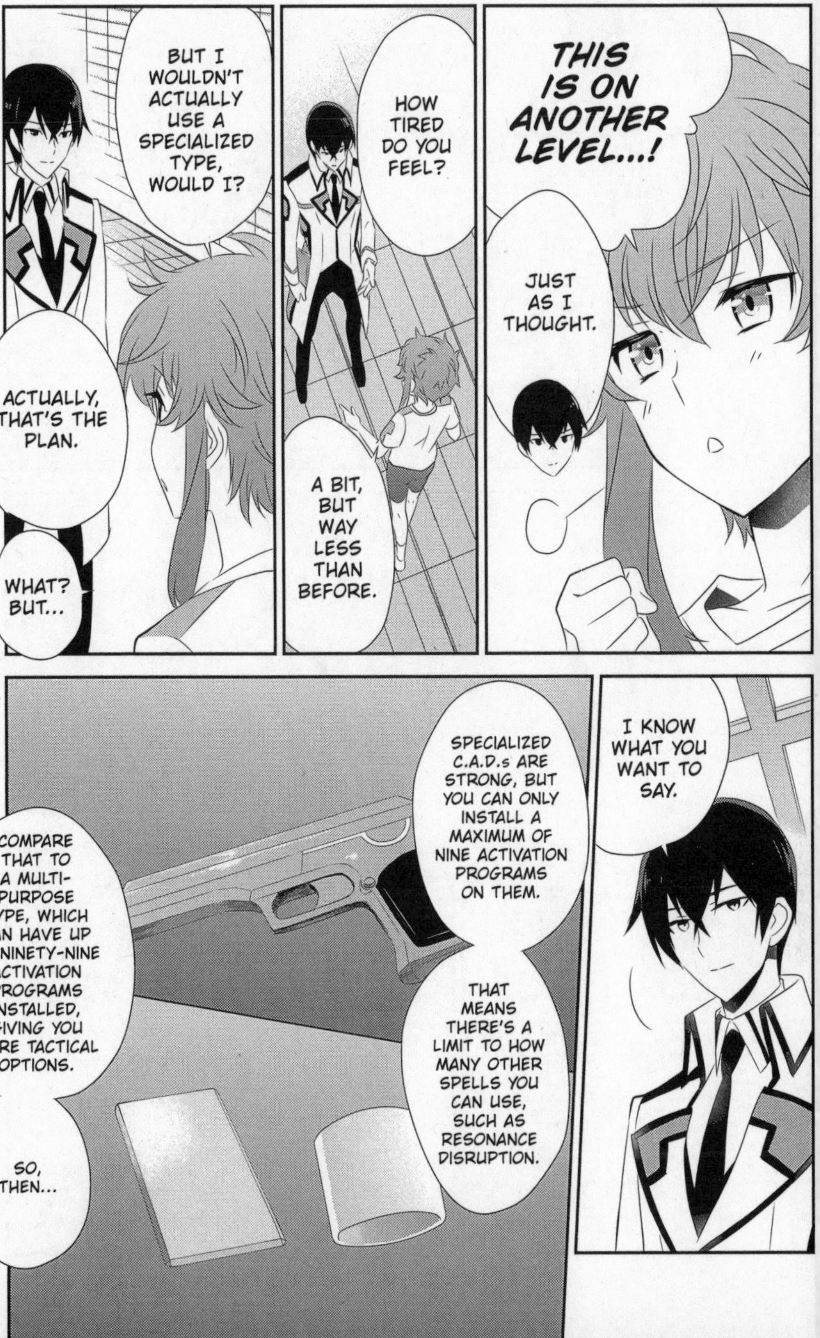
THIS IS ON ANOTHER LEVEL...!
JUST AS I THOUGHT.
HOW TIRED DO YOU FEEL?
A BIT, BUT WAY LESS THAN BEFORE.
BUT I WOULDN'T ACTUALLY USE A SPECIALIZED TYPE, WOULD I?
ACTUALLY, THAT'S THE PLAN.
WHAT? BUT...
I KNOW WHAT YOU WANT TO SAY.
SPECIALIZED C.A.D.s ARE STRONG, BUT YOU CAN ONLY INSTALL A MAXIMUM OF NINE ACTIVATION PROGRAMS ON THEM.
THAT MEANS THERE'S A LIMIT TO HOW MANY OTHER SPELLS YOU CAN USE, SUCH AS RESONANCE DISRUPTION.
COMPARE THAT TO A MULTI-PURPOSE TYPE, WHICH CAN HAVE UP TO NINETY-NINE ACTIVATION PROGRAMS INSTALLED, GIVING YOU MORE TACTICAL OPTIONS.
SO, THEN...

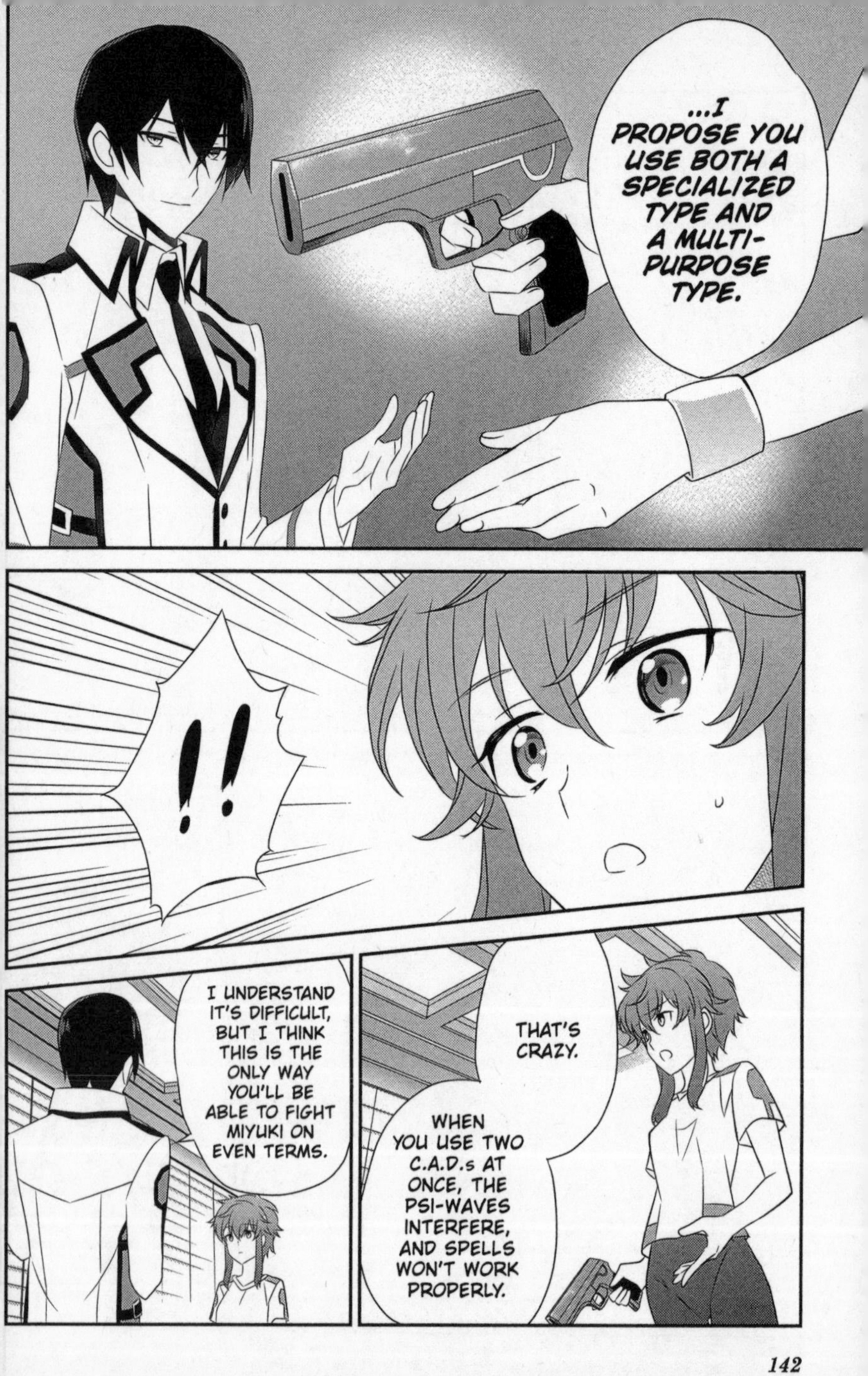
...I PROPOSE YOU USE BOTH A SPECIALIZED TYPE AND A MULTI-PURPOSE TYPE.
!!
THAT'S CRAZY.
WHEN YOU USE TWO C.A.D.s AT ONCE, THE PSI-WAVES INTERFERE, AND SPELLS WON'T WORK PROPERLY.
I UNDERSTAND IT'S DIFFICULT, BUT I THINK THIS IS THE ONLY WAY YOU'LL BE ABLE TO FIGHT MIYUKI ON EVEN TERMS.

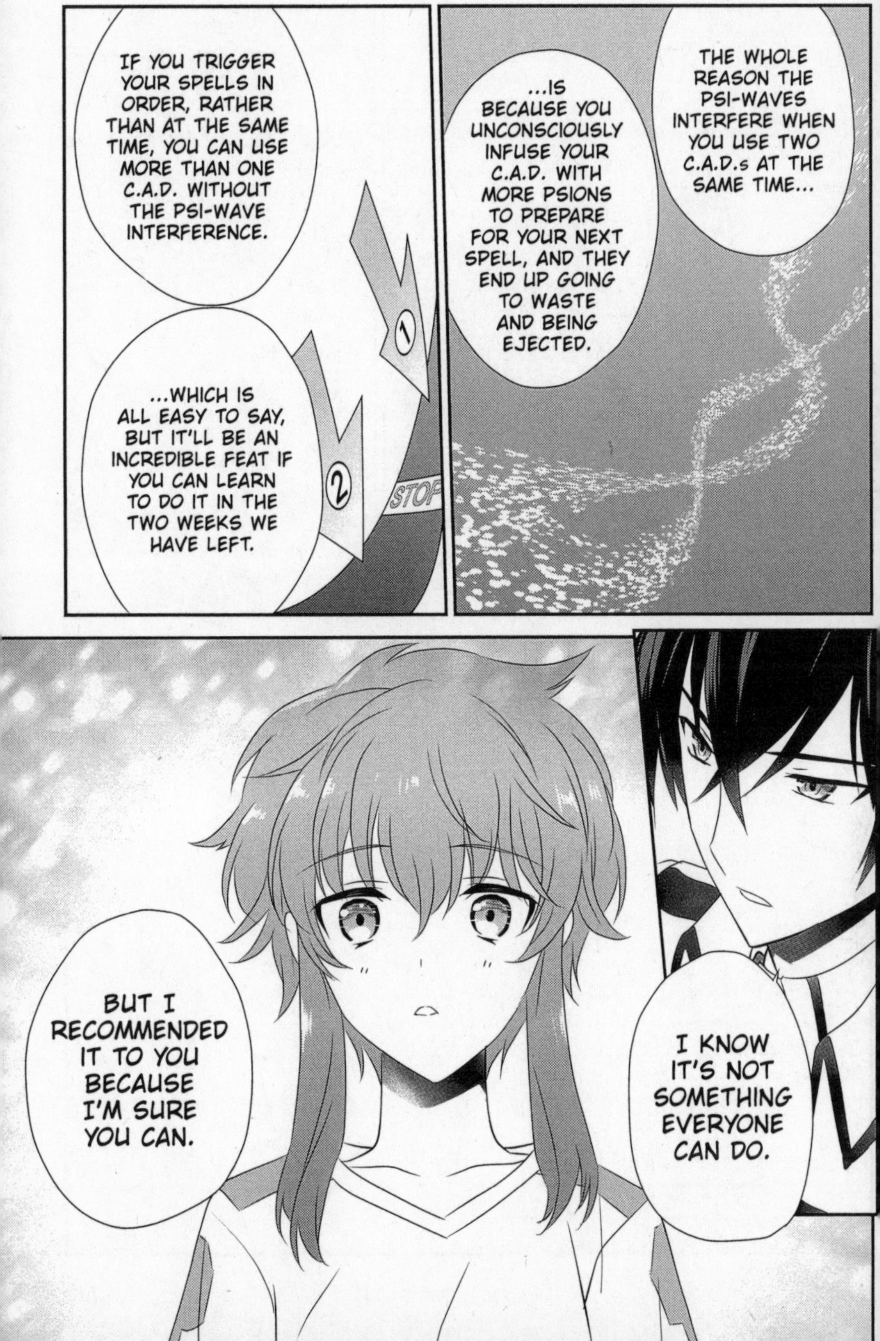
THE WHOLE REASON THE PSI-WAVES INTERFERE WHEN YOU USE TWO C.A.D.s AT THE SAME TIME...
...IS BECAUSE YOU UNCONSCIOUSLY INFUSE YOUR C.A.D. WITH MORE PSIONS TO PREPARE FOR YOUR NEXT SPELL, AND THEY END UP GOING TO WASTE AND BEING EJECTED.
IF YOU TRIGGER YOUR SPELLS IN ORDER, RATHER THAN AT THE SAME TIME, YOU CAN USE MORE THAN ONE C.A.D. WITHOUT THE PSI-WAVE INTERFERENCE.
1
2
STOP
...WHICH IS ALL EASY TO SAY, BUT IT'LL BE AN INCREDIBLE FEAT IF YOU CAN LEARN TO DO IT IN THE TWO WEEKS WE HAVE LEFT.
I KNOW IT'S NOT SOMETHING EVERYONE CAN DO.
BUT I RECOMMENDED IT TO YOU BECAUSE I'M SURE YOU CAN.

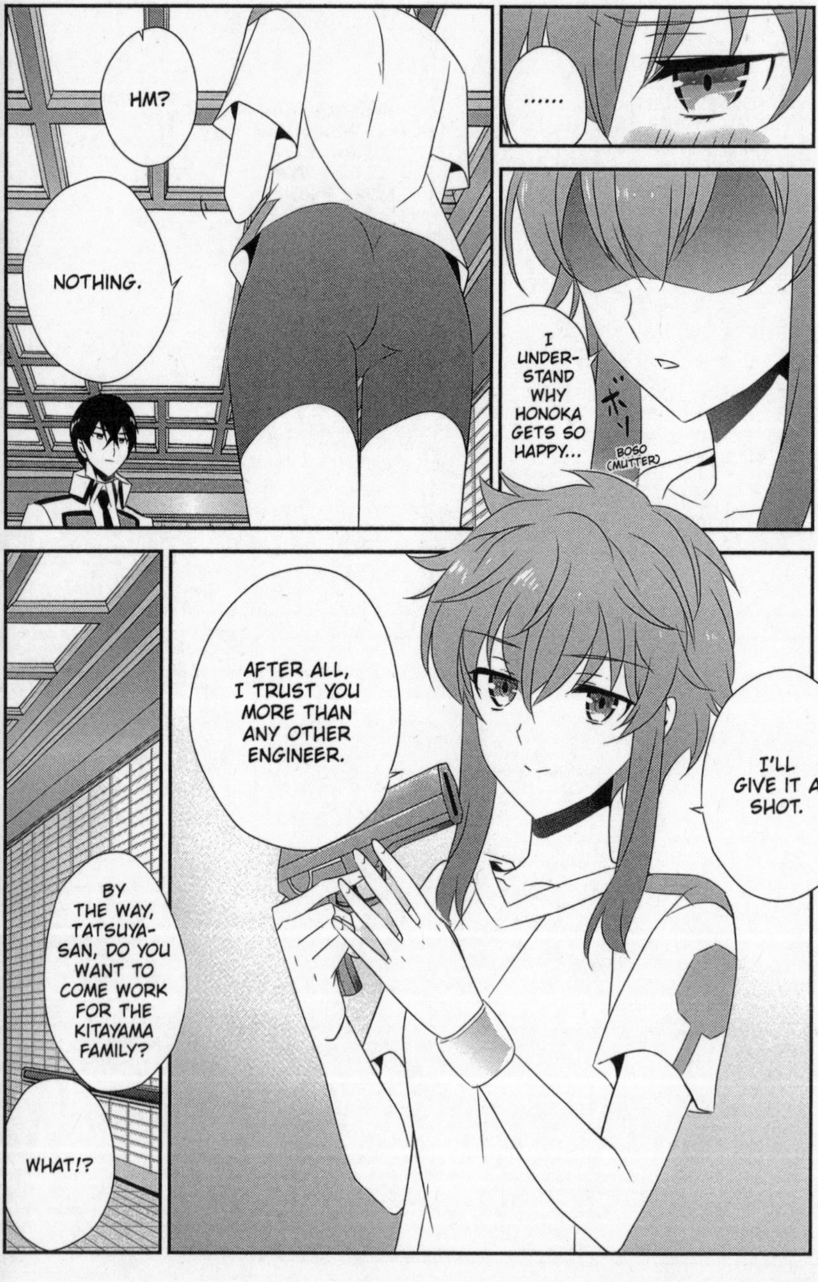
......
I UNDERSTAND WHY HONOKA GETS SO HAPPY...
ボソ
BOSO (MUTTER)
HM?
NOTHING.
I'LL GIVE IT A SHOT.
AFTER ALL, I TRUST YOU MORE THAN ANY OTHER ENGINEER.
BY THE WAY, TATSUYA-SAN, DO YOU WANT TO COME WORK FOR THE KITAYAMA FAMILY?
WHAT!?

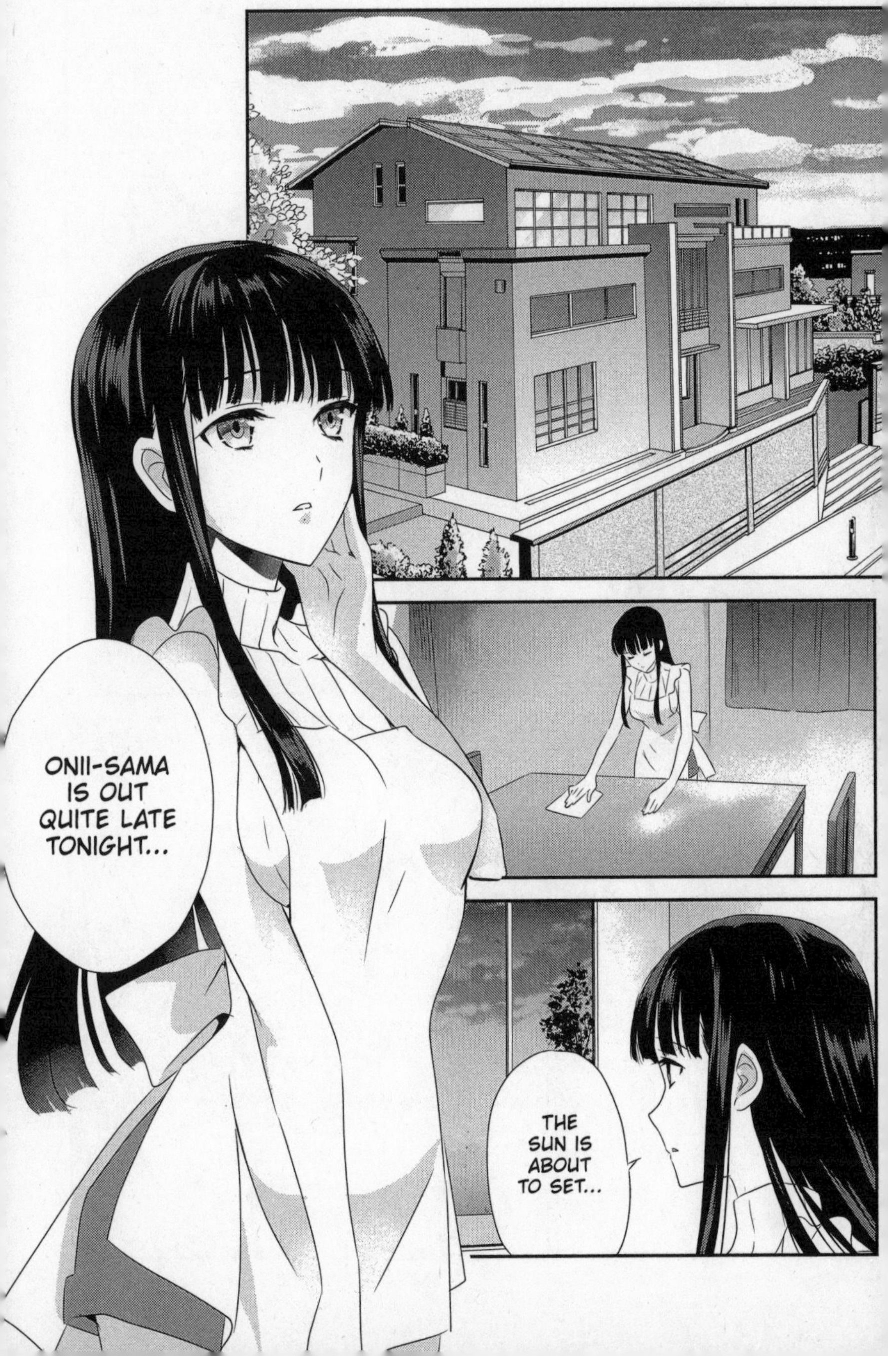
THE SUN IS ABOUT TO SET...
ONII-SAMA IS OUT QUITE LATE TONIGHT...

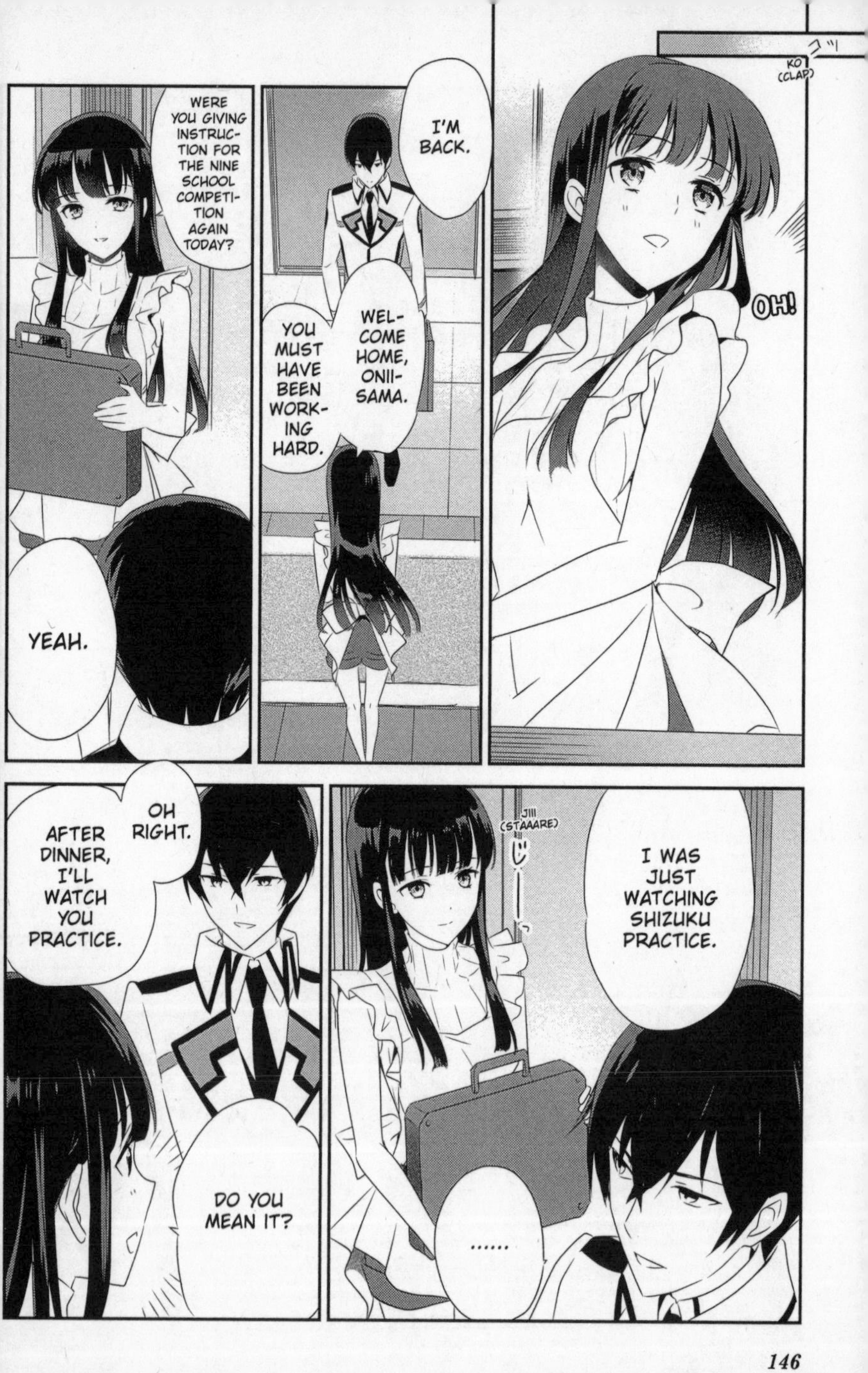

コツ
KO (CLAP)
OH!
I'M BACK.
WEL-COME HOME, ONII-SAMA.
YOU MUST HAVE BEEN WORK-ING HARD.
WERE YOU GIVING INSTRUC-TION FOR THE NINE SCHOOL COMPETI-TION AGAIN TODAY?
YEAH.
I WAS JUST WATCHING SHIZUKU PRACTICE.
JIII (STAAARE)
じーーっ
......
OH RIGHT.
AFTER DINNER, I'LL WATCH YOU PRACTICE.
DO YOU MEAN IT?

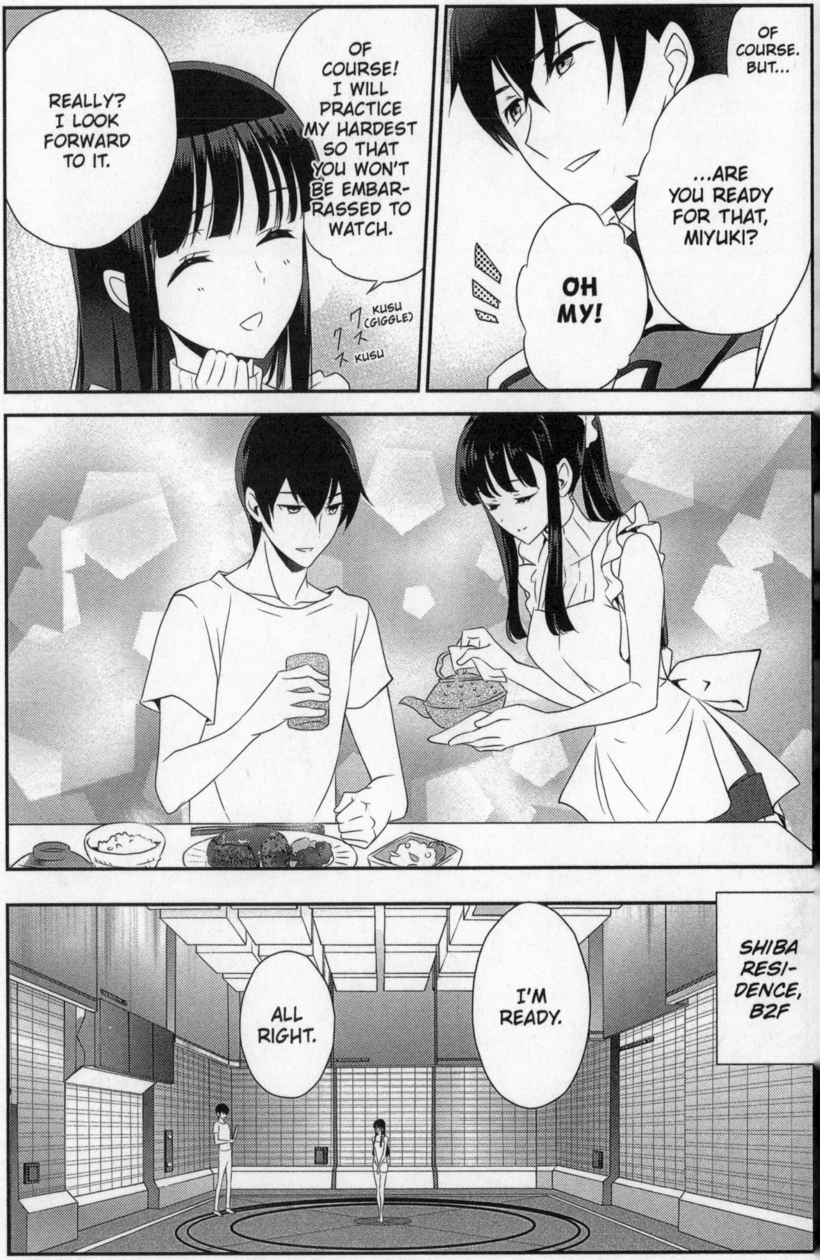
OF COURSE. BUT...
...ARE YOU READY FOR THAT, MIYUKI?
OH MY!
OF COURSE! I WILL PRACTICE MY HARDEST SO THAT YOU WON'T BE EMBARRASSED TO WATCH.
KUSU (GIGGLE) KUSU
REALLY? I LOOK FORWARD TO IT.
SHIBA RESIDENCE, B2F
I'M READY.
ALL RIGHT.

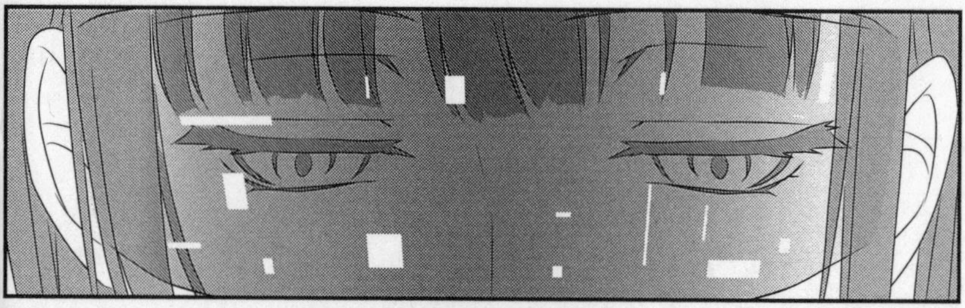

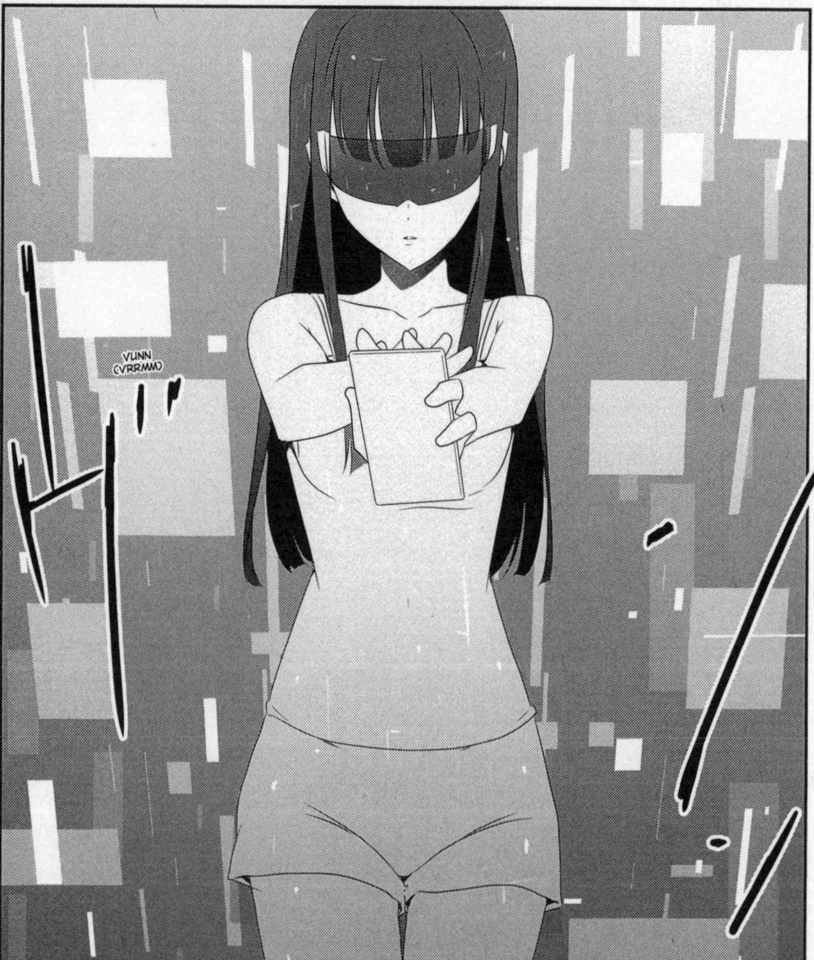
VUNN
(VRRMM)

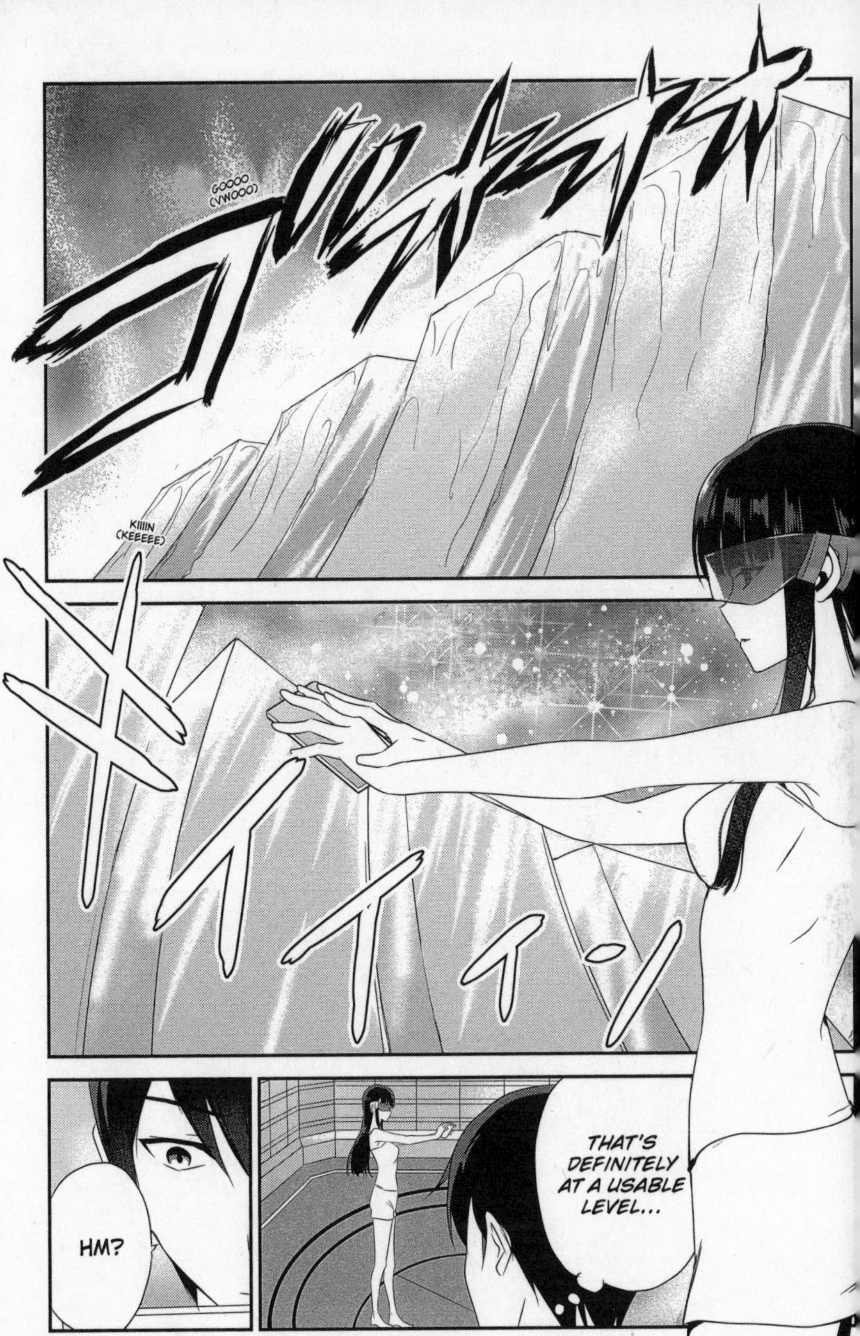
GOOOO (VWOOO)
KIIIIN (KEEEEE)
THAT'S DEFINITELY AT A USABLE LEVEL...
HM?

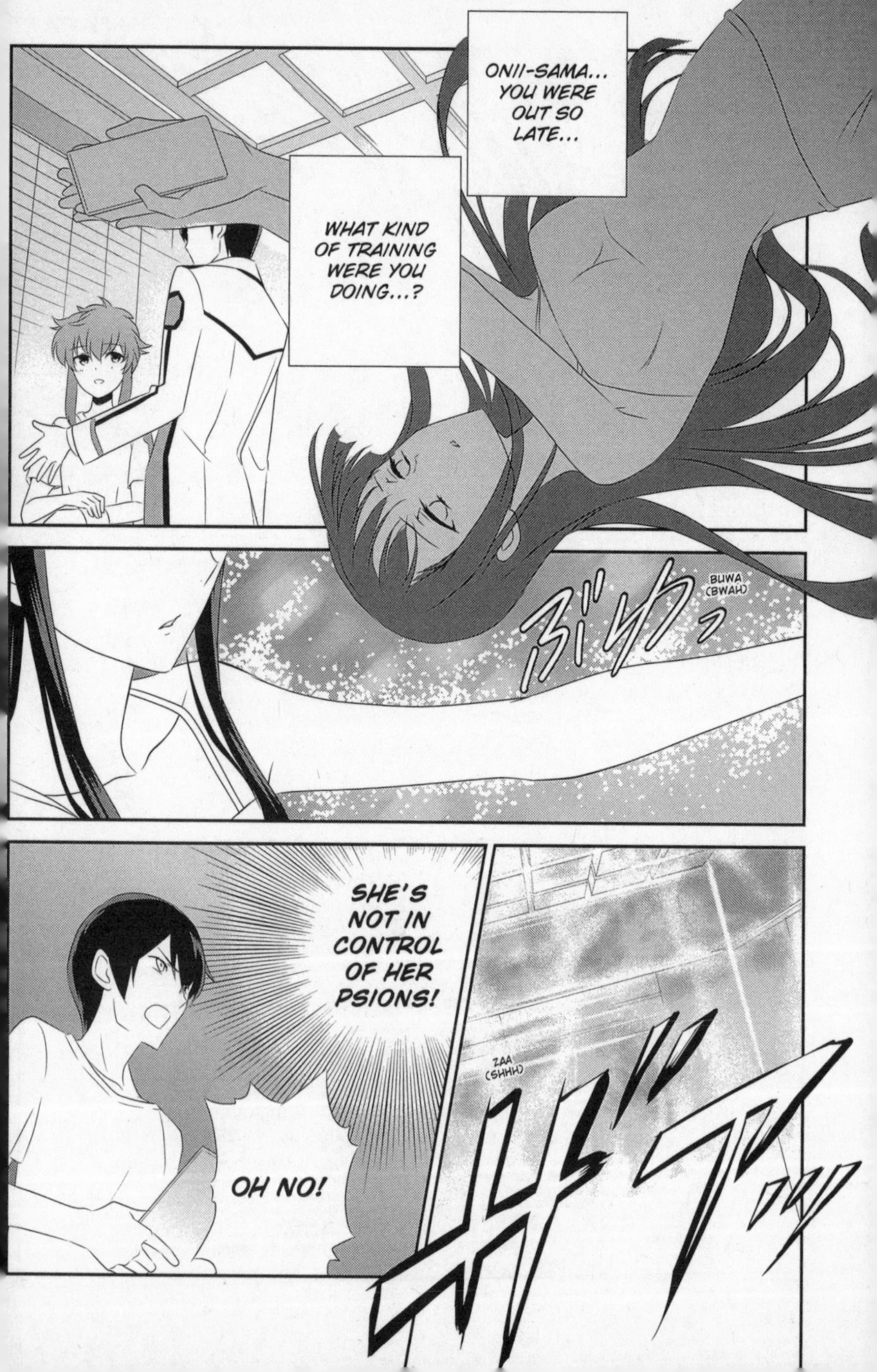
ONII-SAMA... YOU WERE OUT SO LATE...
WHAT KIND OF TRAINING WERE YOU DOING...?
BUWA (BWAH)
SHE'S NOT IN CONTROL OF HER PSIONS!
ZAA (SHHH)
OH NO!

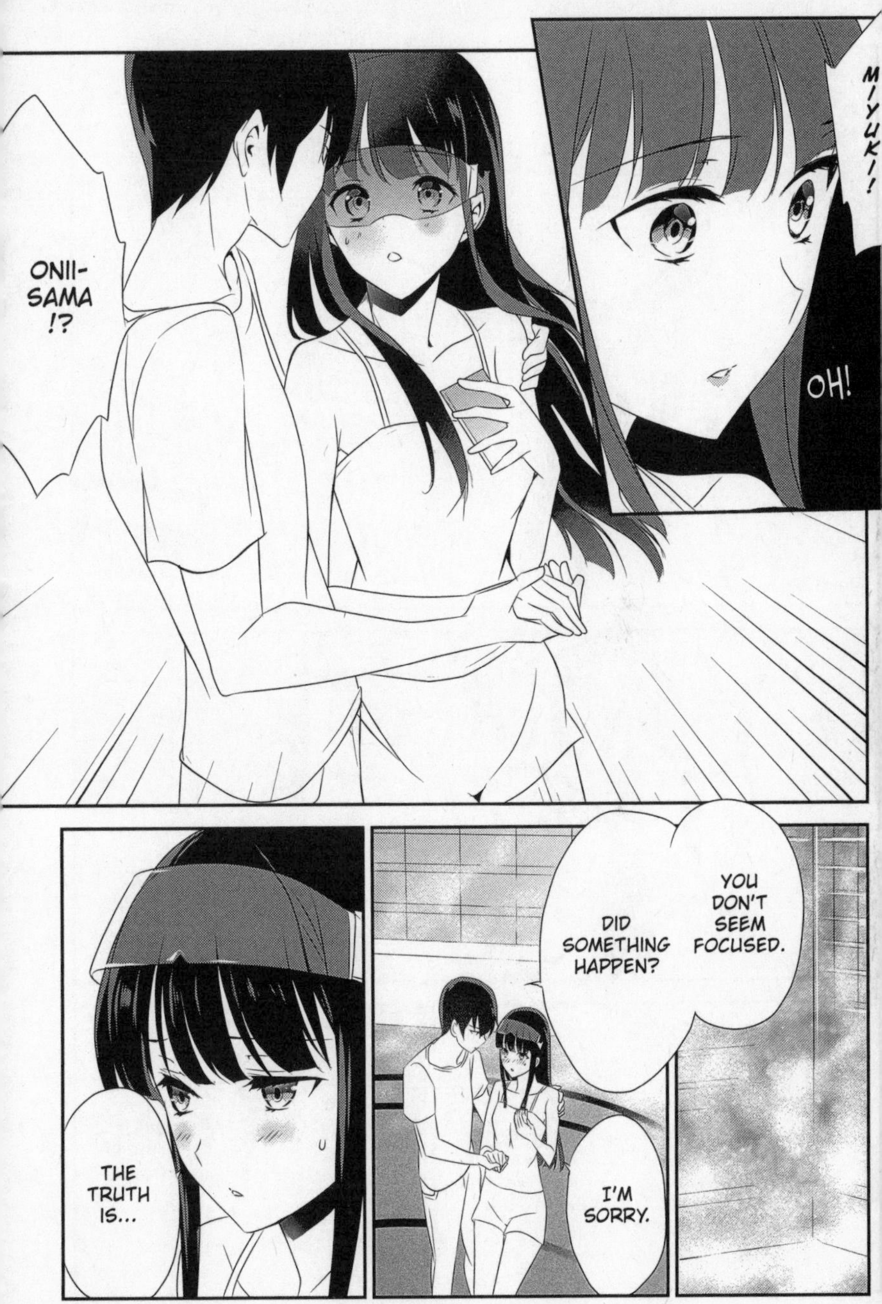
MIYUKI!
OH!
ONII-SAMA!?
YOU DON'T SEEM FOCUSED.
DID SOMETHING HAPPEN?
I'M SORRY.
THE TRUTH IS...

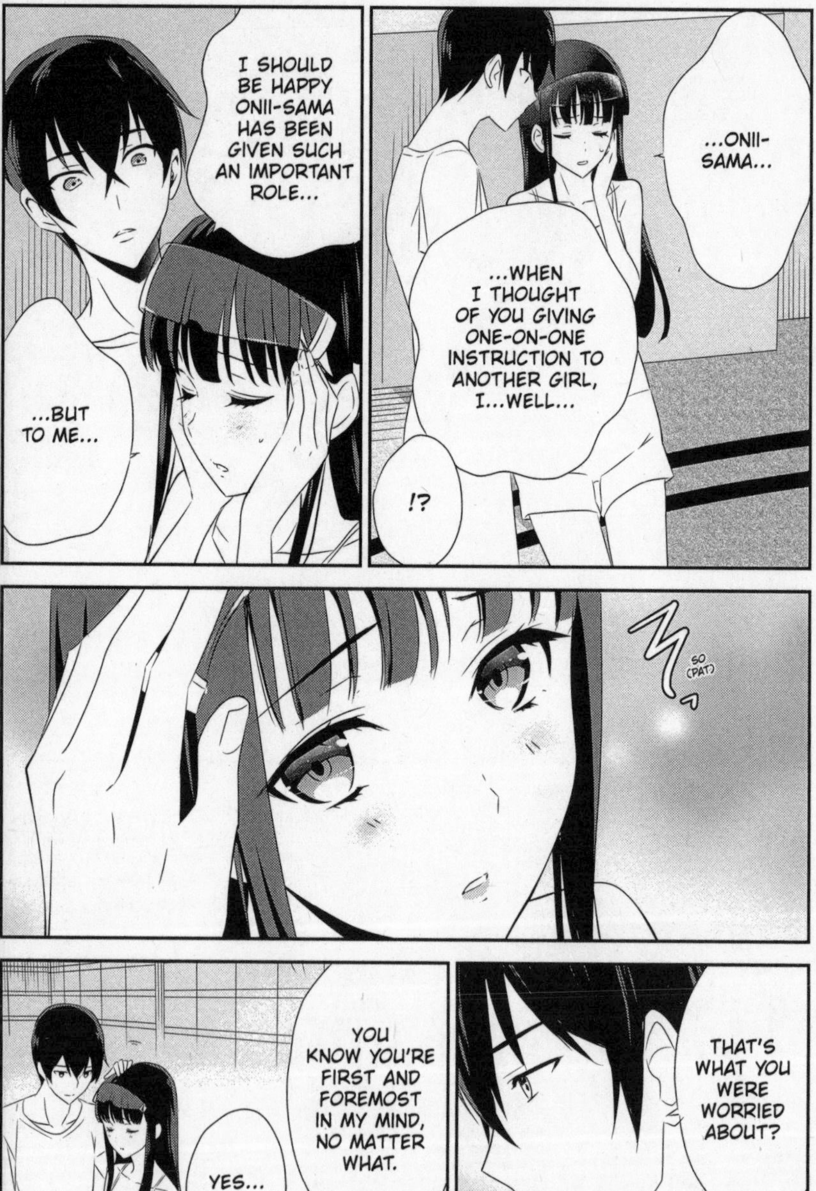
...ONII-SAMA...
...WHEN I THOUGHT OF YOU GIVING ONE-ON-ONE INSTRUCTION TO ANOTHER GIRL, I...WELL...
!?
I SHOULD BE HAPPY ONII-SAMA HAS BEEN GIVEN SUCH AN IMPORTANT ROLE...
...BUT TO ME...
SO (PAT)
THAT'S WHAT YOU WERE WORRIED ABOUT?
YOU KNOW YOU'RE FIRST AND FOREMOST IN MY MIND, NO MATTER WHAT.
YES...

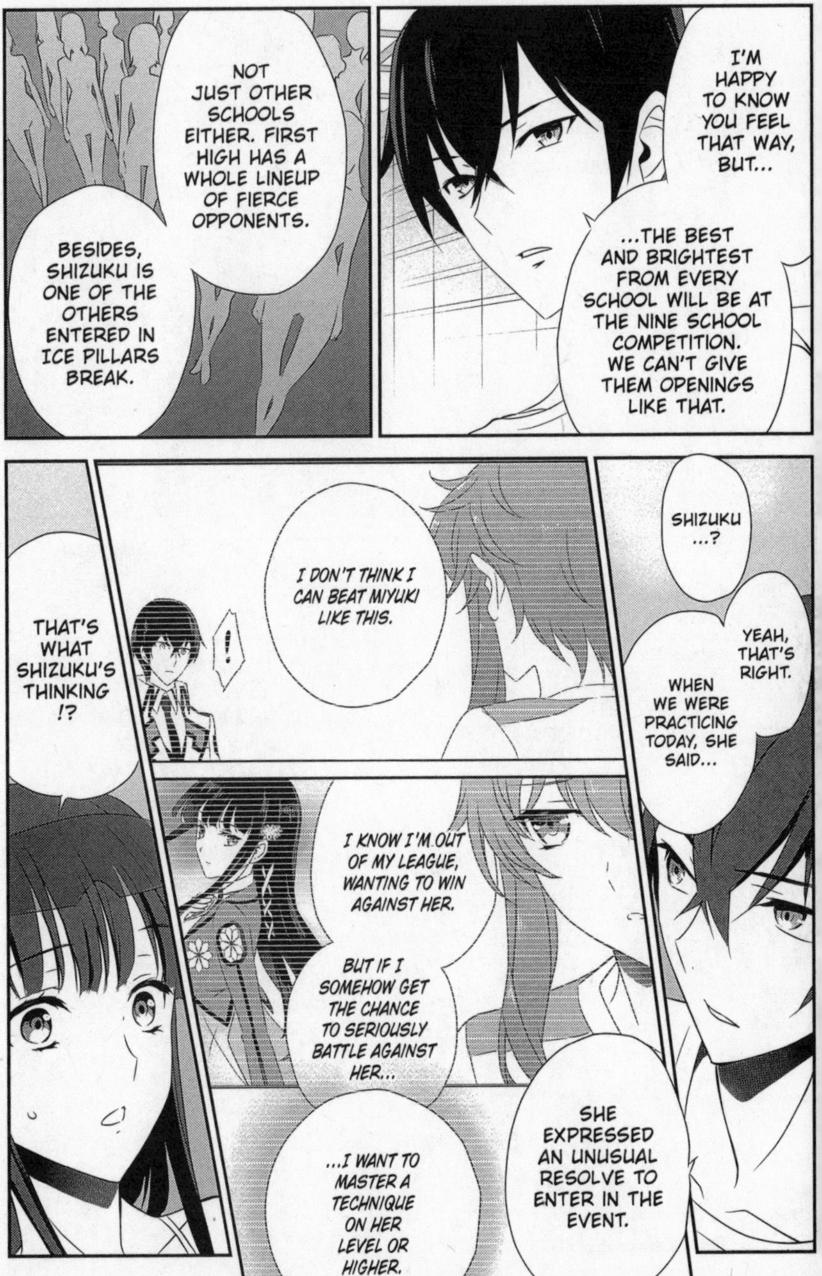
I'M HAPPY TO KNOW YOU FEEL THAT WAY, BUT...
...THE BEST AND BRIGHTEST FROM EVERY SCHOOL WILL BE AT THE NINE SCHOOL COMPETITION. WE CAN'T GIVE THEM OPENINGS LIKE THAT.
NOT JUST OTHER SCHOOLS EITHER. FIRST HIGH HAS A WHOLE LINEUP OF FIERCE OPPONENTS.
BESIDES, SHIZUKU IS ONE OF THE OTHERS ENTERED IN ICE PILLARS BREAK.
SHIZUKU ...?
YEAH, THAT'S RIGHT.
WHEN WE WERE PRACTICING TODAY, SHE SAID...
I DON'T THINK I CAN BEAT MIYUKI LIKE THIS.
!
I KNOW I'M OUT OF MY LEAGUE, WANTING TO WIN AGAINST HER.
BUT IF I SOMEHOW GET THE CHANCE TO SERIOUSLY BATTLE AGAINST HER...
...I WANT TO MASTER A TECHNIQUE ON HER LEVEL OR HIGHER.
SHE EXPRESSED AN UNUSUAL RESOLVE TO ENTER IN THE EVENT.
THAT'S WHAT SHIZUKU'S THINKING !?

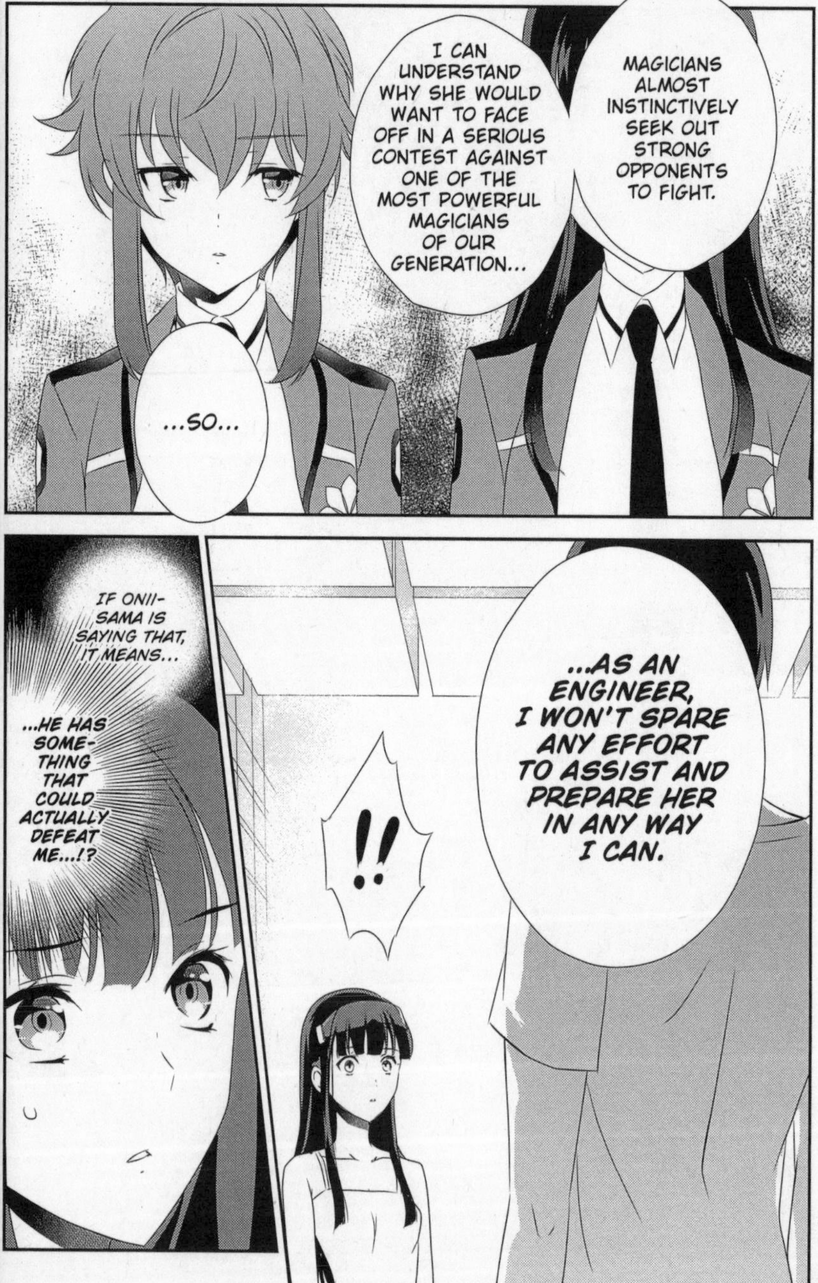
MAGICIANS ALMOST INSTINCTIVELY SEEK OUT STRONG OPPONENTS TO FIGHT.
I CAN UNDERSTAND WHY SHE WOULD WANT TO FACE OFF IN A SERIOUS CONTEST AGAINST ONE OF THE MOST POWERFUL MAGICIANS OF OUR GENERATION...
...SO...
...AS AN ENGINEER, I WON'T SPARE ANY EFFORT TO ASSIST AND PREPARE HER IN ANY WAY I CAN.
!!
IF ONII-SAMA IS SAYING THAT, IT MEANS...
...HE HAS SOME-THING THAT COULD ACTUALLY DEFEAT ME...!?

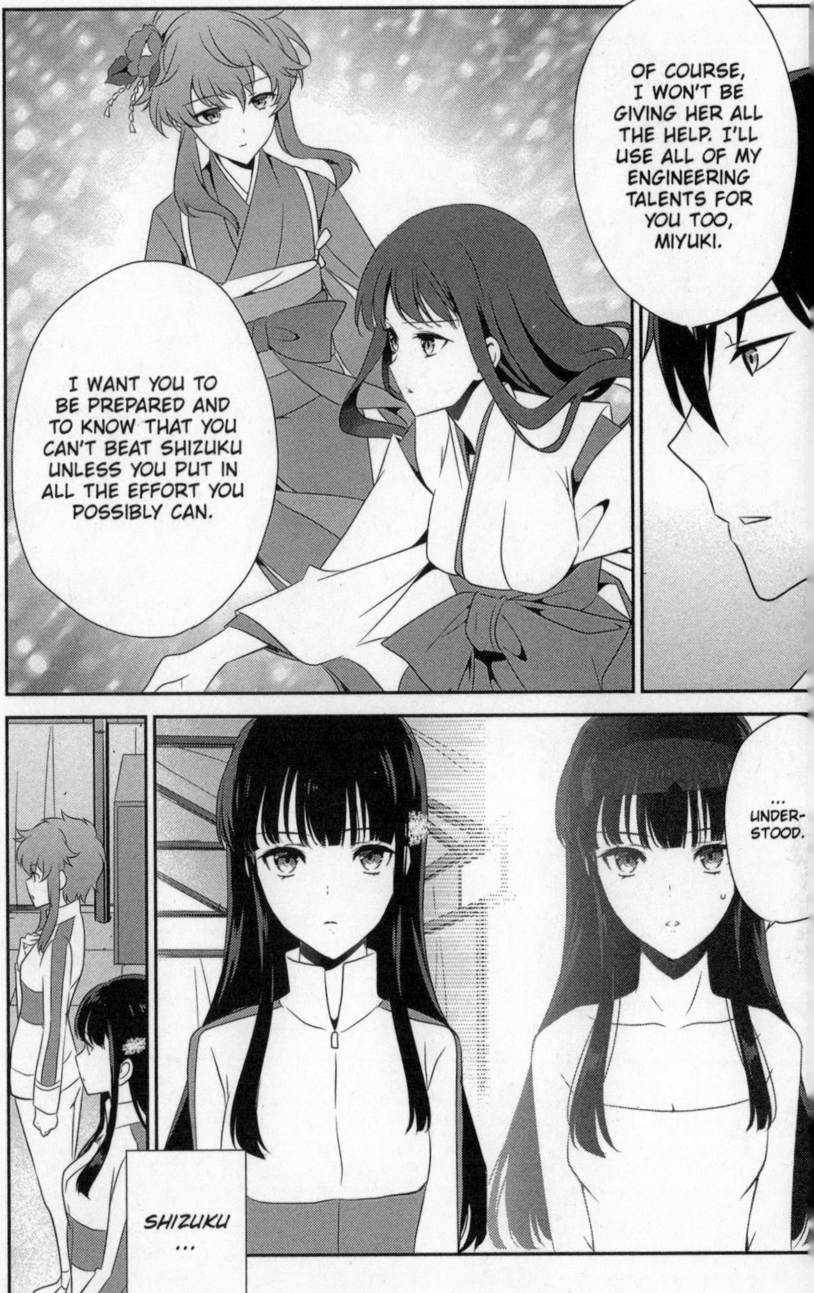
OF COURSE, I WON'T BE GIVING HER ALL THE HELP. I'LL USE ALL OF MY ENGINEERING TALENTS FOR YOU TOO, MIYUKI.
I WANT YOU TO BE PREPARED AND TO KNOW THAT YOU CAN'T BEAT SHIZUKU UNLESS YOU PUT IN ALL THE EFFORT YOU POSSIBLY CAN.
... UNDER-STOOD.
SHIZUKU ...

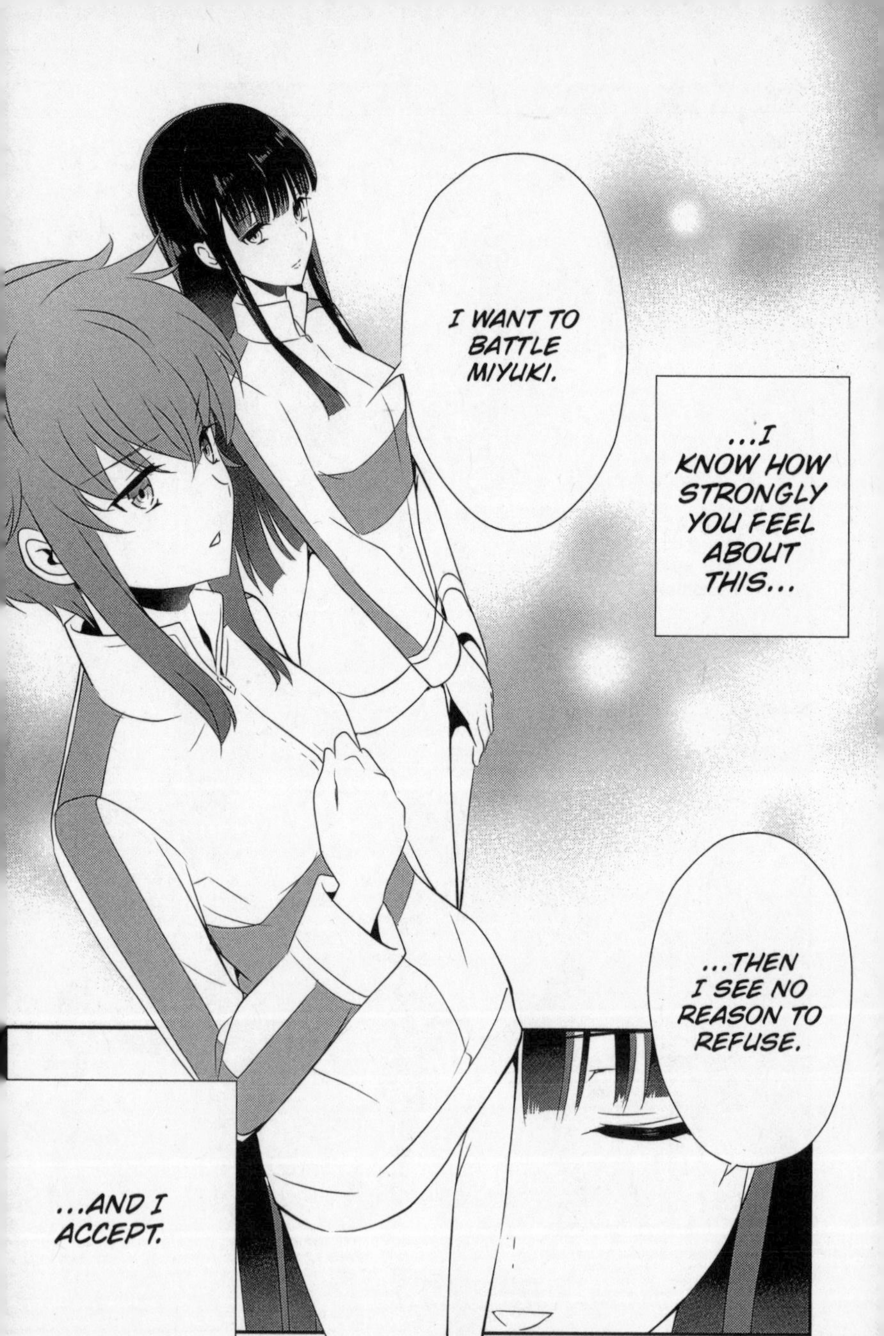
I WANT TO BATTLE MIYUKI.
...I KNOW HOW STRONGLY YOU FEEL ABOUT THIS...
...THEN I SEE NO REASON TO REFUSE.
...AND I ACCEPT.

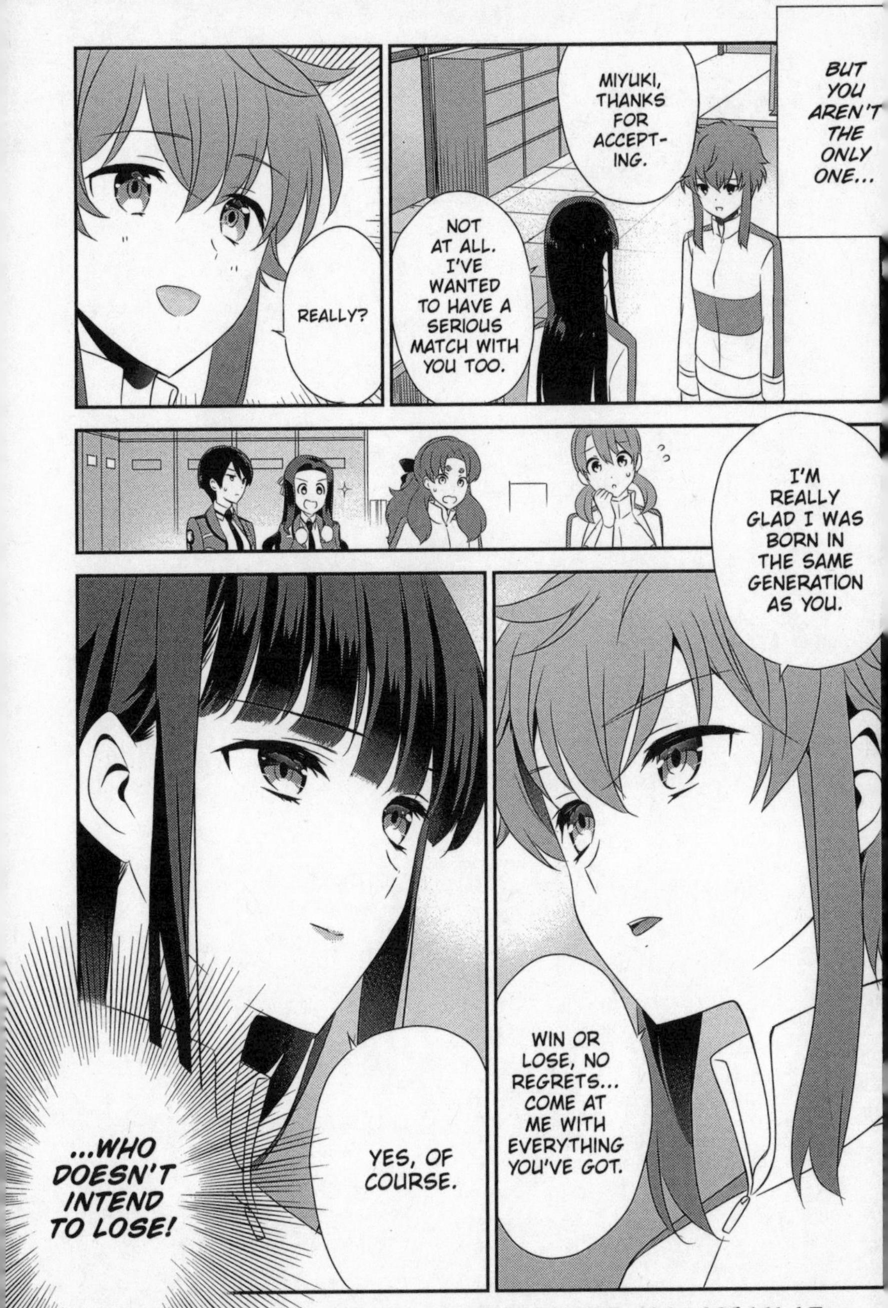
BUT YOU AREN'T THE ONLY ONE...
MIYUKI, THANKS FOR ACCEPT-ING.
NOT AT ALL. I'VE WANTED TO HAVE A SERIOUS MATCH WITH YOU TOO.
REALLY?
I'M REALLY GLAD I WAS BORN IN THE SAME GENERATION AS YOU.
WIN OR LOSE, NO REGRETS... COME AT ME WITH EVERYTHING YOU'VE GOT.
YES, OF COURSE.
...WHO DOESN'T INTEND TO LOSE!

TO BE CONTINUED IN VOLUME 8

Activation sequence
The blueprints for magic and the programs used to construct it. Activation sequence data is stored in a compressed format in C.A.D.s. Design waves are sent from the magician to the device, where they're converted into a signal according to the decompressed data and returned to the magician.

Antinite
A military-grade commodity only produced in lands where ancient alpine civilizations prospered, such as part of the Aztec Empire and the Mayan countries and regions. Extremely valuable due to its limited production quantity and impossible for civilians to acquire.

Blanche
A national anti-magic political organization with the objective of uprooting discrimination in society based on magical ability. They hold protest activities based on the criticism of the fictional concept of the current system giving special political treatment to magicians. Behind the scenes, they engage in terrorism and other illegal activities and are strictly watched by the public peace agency.

Blooms, Weeds
Terms displaying the gap between Course 1 students and Course 2 students in First High. The left breast of Course 1 student uniforms is emblazoned with an eight-petaled emblem, but it is absent from the Course 2 uniforms.

Cabinets
Small, linear vehicles holding either two or four passengers and controlled by a central station. Used for commuting to work and school as a public transportation replacement for trains.

Cardinal George
Shinkurou Kichijouji's nickname. Given to him for having discovered one of the Cardinal Codes, which only existed in theory beforehand, at the young age of thirteen.

Cast jamming
A variety of typeless magic that obstructs magic sequences from exerting influence on Eidos. It weakens the process by which magic sequences affect Eidos by scattering large amounts of meaningless psionic waves.

C.A.D. (Casting Assistant Device)
A device that simplifies the activation of magic. Magical programming is recorded inside. The main types are specialized and multi-purpose.

Crimson Prince
Masaki Ichijou's nickname. Given to him for having fought through a battle "drenched in the blood of enemy and ally alike" during the Sado Invasion of 2092 as a volunteer soldier on the defensive line at the young age of thirteen.

Égalité
A branch organization of Blanche. They take in young people who hate politics, so they don't reveal that they're directly related to Blanche.

Eidos (Individual information body)
Originally a term from Greek philosophy. In modern magic, Eidos are the bodies of information that accompany phenomena. They record the existence of those phenomena on the world, so they can also be called the footprints that phenomena leave on the world. The definition of "magic" in modern magic refers to the technology that modifies these phenomena by modifying Eidos.

Four Leaves Technology (F.L.T.)
A domestic C.A.D. manufacturer. Originally famous for its magic engineering products, rather than finished C.A.D.s, but with the development of its Silver line of models, its fame skyrocketed as a C.A.D. manufacturer.

Goldie family
A famed family of modern magic in England. Amy is part of their bloodline, and her grandmother is the aunt of the current head.

Idea (Information body dimension)
Pronounced "ee-dee-ah." Originally a term from Greek philosophy. In modern magic, "Idea" refers to the platform on which Eidos are recorded. Magic's primary form is a technology wherein a magic sequence is output onto this platform, thus rewriting the Eidos recorded within.

The Index
A table of the proper names of spells recorded in the encyclopedia of magic created by the National Magic University. Its full name is the "National Magic University's Compiled Magic Encyclopedia Name Index." Researchers in Japan who are involved in magical research and development work hard every day with the grand goal of being

chosen for the Index.

◉ I.S. Magic
Unique abilities that are difficult to systematize as magic. "I.S." stands for "innately specialized."

◉ Loopcast system
Activation sequences made so that a magician can continually execute a spell as many times as their calculation capacity will permit. Normally, one must re-expand activation sequences from the C.A.D. every time one executes the same spell, but the loopcast system makes it possible by automatically duplicating the activation sequence's final state in the magician's magic calculation region.

◉ Magician
An abbreviation of "magical technician," referring to anyone with the skill to use magic at a practical level.

◉ Magic Association of Japan
A social group of Japanese magicians based in Kyoto. The Kantou branch location is established within Yokohama Bay Hills Tower.

◉ Magic calculation region
A mental region for the construction of magic sequences. The substance, so to speak, of magical talent. It exists in a magician's unconscious, and even if a magician is normally aware of using his or her magic calculation region, he or she cannot be aware of the processes being conducted within. The magic calculation region can be called a "black box" for the magician himself.

◉ Magic engineer
Refers to engineers who design, develop, and maintain apparatuses that assist, amplify, and strengthen magic. Their reputation in society is slightly worse than that of magicians. However, magic engineers are indispensable for tuning the C.A.D.s, indispensable tools for magicians, so in the industrial world, they're in higher demand than normal magicians. A first-rate magic engineer's earnings surpass even that of first-rate magicians.

◉ Magic high school
The nickname for the high schools affiliated with the National Magic University. There are nine established throughout the country. Of them, the first through the third have two hundred students per grade and use the Course 1/Course 2 system.

◉ Magic sequence
An information body for the purpose of temporarily altering information attached to phenomena. They

are constructed from the psions possessed by magicians.

◉ Nine School Competition
An abbreviation of "National Magic High School Goodwill Magic Competition Tournament." Magic high school students across the country, from First through Ninth High, are gathered to compete with their schools in fierce magic showdowns. There are six events: Speed Shooting, Cloudball, Battle Board, Ice Pillars Break, Mirage Bat, and Monolith Code.

◉ Psions
Non-physical particles belonging to the dimension of psychic phenomena, psions are elements that record information on consciousness and thought products. Eidos—the theoretical basis for modern magic—as well as activation sequences and magic sequences—supporting its main framework—are all bodies of information constructed from psions. Also referred to as "thought particles."

◉ Pushions
Non-physical particles belonging to the dimension of psychic phenomena. Their existence has been proven, but their true form and functions have yet to be elucidated. Magicians are generally only able to "feel" the pushions being activated through magic. Also referred to as "spirit particles."

◉ Tactical-class magician
A magician who can use tactical-class magic—magic with the power to destroy an entire city or fleet in a single attack. Thirteen such tactical magicians have been made internationally public, and these are called the Thirteen Apostles.

◉ The Ten Master Clans
The strongest group of magicians in Japan. Ten families from a list of twenty-eight are chosen during the Ten Master Clans Selection Conference that happens every four years and are named as the Ten Master Clans. The twenty-eight families are Ichijou, Ichinokura, Isshiki, Futatsugi, Nikaidou, Nihei, Mitsuya, Mikazuki, Yotsuba, Itsuwa, Gotou, Itsumi, Mutsuzuka, Shippou, Rokkaku, Rokugou, Roppongi, Saegusa, Shippou, Tanabata, Nanase, Yatsushiro, Hassaku, Hachiman, Kudou, Kuki, Kuzumi, Juumonji, and Tooyama.

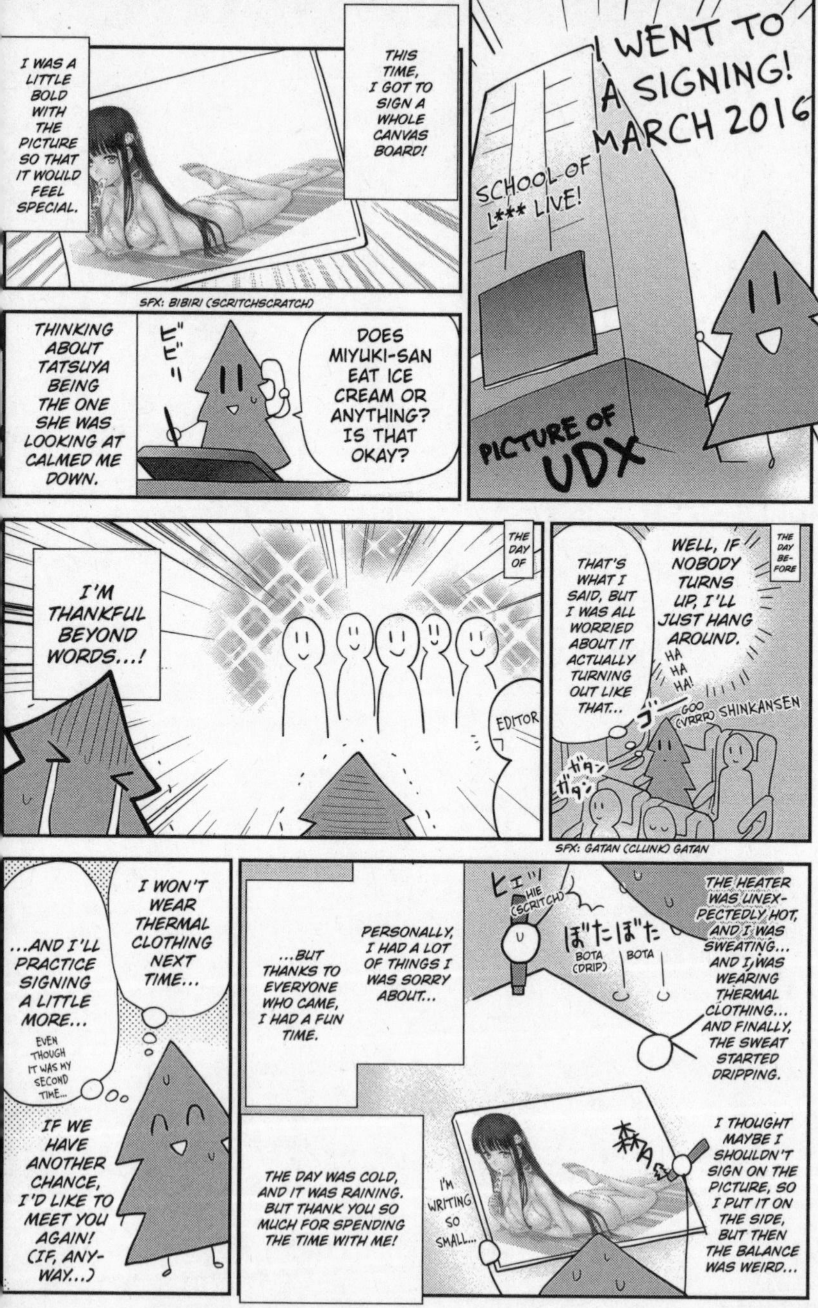
I WENT TO A SIGNING!
MARCH 2016
SCHOOL-OF L*** LIVE!
PICTURE OF UDX
THIS TIME, I GOT TO SIGN A WHOLE CANVAS BOARD!
I WAS A LITTLE BOLD WITH THE PICTURE SO THAT IT WOULD FEEL SPECIAL.
SFX: BIBIRI (SCRITCHSCRATCH)
DOES MIYUKI-SAN EAT ICE CREAM OR ANYTHING? IS THAT OKAY?
THINKING ABOUT TATSUYA BEING THE ONE SHE WAS LOOKING AT CALMED ME DOWN.
THE DAY BE-FORE
WELL, IF NOBODY TURNS UP, I'LL JUST HANG AROUND.
HA HA HA!
THAT'S WHAT I SAID, BUT I WAS ALL WORRIED ABOUT IT ACTUALLY TURNING OUT LIKE THAT...
GOO (VRRR) SHINKANSEN
SFX: GATAN (CLUNK) GATAN
THE DAY OF
I'M THANKFUL BEYOND WORDS...!
EDITOR
HIE (SCRITCH)
BOTA (DRIP) BOTA
THE HEATER WAS UNEX-PECTEDLY HOT, AND I WAS SWEATING... AND I WAS WEARING THERMAL CLOTHING... AND FINALLY, THE SWEAT STARTED DRIPPING.
I THOUGHT MAYBE I SHOULDN'T SIGN ON THE PICTURE, SO I PUT IT ON THE SIDE, BUT THEN THE BALANCE WAS WEIRD...
I'M WRITING SO SMALL...
PERSONALLY, I HAD A LOT OF THINGS I WAS SORRY ABOUT...
...BUT THANKS TO EVERYONE WHO CAME, I HAD A FUN TIME.
THE DAY WAS COLD, AND IT WAS RAINING. BUT THANK YOU SO MUCH FOR SPENDING THE TIME WITH ME!
I WON'T WEAR THERMAL CLOTHING NEXT TIME...
...AND I'LL PRACTICE SIGNING A LITTLE MORE...
EVEN THOUGH IT WAS MY SECOND TIME...
IF WE HAVE ANOTHER CHANCE, I'D LIKE TO MEET YOU AGAIN! (IF, ANY-WAY...)

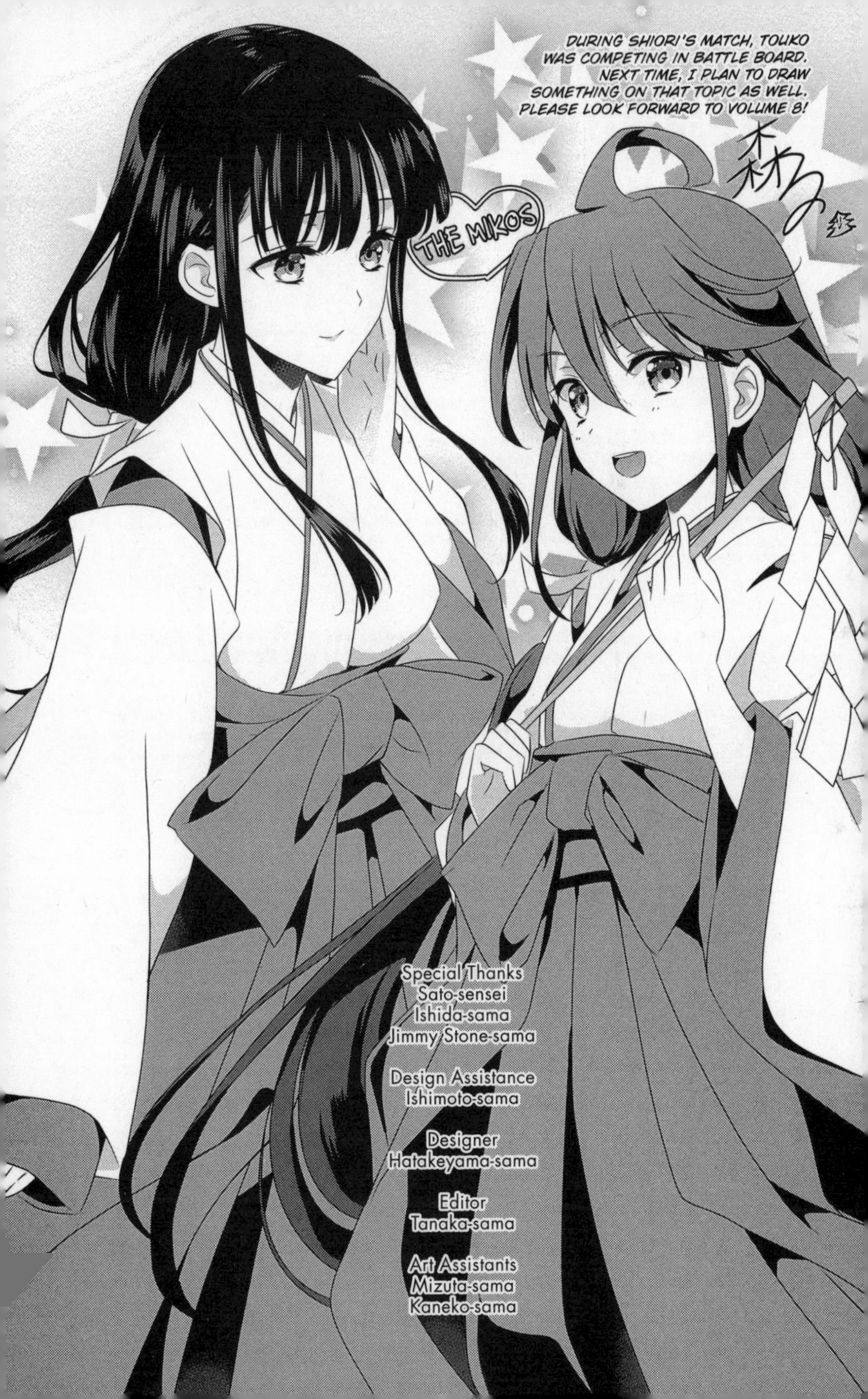
DURING SHIORI'S MATCH, TOUKO WAS COMPETING IN BATTLE BOARD. NEXT TIME, I PLAN TO DRAW SOMETHING ON THAT TOPIC AS WELL. PLEASE LOOK FORWARD TO VOLUME 8!
THE MIKOS
Special Thanks
Sato-sensei
Ishida-sama
Jimmy Stone-sama
Design Assistance
Ishimoto-sama
Designer
Hatakeyama-sama
Editor
Tanaka-sama
Art Assistants
Mizuta-sama
Kaneko-sama

THE HONOR STUDENT
AT MAGIC HIGH SCHOOL ⑦

YU MORI
Original Story: TSUTOMU SATO
Character Design: KANA ISHIDA

Translation: Andrew Prowse
Lettering: Phil Christie

MAHOUKA KOUKOU NO YUUTOUSEI Volume 7
© TSUTOMU SATO / YU MORI 2016
All rights reserved.
Edited by ASCII MEDIA WORKS
First published in Japan in 2016 by KADOKAWA CORPORATION, Tokyo.
English translation rights arranged with KADOKAWA CORPORATION, Tokyo, through Tuttle-Mori Agency, Inc., Tokyo.

English translation © 2017 by Yen Press, LLC

Yen Press
1290 Avenue of the Americas
New York, NY 10104

Visit us at yenpress.com
facebook.com/yenpress
twitter.com/yenpress
yenpress.tumblr.com
instagram.com/yenpress

First Yen Press Edition: June 2017

Yen Press is an imprint of Yen Press, LLC.
The Yen Press name and logo are trademarks of Yen Press, LLC.

The publisher is not responsible for websites (or their content) that are not owned by the publisher.

Library of Congress Control Number: 2016932699

ISBNs: 978-0-316-47184-8 (paperback)
        978-0-316-47416-0 (ebook)

10 9 8 7 6 5 4 3 2

BVG

Printed in the United States of America